Legal Socialization

Ellen S. Cohn Susan O. White

Legal Socialization

A Study of Norms and Rules

Springer-Verlag
New York Berlin Heidelberg
London Paris Tokyo Hong Kong

Ellen S. Cohn, PhD
Department of Psychology, University of New Hampshire
Durham, New Hampshire 03824-3567, USA

Susan O. White, PhD
Department of Political Science, University of New Hampshire
Durham, New Hampshire 03824-3567, USA

Library of Congress Cataloging-in-Publication Data
Cohn, Ellen S.
Legal socialization: a study of norms and rules/Ellen S. Cohn, Susan O. White.
p. cm.
Includes bibliographical references.
ISBN-13: 978-1-4612-7989-1 e-ISBN-13: 978-1-4612-3378-7
DOI: 10.1007/978-1-4612-3378-7
1. Sociological jurisprudence. I. White, Susan O. II. Title.
K270.C64 1990
340'.115—dc20 89-49256

Printed on acid-free paper

Typeset by Best-set Typesetter, Ltd., Hong Kong.

9 8 7 6 5 4 3 2 1

To David and Erica

E. S. C.

To Ellen

S. O. W.

Preface

This book began with a meeting of the minds between two people from different disciplines. Each of us had a long-time interest in the role of law in political and social life, particularly its influence on the normative order. Ellen Cohn, a psychologist, had done research on the social psychology of perceptions of crime and other law-related issues. Susan White is a political scientist who had studied compliance behavior and socialization to rules. Fortuitously, one of us was a member of our university's student conduct board, which provides a view of student life that faculty seldom see. This view provided the basis for our early discussions of the kinds of behaviors that occurred on campus, the attitudes of student board members toward judging their peers, and the effects of enforcement practices.

It became clear that we were observing the political, social, and psychological dynamics of a legal culture. Incoming students were learning both the norms of behavior that prevailed among their peers and the enforcement practices of those in authority. The constant interplay between norms and rules created a fertile environment for legal socialization in which each occasion for enforcing a rule became an occasion for testing one's values and beliefs. When asked informally, students usually offered well-formed reasons for their actions and judgments. At the same time, strong environmental pressures were clearly apparent. We discussed the unresolved gap in the literature between social learning and legal development explanations of legal socialization and decided that our student community was a perfect natural setting in which to test these competing hypotheses.

The result was an interdisciplinary research design and collaboration that received the financial support of our university and the National Science Foundation. We are grateful to Dean Stuart Palmer of the College of Liberal Arts and to President Gordon Haaland of the University of New Hampshire for their early support and encouragement. National Science Foundation Grant SES-8112020 provided the funding for managing the quasi-experiment and the data collection and analysis. Ellen Cohn received a Summer Faculty Fellowship from the Graduate School of the University of New Hampshire to support her work on the project. Susan White was released from teaching responsibilities by the University of New Hampshire through its Faculty Scholar program.

Support from the Division of Student Affairs at the University of New Hampshire was essential for conducting the study. We wish to express our appreciation to J. Gregg Sanborn, associate vice president and dean for student affairs; Carol Bischoff, director of residential life; Scott Chesney, associate director of residential life; and the many hall directors who helped us, especially Dan Slattery and Karen Rowe. Marianna Grimes provided invaluable assistance during the data collection process. Sibylle Carlson helped in the early stages of coding and analyzing the data. The study could not have been completed without extensive help from many RAs, who must remain unnamed, although much appreciated. Finally, we must thank the many members of the residential community whose role as subjects provided the data for this research.

Research assistance came in several forms. Psychology graduate students Susan Newman, Danny Malloy, Mae Lynn Neyhart, and Saul Rosenthal assisted in both the data collection and the quantitative data analysis stages. Psychology undergraduate students Jesse LaCrosse, Patricia Smigielski, and Kirsten Gannon helped with the data coding and analysis and the typing of the manuscript. Students in Susan White's seminars contributed invaluable observational data. We especially thank Linda Foulsham and Alison Porteous for their help in data collection and qualitative data analysis. Both Anna Moses and Donna Hardy are to be commended for their help in the final preparation of the manuscript.

Many colleagues and students contributed helpful comments on early papers and the text of this book. We want to thank Joan McCord, David Sugarman, Felice Levine, June Louin Tapp, Rebecca Warner, Kathleen McCartney, Victor Benassi, Ann Diller, Susan Newman, Marcy Kraus, James Grosch, Mae Lynn Neyhart, and Nancy Asdigian. We also appreciate the warm support of Dr. Robert Kidd of Springer-Verlag throughout the process of writing this book.

Finally, we want to thank Ellen Corcoran, a colleague and third collaborator in the data collection process. Ellen would never write this kind of book, so we take pains to relieve her of any responsibility for the analysis we have presented. But we note with gratitude that the book could not have been written at all without her extensive interviewing skills and her capacity to inspire the trust and confidence of students and staff.

Contents

Prologue

"I guess people do respond best when the rules and guidelines are clear-cut. It seems to me, though, that it would be better to have people thinking themselves about what is right and wrong and make their decisions accordingly."

"I mean, so what if they're being responsible, they're still breaking the rules."

On a Thursday evening in November Carol and Steve, the two RAs (hall staff) on duty, were walking the corridors of H—— Hall on their hourly rounds. They smelled a familiar odor in the air. After some investigation, including sniffing under the doors of several rooms, they determined that the marijuana odor was coming from a room where a party was underway. Behind the closed doors, a stereo was blaring loudly. Steve knocked on the door. There was no response from inside, so Steve banged heavily on the door and shouted to get someone's attention.

After several minutes of banging, the door opened and two people walked out casually. They had not answered the door but instead were just leaving the party. Steve and Carol stood unnoticed in the open doorway, sharply scanning the room. Finally, Steve banged on the wall and yelled out, "Bob!" to someone sitting on the sofa. Bob looked around and the nine people in the room grew silent. Bob got up and turned down the stereo. "Bob and Joe, will you come outside for a minute?" Carol requested.

Out in the hall, Steve asked, "Are you smoking pot in there?" Joe said, "There's been some pot smoked, but what right do you have walking in on us?" Carol said, "We have to write you up for Jud Board." Bob replied, angrily, "Has anyone complained? Go ahead and write us up. We'll see what happens."

The case was scheduled for a hearing before the student Judicial Board on the following Tuesday. The penalty for a finding of guilty would be eviction from the residence hall.

An Introduction to Legal Socialization

Rules are pervasive in human experience. They define much of our public life and reach extensively into our private relationships. The institutions within which we carry on our daily lives are both sources and enforcers of rules. Family, place of worship, school, workplace are all settings in which rules structure and compel the behavior of participants. But rules are not only pervasive; they are largely successful. Much of the time we obey them without thinking because we have learned to do so and our behavioral routines require it. It is seldom necessary to use force, although invoking authority is common. Distinctions are necessary in order to understand rule-governed behavior, however, because compliance does vary considerably across both individuals and situations. Some rules are self-imposed or voluntarily agreed to, whereas others are promulgated and enforced by governmental authority. And despite the efficacy of rules for most of us, some individuals seem impervious to their power.

Whatever the basis for our compliance, it is clear that rules carry some kind of psychological imperative, and often a moral obligation, to which human beings in general respond. Indeed, more interesting than the rules themselves are the ways in which rules are enforced and our varied responses to that enforcement. Rules are the tools of authority, and their means of enforcement are prime indicators of legitimacy. Our concepts of rights, duties, fairness, and other similar values stem not only from philosophical principles but also from our experiences with rule enforcement. The fact that these concepts may differ from individual to individual and group to group is in part a function of our different experiences with authority. These prescriptive values are products of both personal and historical learning because they represent the exercise of authority over time at various levels of social and political life. Legal socialization is the study of how these concepts and related behavioral responses are learned. It is, therefore, fundamentally the study of rule enforcement and its surrounding attitudes and behaviors.

Our responses to rule enforcement may be positive or negative. Feelings of attachment to figures of authority or to the nation and "commitment to the rule of law" are two examples of positive response. But enforcement also reveals the coercive nature of authority. Negative responses to authority—from rebellion to civil disobedience to crime—are common in the face of coercion, whether by police or by parents. Understanding these varying responses, their genesis, and the conditions under which they occur is the subject of this book. The obvious complexity of the subject poses a special challenge to empirical analysis. The very pervasiveness of rule enforcement, however, suggests that behavioral generalizations are possible despite the variety of circumstances in which it occurs. The study reported here was launched in that belief.

The Study

We start with three premises. The first has to do with theoretical complexity, the second with empirical validity, and the third with methodological demands. Each premise represents a choice of alternative approaches to the study of legal socialization, a choice forced by the complexity of the subject matter. They are to some extent unhappy choices because they exclude other, often intriguing, possibilities. But they also reflect our judgment about the need to advance research in this field by interdisciplinary means. In this respect, they are truly happy choices because they are driven by the questions intrinsic to the subject matter rather than by the requirements of a particular discipline. Our reasoning follows.

Socialization and Multiple Learning Dimensions

Legal socialization is a form of social learning, but it is theoretically complex because there are at least three learning dimensions. Figuratively speaking, one of these dimensions is vertical, another horizontal, and a third longitudinal. The vertical dimension refers to the multiple levels of rule-governed behavior within a society. Depending on the complexity of a society, an individual may encounter many levels of authority in the same day. The question is: Does contact with authority and rule enforcement at one level (e.g., the family) generate the same behavioral response as similar contact at another level (e.g., a state's criminal laws)? If yes, then what behavioral mechanism accounts for such a complex response pattern? If no, then what are the different behavioral linkages between the individual and the multiple levels of authority in a society (Easton & Dennis, 1969; Jennings & Niemi, 1974, 1981; Krislov, Boyum, Clark, Shaefer, & White, 1972; Merelman, 1969; Sears, 1975)? Equally perplexing is the horizontal range of situational and cultural variation in rule enforcement. Studying the extent of subcultural and other group variation in a pluralistic society discourages a theoretical reach for a single behavioral mechanism (Geertz, 1973). Cross-cultural variation only expands the problem (Renshon, 1977).

The third learning dimension of legal socialization, the longitudinal, poses a different set of questions. Here the focus is on the individual's path through the variety of perspectives on authority and experiences with rule enforcement that occur during a lifetime. This approach is most adaptable to the study of socialization because at any point along that path one can test hypotheses drawn from either social learning theory or developmental theory. The search for a behavioral mechanism remains the theoretical imperative, but the need to explain all the political and societal linkages is not paramount. The theoretical choice among these three learning dimensions thus becomes clear. Although the issues underlying legal socialization are both microstructural and macrostructural, the microstructural level is more amenable to rigorous empirical analysis. The key is to define the political and societal linkages in behavioral terms so that the behavioral mechanism that is identified as the catalyst for legal socialization can provide the theoretical basis for macrostructural statements as well as microstructural level explanation.

We want to stress that, in choosing the longitudinal dimension, we by no means abandon the search for a behavioral mechanism or our interest in its application across multiple levels of authority and cultural variation. These are inherent in the concept of legal socialization. But the first premise of this study is that legal socialization is best approached in terms of a longitudinal learning dimension. This strategy makes it possible to test hypotheses drawn from social learning theory and developmental theory while not precluding the availability of a full range of rule enforcement experience for micro-level analysis. These two theories differ significantly in the role each accords to the social environment in shaping individual attitudes and behaviors in rule-governed settings. The strategy we have chosen, therefore, permits us to test competing hypotheses about legal socialization.

Natural Setting

Our second premise is that legal socialization is most appropriately studied in a natural setting. This point has been made about general political socialization by Renshon (1977) in the *Handbook of Political Socialization* and about legal socialization in particular by June Louin Tapp (1980) in her presidential address for the Society for the Psychological Study of Social Issues. These two leaders in the socialization field were both commenting on the limitations inherent in standard paper-and-pencil tests of subjects' responses to experiences with the public arena. The fact that such tests are necessarily remote from the subjects' experiences and the settings in which they took place casts some doubt on the validity of the responses when inferences are being drawn about specific arenas of application. The experimental nature of most of these research designs are their strength but also their weakness when the research questions are rooted in substantive problems of the public arena rather than in human behavior that is not situationally specific.

This issue has been debated among behavioral scientists for many years, of course, and we do not wish to extend that debate. In our view, the call for more research in natural settings is a consequence of the realization that the existing work on legal socialization has reached something of an impasse, or at least a rather sterile pause. This is in part because it has not been possible to encompass measures of the full range of legal socialization effects—reasoning, attitudes, and behaviors—in a single study. This limitation stems in part from the difficulty of field experimentation (or, more properly, quasi-experimentation) and in part from the scarcity of natural settings in which this range of data collection is possible. One reason for undertaking the current study was precisely the fact that we could overcome these limitations.

The natural setting we have chosen is a university residential community. It is large enough to provide distance between rule enforcers and residents so that normative consensus alone is insufficient to maintain conformity. It is also small enough to provide variables of common meaning, so that everyone in the community knows what enforcement looks like, what behaviors are likely to provoke enforcement, and what the rules mean when they proscribe certain behaviors. There are prevailing norms, which are well understood by community members although often obscure to outsiders, and there are counter norms distributed among small groups here and there. There is variation in enforcement depending on seriousness and location, and variation in rule-violating behavior across individuals and residence halls. In short, it is a natural laboratory for studying legal socialization.

Multimethodological

Our third premise is that multiple methods are needed in order to take best advantage of the opportunities offered by the natural setting. We were reluctant to abandon the experimental approach entirely, so the heart of the research design is a field experiment involving four residence halls. In order to test the relative validity of hypotheses from social learning theory and developmental theory, we varied the conditions for legal socialization, the rule-enforcing environment. Attitudinal data on rule-violating behaviors and enforcement and self-reports of rule-violating behavior were collected from the experimental residence halls and from a wider sample. Data collection took place at the beginning of fall semester and near the end of spring semester.

We also followed three other strategies of data collection: records of the incidence of rule violation from official incident reports and from the daily duty logs of residence hall staff; observational data from participant observers; and a case study of rule enforcement by a peer judicial board. These various data sources provided a systematic descriptive record of our independent variable, the varying conditions in the residential community:

descriptions of enforcement practices, both in terms of the type of enforcement and its relative frequency, and descriptions of the procedures used to resolve disputes and impose sanctions. Secondly, they provided a systematic descriptive record of our dependent variables: descriptions of the range of behaviors that occur, especially the relative frequency of rule-violating behaviors over time, toleration of rule-violating behaviors, responses to enforcement, and willingness to support or engage in enforcement.

These various data enabled us to examine the complex fabric of behavioral interaction that surrounds issues of rule enforcement in a developing community. With the survey data we measured specific attitudinal and behavioral changes under two conditions for legal socialization. The observational data provided a detailed contextual picture of these socialization effects, and especially of the dynamic process involved in the interaction between norms of behavior and rule enforcement.

Part I

Legal Socialization Theory

In the first section, we introduce the research questions being addressed in the book. We present the major theoretical approaches to studying legal socialization: cognitive development theory (Levine & Tapp, 1977; Tapp & Kohlberg, 1977) and social learning theory (Akers, 1985; Akers, Krohn, Lonza-Kaduce, & Radosevitch, 1979; Bandura, 1969b, 1977). Finally we describe in detail the research design, including the setting, the population, the variables, hypotheses, and experimental manipulations.

In Chapter 1, we present the major issues involved in understanding legal socialization and the specific questions that will be answered in the current study. Specifically we focus on the cognitive developmental (Levine & Tapp, 1977; Tapp & Kohlberg, 1977) versus the social learning (Akers, 1985; Akers et al., 1979; Bandura, 1969b, 1977) explanation of legal socialization. Related to these two theoretical explanations is a consideration of the relative influence of internal and external factors. We also examine whether the relationship between reasoning and behavior is direct or mediated by situational attitudes, i.e., the enforcement status of the rule and the normative status of the behavior. At the end of the chapter, we briefly present the operationalization of the theories, setting, population, variables, and experimental manipulation.

Chapter 2 compares the two major legal socialization theories: legal developmental theory (Levine & Tapp, 1977; Tapp & Kohlberg, 1977) and social learning theory (Akers, 1985; Akers, et al., 1979; Bandura, 1969b, 1977). The two theories vary in their view of the nature and function of cognitive structures, the role of norms of behavior and other situational factors, and the effects of the rule-enforcing environment. Both theories emphasize the importance of cognitive structures, but neither explains how these structures and norms of behavior are related to each other and the behaviors.

Finally in Chapter 3, we explain the research design in detail. We describe the two populations studied, a random sample of entering freshmen students and a representative sample of freshmen and upperclass students living in the four residential halls under study. The three primary variables being studied are legal reasoning, attitudes toward rules (enforcement status) and rule-violating behaviors (normative status), and the frequency of engaging in rule-violating behaviors. Finally the experimental manipulation consisted of two control residence halls and two experimental halls, Peer Authority and External Authority residence halls. In the Peer Authority residence hall, students have a student run internal Judicial Board. In the External Authority residence hall, all rule violations are strictly enforced by the hall staff with no involvement on the part of hall residents.

1

Studying Legal Socialization

Chapter 1 sets forth some issues underlying the study of legal socialization and defines the specific questions to be addressed. The questions include the normative implications of legal socialization, the relative influence of internal and external factors in the learning process, the relationship between reasoning and behavior, the role of attitudes as mediators between reasoning and behaviors, and the relationship between legal reasoning and legal culture. We end the chapter with a brief delineation of the scope of the study, including the two leading theories and their operationalization and a description of the empirical setting.

The Normative Implications of Legal Socialization

As a field of study, legal socialization has a dual nature. It combines substantive concerns about the role of law in social life with the empirical analysis of human behavior in rule-governed settings. The substantive or jurisprudential concerns are broad-stroked and largely normative in character. They include the legitimacy of laws and law enforcement, the values of justice and fairness, and judgments about criminal responsibility and punishment (see, for example, Austin, 1954; Fuller, 1964; Hart, 1961, 1968; Kelson, 1945). Traditional legal scholarship approached these jurisprudential concerns as questions for philosophical argumentation and debate (Holmes, 1897; Kant, 1949, 1965; Mill, 1950). They were understood to be normative and therefore not appropriate for the hypothesis-testing techniques of social science.

In recent years, students of the law have been restating these normative concerns as empirical questions (e.g., Kelman & Hamilton, 1989; Krislov, et al., 1972; Lerner, 1980). Instead of asking, for example, why people ought to obey the law, they have asked why do people obey the law? Is it because they fear punishment or because they believe that an essential social purpose is being served by the law? Or is it simply because they believe that laws should be obeyed? Not satisfied with the jurisprudential answers provided by traditional legal scholarship, current researchers have turned to the theories and methodologies of social science. Empirical analysis, it was thought, would permit scholars to answer the substantive questions without stumbling over their normative character. Particularly intriguing for this purpose has been an interdisciplinary tradition of empirical research that focuses on the processes of socialization.

The concept of socialization refers to the acquisition of a society's values and norms by its members. The process of acquiring values and norms is the fundamental link between the individual and social and political life. The primary socializing agents are assumed to be the family, schools, and religious institutions (Connell, 1972; Dennis, 1973; Greenstein, 1965; Hess & Easton, 1960; Hess & Torney, 1967). Socialization is used to explain both how individuals become attached to a culture and how the culture and institutions of a society are then maintained over time (Almond & Verba, 1965; Easton, 1965; Parsons & Shils, 1951). It is usually assumed that a process of generational transference takes place whereby individuals learn attitudes and modes of behavior that conform to the values and traditions of the society (Jennings & Niemi, 1974, 1981). In this way the normative structure is passed on as the new members learn from (are socialized by) the old. This process is probably more complex than theorists have assumed, however. Peer influence has long been known to be important in the socialization process (Brim & Wheeler, 1966; Hirschi, 1969; Langton, 1967; Sutherland & Cressey, 1978) and recent research has shown that the relationship between parent and child is not always unilateral (McCartney, Robeson, Jordan & Mouradian, 1989).

Because socialization provides the behavioral linkage between the individual and society, students of the role of law in society have found legal socialization to be a helpful and provocative framework for their empirical questions (Hogan, 1976; Kelman, 1958; Levine, 1979; Levine & Tapp, 1977; Tapp, Finckenauer, & Yakovlev, 1988; Tapp, Gunnar, & Keating, 1983; Tapp & Kohlberg, 1977). The nature of that linkage can be characterized in different ways, however, depending on whether one focuses on the internal capacities of the individual or the external influence of the environment. The autonomy of the individual relative to the power of the shaping environment is a major theme in socialization literature. The term "socialization" seems to imply that the individual is passive, a receptor of norms and values and an object to be molded by the social environment. As we shall see, however, the major debate within legal socialization is between an individualistic theoretical perspective, which denies the direct influence of the environment, and theories that attempt to explain how the environmental influence functions.

As these concerns indicate, turning to the empirical analysis of socialization in order to understand the role of law in society has not exorcised the normative debate. It is there at the level of general theory, where the concept of socialization provides the linkage between the individual and institutions over time. Critics argue that equating socialization with the function of maintaining a society in this way implies that the study of socialization is biased toward conserving the old by shaping the new in its own image (Renshon, 1977; Schwartz & Schwartz, 1975). Law in particular is often the instrument of order rather than a creative force in the process of change. Some would also argue that the literature is predominantly concerned with "successful socialization," whether by parents to bend children to their bidding or by institutions to bind people to a supportive and compliant life.

Even the process by which these values and norms are acquired is not free of ideological import. Students of socialization (Goslin, 1969) define it as a learning process, although they then disagree about the nature of learning. Explaining how people learn, especially how they learn social competencies and behaviors, is the subject of continuing debate among behavioral scientists. Part of that debate has to do with direct policy implications, which are controversial both inside and outside the scientific community. For example, the Law Enforcement Assistance Administration (1974, February), a federal agency, was not permitted to provide funds for behavior modification programs, which were based on social learning theory; and according to academic critics, moral/legal development theory implies that women, lower-class populations and non-Western cultures cannot reach the highest levels of reasoning (Broughton, 1986; Gilligan 1982). When one adopts a socialization perspective, one must first choose between different models of the learning process. That choice, which is a major focus of the current study, has important implications for the role of law in society (Emler & Hogan, 1981; Hogan, 1976; Mancuso & Sarbin, 1976; Mischel & Mischel, 1976; Tapp & Kohlberg, 1977).

The two leading research traditions in the field of legal socialization take entirely different views of the process of socialization to rules. Cognitive developmental theory focuses primarily on the individual and invariant stages of development (Kohlberg, 1969, 1984; Levine & Tapp, 1977; Piaget, 1932; Tapp & Kohlberg, 1977). Social learning theory focuses primarily on the conditioning effects of the environment (Akers, 1985; Akers et al., 1979; Aronfreed, 1968, 1969; Bandura, 1969b; Mischel & Mischel, 1976). As approaches to legal socialization, the two theories therefore give quite different answers to the question: Why do people obey rules? Legal development theory (Levine & Tapp, 1977; Tapp & Kohlberg, 1977) postulates the dominant role of cognitive processes, specifically legal reasoning, in such decisions. Most versions of social learning theory suggest that compliance is controlled more by factors in the social environment. In short, the model of the learning process put forward by legal development theory leads toward individualistic values, whereas the model of the learning process inherent in social learning theory suggests that individuals may become subordinate to groups and ultimately to communitarian values.

In an important sense, a focus on legal socialization links the learning process with the particular content that is being learned. For example, learning traditional values through generational transference may be inherently repressive because maintaining a society's normative structure in this way is necessarily biased against individualized response and social creativity. On the other hand, learning individualistic values may foster individual autonomy at the expense of communitarian goals. Studying attitudes toward rule-governed behaviors and toward the enforcement of those rules necessarily encompasses the social content of those behaviors and rules. The socialization literature is filled with content-based studies; examples include "Socialization in Correctional Communities" (Wheeler, 1961), "Persuasion to Virtue" (Tapp & Levine, 1970), "Socialization into Child Abuse" (Parke, 1977), and "Socialization into Criminality" (Haney & Zimbardo, 1977). However one goes about studying legal socialization, focusing on the learning process will not allow one to avoid the content of what is learned.

For all of these reasons, we have designed this study to incorporate competing theories of legal socialization. We will first consider their validity as explanations of legal socialization, but we will not ignore their substantive meaning and normative implications. We will explore what each theory implies about the content of what is learned, that is, about attitudes toward rules and rule enforcement, and about rule-violating behaviors. These attitudes necessarily include social content, specifically, the social meaning of the behaviors prohibited by the rules, whether or not individuals approve of engaging in these rule-violating behaviors and whether or not they approve of enforcing the rules that prohibit the behaviors. We also consider how these attitudes are related to legal reasoning and actual behaviors and under what conditions these relationships hold. Another consideration is whether rule-governed behavior is a constant, i.e., is there a generalized propensity to follow or violate rules or do individuals choose to follow some rules and violate others? Our eventual aim is to develop a theory of legal socialization—not a theory of process alone or of content alone, but rather one that accounts for the acquisition of different kinds of legal values and behaviors under varying conditions.

The Relative Influence of Internal and External Factors

A primary question to be addressed in studying legal socialization is the relative influence of internal and external factors in the learning process. Treating this for the moment as an epistemological question rather than a statement of empirical theory, one can see that logically there are three possible perspectives on the socialization process. The first would emphasize the innate capacities of the individual learner. The second would focus primarily on the effects of environmental conditions on the learning process. The third would look beyond these internal and external factors *per se* to the interaction between them. It is important to see the particular virtues of each perspective in order to appreciate the theoretical choices available for studying legal socialization.

A model of the learning process from the perspective of internal factors begins with an assumption of innate capacities. This is because whatever the relationship with the environment, the source or generator of learning is the self. The logic of innate capacities is often developmental, either in the teleological sense, as favored by Aristotelian science, or simply in the sense that maturation produces changes in how the self deals with its environment. Either way, learning is controlled by a cognitive structure and faculties that are internal to the individual. For the purposes of studying legal socialization, this focus on the self means that one's beliefs about rules, fairness, and being responsible for one's actions are determined by individual choice.

There is a strong tradition in legal and political philosophy that argues for the primacy of internal factors in the socialization process. This tradition holds that social control is not the primary purpose of law because the makings of a good citizen, a good democrat, are innate. Legal constraints may offer guidance and structure to the citizenry but should not be used to repress the natural development of the individual. Theories of government, particularly of democracy, as well as theories of political and legal obligation have been based on the efficacy of individual choice (Kant, 1949, 1965; Locke, 1960; Mill, 1950).

For example, natural rights theory holds that laws, indeed all of government, exist for the purpose of making secure the natural rights of human kind. Because rights are "natural," meaning an inherent part of human nature, they are logically prior to any constraints of the law. The law does not, and cannot, create these natural rights. But in order for natural rights to be something other than a figment of political imagination they have to be grounded in actual or potential human faculties. Natural rights theorists believe that people are guided by what the Enlightenment called "right reason," or the capacity of the individual to find morality by following the rational dictates of self-interest (Locke, 1960). Many of the values of democratic theory spring from this concept of the self-directed individual (Mill, 1950). In the language of social contract, the legitimacy of laws derives from autonomous consent. Without the possibility of individual autonomy, the argument goes, democratic theory would have no basis in the real world of laws and politics (Barker, 1960; Benn & Peters, 1959)

Despite the optimism that characterizes these individualistic assumptions, they are deficient in two ways when used as a basis for legal socialization. The first has to do with the developmental logic of a theory based on innate capacities. When understood in teleological terms, self-realization can be construed as deterministic because the self is imprisoned in its unfolding and can never be other than its innate characteristics. One might even argue that socialization is irrelevant to this conception of the individual. Maturational development is less deterministic and less closed to the environment but learning does not take place unless the self has reached the appropriate developmental stage. Even though the individual is the locus of control, the developmental level cannot be transcended. Most would argue that an exclusively internal perspective cannot account for nondevelopmental influences on individual views of law (Broughton, 1986; Emler, 1983; Loevinger, 1986).

It is difficult, also, to accommodate communitarian values in a theory based on individualistic assumptions. Rules, fairness, and being responsible for one's actions are issues for the collectivity, and it might be argued that stress on individual autonomy and self-realization would tend to impede learning that is directed toward collective harmony. Legal socialization is about collective responsibilities. It pertains, by definition, to constraints on individual license. Therefore, a model of the learning process that is confined to internal factors provides an insufficient basis for studying legal socialization, despite the auspicious assumptions associated with natural rights theory.

A focus on external factors raises a different set of questions for the study of legal socialization. If the process of socialization is controlled by external factors, attitudes and behaviors are shaped not by individual choice but by the social environment. The inevitable consequence is that substantive issues concerning the role of law enter the picture. The social environment includes rules, the exercise of authority, and norms of community responsibility. Since these factors vary from society to society, it follows that beliefs about rules, fairness, and being responsible for one's actions will vary as well. As we argued earlier, the content of legal socialization, the implications for social and political life of what is learned by those being socialized to rules, becomes as significant for our analyses as the process itself.

This conjunction of process and content suggests several different dimensions of legal socialization that extend beyond personal development and constrain individual choice. The agents of socialization deserve attention because they are in a position to manipulate legal content. Such agents include the major socializing institutions of family, school, and religion, with the addition of any specialized institutions of law enforcement (e.g., Goslin, 1969; Jennings & Niemi, 1974; Krislov et al., 1972; Levine & Tapp, 1977; Renshon, 1977; Schwartz & Schwartz, 1975; Tetin, 1980; Torney, 1971, 1977). Agency is particularly important because the manner in which legal content is conveyed provides an essential link between that content and the process of socialization. For example, the exercise of authority can be more or less coercive, creating varying conditions for the acceptance of messages about the nature of law. The imitative or modeling process is well known to be an effective socializer, as social learning theories agree (Bandura, 1969b, 1973, 1977, 1986).

It is also illuminating to compare authority that is exercised formally, through specialized institutions of law enforcement such as police and courts, to authority that is exercised informally, through the invocation of norms. In some societies normative definition is so distinct and response so strong that forbidden acts are self-punishing, i.e., the violator immediately feels disgraced without any overt action by law enforcers. At the other end of this continuum, only coercion or the threat of coercion can make laws authoritative. While legitimacy may lie more with the former than with the latter, both might be characterized as repressive. Most uses of law lie between these extremes and combine formal and informal ways of exercising authority. But however the social control process works in any society, it is clearly a significant means of legal socialization as well. And as it contributes to maintaining the normative structure, it tends to reinforce the prevailing ideological bias towards either consensus or command as the proper model of authority (Durkheim, 1952, 1984; Goode, 1986; Hobbes, 1960; Lemert, 1972; Weber, 1939).

Another dimension of legal socialization has to do with societal structure, particularly the extent to which any society exhibits enough differentiation to undermine the existence of "shared values." An obvious example is class structure and the role of law as an instrument to secure the interests of the more powerful (Black, 1976). One does not have to accept the Marxist thesis to feel its power in this legal context (Humphries & Greenberg, 1984). Several studies have shown that class differences account for significant variation in attitudes related to legal socialization: (a) individuals' willingness to trust government (Lane, 1962; McClosky, 1964), (b) their basis for accepting authority (Lipset, 1960; Lipset & Raab, 1970); (c) their acceptance of other racial and ethnic groups (Lane, 1962; Lipset, 1960; Lipsitz, 1964); and (d) their basis for attributing responsibility to people of different socioeconomic backgrounds (Sanders, Regulus, & Hamilton, 1980). These studies found that lower-class respondents have a greater tendency to distrust government, fear other racial and ethinic groups, and think in terms of consequences rather than intentions in holding others responsible for harmful conduct.

There are two kinds of inferences one could draw from these findings. First, one could make the normative judgment that elites are better qualified than lower-class individuals to control human affairs because the latter exhibit "antidemocratic" tendencies. Or second, one could look more closely at the rule-enforcing environment and conclude that the seeming antidemocratic tendencies of lower-class individuals are in fact a rational response to the circumstances of powerlessness in which they find themselves. That is, people in lower-class situations have good reason to distrust government, are more likely to experience ethnic and racial conflict because of their life situations, and are more accustomed to being held accountable in terms of the consequences of their actions regardless of their intentions or any other moral state. In short, the conditions for legal socialization shape attitudes toward the exercise of authority and the values that individuals extract from their experiences of the use of law in society.

To conclude that lower-class individuals have less political or moral capacity than those in middle- and upper-class situations (e.g., Kornhauser, 1959; Lane, 1962; Lipset, 1960) would be to ignore the very real impact of the conditions under which these attitudes and values are formed. Other structural features of a society can produce similarly consequential conditions for legal socialization, most obviously gender and race. Women in all societies (Klein, 1984) and racial minorities in many (Patterson, 1982) experience the exercise of authority differently than do men and dominant racial groups. Whether the law is involved directly or only indirectly, as in families and schools, the conditions under which authority is exercised and the individual's relationship to that authority are powerful factors in legal socialization (Adelson & O'Neill, 1966; Jaros, Hirsh, & Fleron, 1968; Searing, Schwartz, & Lind, 1973).

It is clear, therefore, that the study of legal socialization cannot ignore external factors. But the question then arises: How does one take account of innate capacities and individual choice in a socialization process that is so subject to environmental pressures (Cook, 1985; Rosenberg, 1985)? Can anyone be shaped into a rule violator or is there room for individual autonomy in making moral and legal decisions? Our solution is to lay the ideological issues aside, at least for the time being, and to treat this as an empirical question. That is, we choose to formulate the issue of the relative weight of internal and external factors in legal socialization as a test of competing hypotheses rather than as an argument over substantive priorities. This formulation also enables us to pursue what we believe to be a fruitful line of inquiry about legal socialization, namely, that both individual choice and environmental influence affect the socialization process (Gibbs & Schnell, 1985).

In our view, it is the interaction between the two kinds of factors, internal and external, that brings about the learning we call socialization. As will be discussed later, this is not a new argument. Both of the leading theories of legal socialization suggest an essential linkage between cognitive processes and the social environment (Bandura, 1986; Levine & Tapp, 1977; White & Cohn, 1989). But our strategy of testing competing hypotheses allows us to go beyond earlier studies and begin to determine empirically the nature of that interaction. In particular, we can examine the processes of socialization, the linkage of internal and external factors, in a context that includes norms and rules and the exercise of authority. Combining process and content in this way makes accessible the additional goal of exploring empirically the interaction between person and environment in legal socialization (Cohn & White, 1986).

Relationship between Reasoning and Behavior

Any study of socialization must address the well-known inability of social science to succeed in specifying relationships between reasoning and behavior. We tend to assume that a person's ideas (opinions, attitudes) are a guide to that person's behaviors. This conventional assumption covers a complex circuitry, however, that includes connections between the general and the specific, the ought and the is, rhetoric and reality, group norms and personal preferences, and principles of action versus behavioral consequences. But human conduct, we like to believe, is not reducible to the physical movements that constitute behaviors (Peters, 1958; Winch, 1958) so we look for the idea, opinion, attitude, or belief that "caused," or at least is associated with, the way in which a person behaves. The ordinary person on the street might ask someone "why did you do that?" expecting an explanation that includes reasons for behaving in a certain way. The social scientist, also assuming a connection, conducts an opinion poll or an attitude survey. But what underlies the social scientist's inquiry is not a need to know why someone did *X* but rather a need to predict the relationship between reasoning and behaviors.

In studying legal socialization, for example, we may have precise and detailed knowledge of beliefs about authority and the enforcement of laws in a particular community but be unable to predict the level of compliance on the basis of that knowledge (Sarat, 1977). The inability to predict then raises legitimate questions about the value of that kind of knowledge. Are these beliefs simply a story that people tell themselves about their collective life that is irrelevant to how they behave? Do a society's legal culture and the process of socialization to rules have no influence on its members' behaviors? Or is the relationship between reasoning and behavior more complex than a simple connection between ideas about rules and how people behave when the rules are enforced?

This problem of prediction has been especially acute in the areas of social science that concern normative behavior (Deutscher, 1973; Dillehay, 1973; LaPierre, 1934). In a classic study, LaPierre found that people would allow a young, foreign born Chinese couple into their hotels and restaurants, although the same people reported that they would not welcome Chinese into their establishments. Additional examples of our lack of success in mastering the relationship between reasoning and actions are the problematic nature of predicting recidivism reliably (Farrington & Tarling, 1985; Monahan, 1978, 1981) and the failure of "educational" efforts to control dangerous behavior from drunken driving to drug use (Sechrest, White, & Brown, 1979). But these defeats are only practical instances of a broader failure to understand how reasoning is connected to behavior. The problem is not impossible to solve, of course, but its difficulty has often led researchers to follow easier paths. For example, because the problem is so difficult, social scientists often follow the conventional assumption and make study of the reasoning process itself into a sufficient goal for their research. As a result, we have numerous studies of opinions or reasoning about certain ideas without any showing of whether or not they have behavioral consequences.

In the study of legal/moral socialization, this approach has produced a large volume of research that is confined to the reasoning process alone (Levine & Tapp, 1977; Tapp & Kohlberg, 1977; Torney, 1971; Zellman & Sears, 1971). We have learned a great deal from that research, in particular about the development of individual capacities to reason through moral dilemmas and legal issues. But we have not learned anything substantial about the connection between reasoning and behavior (Blasi, 1980, 1983; Hogan, 1976). We know the developmental relationship between different formulations of legal principles but we do not know whether and under what conditions the principle will be followed. This intellectualist fallacy, according to one commentator, has produced only "tepid accounts of how children's theoretical legal attitudes change over time" (Hogan, 1976). To avoid the intellectualist fallacy one must put reasoning into a context that engages the moral passions and forces action. Only then will we begin to understand the relationship between reasoning and behavior in legal socialization.

Attitudes as Mediators between Reasoning and Behaviors

Most attempts to link reasoning and behavior have followed a two-stage model, i.e., ideas or opinions or attitudes are surveyed and then correlated with relevant actions. Sometimes the actions are hypothetical and sometimes observed. For example, a number of studies have shown that a large majority of Americans believe in fundamental freedoms such as free speech, but significantly fewer support the application of that principle when applied in controversial situations (McClosky & Brill, 1983; Stouffer, 1955). In a representative study, McClosky's (1964) data show that 90% of the general public agreed with the statement "I believe in free speech for all no matter what their views might be." But only 23% of a comparable population thought that "If a group asks to use a public building to hold a meeting denouncing the government, their request should be granted." Similar gaps between general beliefs and specific applications were found in other areas of civil liberties.

In a recent review of the literature on moral development and behavior, Blasi (1980) looked at research in which attempts were made to link moral cognition to moral action. The only strong evidence of such a relationship was found in research on delinquency where some delinquent populations were found to use lower levels of moral reasoning than matched non-delinquents. Blasi makes the methodological point that "the reasoning structures selected by investigators have a certain degree of remoteness vis-a-vis the action that they are supposed to determine." Indeed, reasoning structures are, by definition, abstractions from specific contexts.

Each of these examples raises important questions about the relationship between reasoning and behavior. The examples are different in obvious ways, but their similarity is more interesting. Both follow the two-stage model, moving from an abstraction to a concrete application. What is missing from the model and from each of these analyses is the social context in which the reasoning is applied. Concrete decisions and behaviors always take place in a social context that provides the actor with social cues and allows the actor to make sense of the situation. This is particularly true in the case of legal socialization because the rules and their enforcement are a public matter. While personal moral values may come into play, the content of behaviors that are governed by laws has a dimension that is not related to personal morality or ideology alone. That dimension is the authority of the community, both formal authority through its laws and informal authority through norms of behavior. The social context for legal behavior is furnished by the dimension of public authority.

Blasi (1980) suggests that the two-stage model, moving from abstraction to concrete application, could be improved by the addition of other factors that might mediate between reasoning and behavior. He specifically suggests personality as a mediating variable. We agree that the two-stage model should be modified to include mediating factors. But we would argue that attitudes grounded in the particular social context are more likely candidates than personality characteristics. It is probably true that individual differences in personality affect how reasoning about abstract ideas is translated into concrete actions. But personality characteristics have been questioned as reliable predictors of behavior (Abelson, 1972; Argyle & Little, 1972; Bem, 1972; Bowers, 1973; Fiske, 1974; Mischel, 1968, 1973; Peterson, 1968; Sarason, Smith, & Diener, 1975) on the grounds that they are remote from particular social contexts, as are abstract ideas. In their review of the personality and social behavior literature, Snyder and Ickes (1985) argue that the current solution to the problem of prediction focuses on situational strategies (e.g., Bem & Funder, 1978; Funder, 1983, 1987). This situational approach also seems appropriate for legal socialization where the mediation function is more likely to be carried out by attitudinal variables that are connected to the situation or the content of the behaviors one is trying to predict. Individuals' attitudes toward rules, rule-violating behaviors, and enforcing rules against those behaviors provide that connection.

In sum, we are proposing a multiple-stage model in which reasoning is linked to behavior by attitudinal factors that serve to convert the abstract generalizations that are typical of reasoning into the concrete applications necessary for actual behaviors. The interaction between person and environment in legal socialization, we will argue, requires this conversion process because legal reasoning *per se* is necessarily abstract and therefore apparently devoid of motive force. It is possible, of course, that legal reasoning is not related to attitudes or behaviors at all and that principles having to do with the logic of general rules and the fairness of their application are simply a textual overlay on a legal culture regardless of whether those principles are taught or otherwise handed down from one generation to another. This study was designed to investigate both that possibility and its more plausible alternative, namely, that the abstractions of legal reasoning are related to the content of the legal culture, and attitudes that embody that content also perform a mediating function linking legal reasoning to relevant behaviors.

Legal Reasoning and the Legal Culture

It could be argued, as suggested earlier, that legal reasoning is devoid of motive force and therefore unrelated to the attitudes and behaviors that constitute a legal culture. Such an argument is superficially persuasive, but only if a strictly Humean causal model of human action is presumed. It is not the purpose of this book to debate philosophy of science issues. There are conceptions of human action other than that embraced by Hume and his positivist successors, however, and they can be particularly helpful in understanding the multivariate relationships produced by legal socialization (Hume, 1955; Winch 1958). The direction of the causal arrow may well be a mistaken point of reference for the kind of complex analysis that the study of legal socialization requires. The following discussion of legal reasoning and the relationship between legal reasoning and other measures of legal socialization is written, and should be read, in this light.

It is important to begin by formulating a behavioral definition of legal reasoning. Legal reasoning differs from legal attitudes in that it typically lacks specific content and a situational reference. In legal reasoning, concepts such as responsibility and fairness as well as rules of various kinds are applied in the process of analyzing particular legal problems: Should I obey this rule? Is this rule being enforced fairly? Should John be held accountable under this rule for his behavior? A primary characteristic of such reasoning is its generalizability. The answers to these questions tend to flow from the process of comparing the particular case to others and analyzing their similarities and differences (Levi, 1948). Through this kind of reasoning by analogy, the reasoner focuses on what about this situation is generalizable to similar situations and what is not.

Empirical studies of legal reasoning have identified another characteristic that links it to the generic category of prescriptive reasoning. According to these studies, moral and legal reasoning are developmental (Kohlberg 1984; Snarey, 1985; Tapp & Kohlberg, 1977; but see Turiel, 1983, 1989), proceeding by stages as individuals both mature and gain access to different kinds of experiences. For legal reasoning, the most important experiences are those that lead individuals to consider the nature of authority and their relationship to various forms of authority. Studies agree that, broadly speaking, there are three stages or levels of reasoning: preconventional or rule-obeying, conventional or rule-maintaining, and postconventional or rule-making (Tapp & Levine, 1977). A preconventional reasoner would answer the question "Should I obey this rule?" by reference to a standard or belief that all rules must be obeyed and that punishment results if they are not. A conventional reasoner answers the question by reference to a need for law and order to prevent a breakdown of society. A postconventional reasoner weighs the reasons for compliance against possible reasons for noncompliance, and otherwise refers to principles that are independent of authority.

According to the developmental theory of moral and legal reasoning, the content of such reasoning is independent of situational factors. Rather, the reasoning process involves the use of criteria (preconventional, conventional, postconventional) to which the analysis of similarity and difference is referred. Situational content, according to developmental theories, may vary but the underlying propensity to follow one set of criteria rather than another in interpreting the legal meaning of a situation and deciding the appropriate response does not vary except as a function of developmental stage change. In other words, each individual's legal reasoning about specific legal problems stems from an internal cognitive structure and not from situational factors. To answer the question "Should I obey this rule?" the individual interprets the rule situation by comparing across personal experiences for similarity and difference (e.g., is this more like jay-walking or shoplifting?) and then applies the criterion determined by the individual's own cognitive structure.

It is important to note two essential characteristics of this formulation. First, cognitive structures are explicitly internal capacities and therefore represent the influence of internal factors in the learning process. We will discuss the specific features of these internal capacities in a later chapter, but for now it should be clear that the multiple-stage model that we are proposing postulates an internal factor as its logical point of departure. Second, cognitive structures concern the ways in which information is organized and not the content of that information. Legal reasoning as we have defined it has to do with cognitive processes. The processes of reasoning about rules, fairness, and responsibility for one's actions differs from reasoning processes about spatial relations, but the difference is between prescriptive reasoning and formal operational reasoning and not between types of content *per se*. While reasoning is never either content-free or unaffected by content, the cognitive structures that organize prescriptive thought are different from the cognitive structures that organize operational thought. Consequently, our multiple-stage model of legal socialization takes account of cognitive structural characteristics and their related processes as well as the specific legal content to which they are applied.

The linkage between the processes of legal reasoning and the content of the legal culture is found in the attitudes and behaviors that are learned and sanctioned in the rule-governed environment. As we have already discussed, this environment defines the collective responsibilities for individuals in a society and sorts out the relative importance of communitarian and individualistic values. While rights and duties are formally defined by the law, the legal meaning of various kinds of social interactions becomes clear through individuals' encounters with authority and with the symbols, both verbal and behavioral, through which authority is expressed in a society. How individuals interpret these legal meanings depends also on their relative status in the society, as determined by class, race and gender. In short, the conditions for legal socialization are embedded in the rule-governed environment.

This environment is inherently prescriptive (or proscriptive) and is therefore experienced by members of a community through the intersection of the two basic normative dimensions of social interaction: rules and behavioral norms. Rules may be formal or informal, i.e., they may be laws promulgated by governmental authority, they may be institutional regulations, or they may simply be the customary practices of some group of people. They are "legitimate" to the extent that they are followed, or at least not visibly and contentiously violated, by most members of the group. We have adopted this broad definition of rules in order to avoid the legalistic implication that rules must be formally promulgated in order to have sufficient prescriptive effect to generate legal socialization. This conception of rules is necessary to represent accurately the close connection between legal socialization and prescriptive experiences of all kinds and levels within a society.

The concept of behavioral norms, on the other hand, must be defined narrowly and precisely because it has been subject to various and often conflicting interpretations (Gibbs, 1981; Pepitone, 1975; Rossi & Berk, 1985). It could be held to mean an individual's judgments about the propriety or morality or acceptability of certain behaviors, or an individual's propensity or willingness to engage in those behaviors, or an individual's expectations of how others will behave, or an individual's beliefs about what others think of the propriety or morality or acceptability of certain behaviors. It could also be held to refer to the predominant judgment among members of a society regarding the propriety or morality of certain behaviors. These discrepant interpretations illustrate the complexity of empirical analysis of normative behavior. They also demonstrate the folly of attempting such analysis in the absence of a precise definition of the term "norm," especially as it is applied to behavior.

We chose to define both rules and norms in behavioral terms, an approach that renders these concepts most useful for the purpose of studying legal socialization (Cohn & White, 1985). By introducing behavioral definitions of rules and norms, the situational linkage between reasoning and behavior can be specified in our multiple-stage model. For example, we find it useful to define rules by reference to the aspect that most directly affects behaviors, i.e., rule enforcement. In order to gauge the behavioral impact of a particular rule, we ask our respondents whether they approve or disapprove of enforcing the rule. This focus on the enforcement situation links the individual's abstract reasoning about rules to a specific example of a situation in which a rule can be enforced against a specific kind of behavior. The response can be termed the *enforcement status of the rule*. Following the same definitional model, we also ask our respondents whether they approve or disapprove of engaging in the behavior that is proscribed by that rule. This response can be termed the *normative status of the behavior*. We can then ask our respondents how frequently they engaged in these rule-violating behaviors, to complete the set of behaviorally defined measures.

This multiple-stage model based on behavioral definitions has the obvious advantage of allowing us to specify a situational linkage between mediating attitudes (the enforcement status of the rule and the normative status of the behavior) and the rule-violating behaviors to which these attitudes refer. Another important advantage is the capacity to analyze the relationship between norms and rules within a population. When we compare the normative status of a behavior with the enforcement status of the rule prohibiting it, we can make statements about the relative enforceability of the rule and the likelihood that enforcement might create instability in the social fabric. We can also detect some degree of disjunction between the socializing function of formal authority and other agencies of legal socialization. To the extent that individuals' norms of behavior agree with the rules, the legal socialization process has been effective in producing a stable society. On the other hand, to the extent that the enforcement status of a rule is significantly lower than the normative status for the proscribed behavior for any significant proportion of the society, one can assume that the legal socialization process is fragmented and expect possible strains within the social fabric.

It is tempting to draw inferences about the stability of a society from this kind of behavioral analysis because it penetrates the political facade that identifies legitimacy with the existence of law. But it is well to remember that legal socialization refers to a learning process, and therefore the existence of disagreement between norms and rules in a society has implications beyond any possible instabilities that might result. A fragmented socialization process may suggest instability, but it may also indicate that the social bonds are strong enough to withstand challenge and that political relationships are flexible enough to allow dissent (Krislov et al., 1972; Rossi & Berk, 1985). A society that exhibits extreme normative consensus is unlikely to be a society of tolerance (Durkheim, 1984). Indeed, normative consensus may be the product of repressive socialization. This point is particularly telling in the case of legal socialization, where the socialization process is vulnerable to the coercive exercise of authority and an instrument for those who seek power. Our model suggests both this vulnerability to coercion and the potential for a free and tolerant society.

Criminologists commonly refer to the difference between those rule-violating behaviors that are understood by most members of a society to be wrong in themselves (*mala in se*) and those that are viewed as wrong only because society has prohibited them (*mala prohibita*). This distinction parallels what we outlined earlier, and it suggests that an important aspect of the study of legal socialization can be made subject to analysis through the use of our behavioral definitions and multiple-stage model. The criminological distinction invites a focus on differences in individuals' orientation to rules depending on how the act itself is perceived, regardless of whether it has been prohibited. The theoretical perspective we propose suggests a view of legal socialization in which the enforceability of the rules is independent of the formal legitimacy of the system and the socialization process is subject to a variety of influences on normative learning. In short, studying legal socialization entails analyzing the forces that lead to both consensus and dissensus (Rossi & Berk, 1985; Zeldich, 1986).

Our multiple-stage model describing the relationship between legal reasoning and behavior is now complete. It includes legal reasoning, defined as cognitive structures that organize an individual's thinking about rules, fairness, and being responsible for one's actions. It also includes attitudes and behaviors that are learned and sanctioned in the rule-governed environment. The behaviors are sanctioned, i.e., they violate rules. The attitudes mediate between the abstract reasoning and specific rule-violating behaviors because they represent the enforcement status of the rules and the normative status of the behaviors. This mediation function reflects a dynamic process in which the extent of agreement or disagreement between rules and norms varies both within individuals and across individuals in a community. The model thus encompasses content as well as process, and internal as well as external factors.

What does the model tell us about legal socialization? It is tempting to assume that one form of socialization is like another, that learning about rules, fairness, and collective responsibility is no different than any other form of social learning. Our model invites analysis of the complexities of the legal culture. The relationship between norms and rules is complicated and often convoluted. Our model selects among the multitude of possible variables and defines them along the same behavioral dimension. The model also links abstract legal reasoning with situational factors, thereby overcoming a major criticism of legal socialization research. Finally, the model permits us to measure the relative influence of cognitive and environmental factors in the learning process and the possible interaction between them. It is, of course, a descriptive model in that it describes but does not itself explain the relationships among the variables affecting legal socialization.

Operationalization

Theories

The theories that purport to explain these relationships are discussed in full in the next chapter. They are legal development theory (Levine & Tapp, 1977; Tapp & Kohlberg, 1977) and social learning theory (Akers, 1985; Akers et al., 1979; Bandura 1969b, 1973, 1977, 1986; Kelman, 1958; Mischel & Mischel, 1976). Both are theories of the learning process. Legal development theory is an adaptation of Kohlberg's (1969, 1976, 1981, 1984, 1986) moral development theory, which in turn is an outgrowth of Piaget's (1932) cognitive developmentalism. There are numerous versions of social learning theory, but they share the central concept that incentive or reinforcement conditions in the social environment control behavior, either directly or through self-regulation processes. On the basis of legal development theory, we would expect that changes in legal socialization effects are primarily related to legal development level instead of the social environment. On the basis of social learning theory, we would expect that changes in legal socialization effects are primarily related to the influence of the social environment instead of legal development.

Setting

We chose a "natural setting" (Tapp & Levine, 1977), which was a residence complex for students at a state university in a small town. There are 23 residence halls on campus, housing approximately 5,000 students during an academic year. Because the activities of the students are centered around the university, a community is formed that involves every aspect of a student's life. Students living in a residence hall are not simply students because for 9 months of the year this community is their home and the base for all of their social relationships. Most of the residence halls include both male and female residents. The community is governed by state criminal laws and the rules promulgated by the university administration. Enforcement is multilayered, carried out by town police, university public safety officers, and resident assistants, who are student employees of the university.

Population

Respondents were drawn from two sources: a random sample of entering freshmen, and a representative sample of residents who participated in an experimental manipulation involving four residence halls.

Variables

The variables were: legal development level, attitudes toward a set of rule-violating behaviors, attitudes toward enforcing rules against those behaviors, and frequency of engaging in those behaviors. These variables provided us with measures of legal reasoning, the normative status of the behaviors, the enforcement status of the rules, and the frequency of rule-violating behavior for each individual. Measures were taken on the opening day of fall semester and in the latter part of spring semester. More detailed information about the measures is provided in Chapter 3.

Experimental Manipulation

Four residence halls were chosen for experimental manipulation. Each was medium-sized and included a representative distribution of residents by age and gender. We varied the rule-governed environment in two of the halls by creating two distinct kinds of rule enforcement. In one case, the rules were heavily and consistently enforced by residence staff and police. In the other case, the rules were enforced by a participant board of residents selected by the group for that purpose. The other two halls served as controls. In one we provided information about the university's rules, and in the other no intervention occurred.

In sum, the study was designed to provide measures of the variables encompassed in our multiple-stage model from members of a community with its own rule-governed environment. Because this was a study of legal socialization, we focused on new members of a community and measured their responses to the rule-governed environment over time. We introduced controlled experimentation procedures to permit us to test hypotheses drawn from the leading theories of legal socialization. Finally, this was a natural setting in which we could reasonably assume that all members of the community had a shared understanding of the meaning of the various rules, rule-violating behaviors, and enforcement practices.

2

Comparing Theories of Legal Socialization

Chapter 2 compares the two leading theories of legal socialization: legal development theory (Levine & Tapp, 1977; Tapp & Kohlberg, 1977), which is a form of cognitive developmental theory (Kohlberg, 1969, 1984, 1986; Piaget, 1932), and social learning theory, a broad theoretical perspective of which several versions are particularly relevant to legal socialization (Akers, 1985; Akers et al., 1979; Bandura, 1969a, 1969b, 1973, 1977; Mischel & Mischel, 1976). The two theories represent two major paradigms in the psychology of learning and entirely different ways of conceptualizing the relationship between person and environment. Although not themselves competing theories, because neither takes the other as its opposite, the two approaches can be understood to generate competing hypotheses about the process of legal socialization (Cohn & White, 1986). The two theories are compared in these terms.

Comparing Two Paradigmatic Theories

Theories of legal socialization are prone to political interpretation because the relative weight of internal and external factors inevitably raises questions about individual autonomy in the face of the rule-enforcing environment. In the present study, we have translated those questions into a three stage model of the empirical processes involved in socialization. The role of theory in this study is to explain the relationships we have posited in our model. By what mechanisms do individuals appropriate the social environment, bend it to their desires, defend themselves against it, cope with it? What role does social interaction play in the development of the person? Our model does not assume an antagonistic relationship between person and environment. We suggest an approach that makes no assumptions other than that the process of social interaction will tell the tale of human development and therefore of legal socialization. It is the nature of this process that is fundamental to our inquiry. Rather than posit, *a priori*, particular roles for internal and external factors in legal socialization, we set out to discover what those roles might be. We shall return to the political implications when those roles are clarified empirically.

With that caveat, we begin by restating what it is we wish to explain. Our three-stage descriptive model of legal socialization includes the following variables: (1) legal reasoning, defined as cognitive structures that organize an individual's thinking about rules, fairness, and being responsible for one's actions; (2) attitudes toward specific rule-violating behaviors and rule enforcement against them; and (3) engaging in those rule-violating behaviors. It is the relationship among these three factors that we wish to explain. That there is a relationship, or multiple relationships, is implied by the model, but the model is formulated as an empirical statement in order to test that implication. Our next task is to specify the relationships as testable hypotheses generated by one or more theories of human behavior.

Different theories should provide a different specification of those relationships. For example, are cognitive structures about being responsible for one's actions related at all to whether or not one engages in rule-violating behaviors? If so, are they related directly or indirectly and does the relationship change over time as one grows older and has different experiences? In what ways are norms of behavior and attitudes toward rule enforcement related to abstract cognitive structures? Do different kinds of experiences with particular rules and rule violations in different enforcement settings affect these relationships? These and other questions are, in a sense, answered differently by different theories, and the validity of each answer is then testable. In sum, our three-stage model of legal socialization assumes relationships among three variables—reasoning, attitudes and behaviors—and particular theories of human learning provide particular versions of that relationship.

What theories are appropriate candidates for explaining legal socialization? There are two major paradigms in behavioral science that bear directly on this question. One is cognitive developmental theory, which is derived from the work of Piaget (1926, 1932) and Kohlberg (1969, 1976, 1981, 1984, 1986) and has spawned an influential theory of legal development (Levine, 1979; Levine & Tapp, 1977; Tapp et al., 1983; Tapp & Kohlberg, 1977). The other paradigm is social learning theory, which originated in what is now called radical behaviorism (Gewirtz, 1969; Hull, 1943; Skinner, 1938, 1953) to distinguish it from the less biologically oriented versions that are currently applied to social learning (Akers, 1985; Akers et al., 1979; Bandura, 1969a, 1969b, 1973, 1977; Kelman, 1958; Mischel & Mischel, 1976). Legal development theory and social learning theory represent conceptually different approaches to the study of legal socialization. They also represent two entirely different ways of looking at the relationship between person and environment or between internal and external factors (Cohn & White, 1986).

The two different approaches are not in themselves competing theories because neither takes the other as its opposite. Each, however, claims a different mechanism for learning. Legal development theory (Levine & Tapp, 1977; Tapp & Kohlberg, 1977) posits cognitive structures that organize prescriptive thinking and that change developmentally, in invariant sequence, through the stages discussed in Chapter 1. Social learning theory (Akers, 1985; Akers et al., 1979; Bandura, 1969a, 1969b, 1973, 1977; Mischel & Mischel, 1976) assumes some form of (usually operant) conditioning process in which the learner behaves in response to anticipated social consequences (Gewirtz, 1969). Variations on the social learning model often stress the role of cognitive processes in a self-regulation pattern of learning (Bandura, 1977, 1986; Mischel & Mischel, 1976), but the mechanism remains an on-going response by the individual learner to the social environment. For legal development theory, the mechanism is rooted in internal factors; for social learning theory, the mechanism is rooted in external factors.

Both theories acknowledge the importance of the other kind of factor. Kohlberg in his writings on moral development (1969, 1976, 1984, 1986) and Levine and Tapp in their formulation of legal development theory (1977) identify role-taking as a necessary experience in the process of developmental learning and change. Role-taking is a means of experiencing the social environment. Aronfreed (1968, 1969), Bandura (1986), Mischel and Mischel (1977), and other leading social learning theorists emphasize the role of cognitive processes in self-regulating behavior. But the stage-determined reasoning from cognitive structures identified by Kohlberg and by Tapp and Levine does not count as cognitive processing in the social learning model; nor does self-regulated response to environmental conditions count as role-taking in the developmental model. Both theories are acknowledging a necessary interaction between the individual and the social environment in order to generate learning, but they disagree entirely about the nature of that interaction.

The two theories represent two major paradigms in the psychology of learning. Comparing them forces one to confront the most fundamental questions about one's subject matter. First, which of these two paradigmatic theories provides the better explanation of legal socialization? To answer this question, we must formulate and test competing hypotheses drawn from the two theories. Second, what can a comparison of these theories tell us about the interaction between the individual and the rule-enforcing environment in the socialization process? Our three-stage model assumes a relationship among three variables—reasoning, attitudes, and behaviors—and each theory provides its own version of that relationship.

The Cognitive Developmental Paradigm

The Influence of Piaget and Mead

Although a number of social thinkers made important contributions, the cognitive developmental paradigm has its primary roots in the work of Jean

Piaget (1926, 1932) with some secondary influence from the philosophy of George Herbert Mead (1934). Both Piaget and Mead represent an older intellectual tradition in which the line between science and philosophy was not so clearly drawn, a fact that is reflected in the breadth of their interests. Although not disciplinary colleagues, they shared a particular way of thinking about human behavior. Rather than being caught up in the biologically oriented perspective of Freud (1925) and the early behaviorists, Mead and Piaget were fascinated by the social bases of human action and by the social interactions that both created and controlled individual behavior. Their psychology was cognitive rather than physiological because of this social focus.

Mead (1934) believed that the human personality, or self, develops through the acquisition of shared social meanings. This is accomplished from the earliest times of a child's life through the learning of language and through entering into other forms of social interaction. In this way, the child learns to see herself and her behavior from the standpoint of someone else. Thus her attitudes are by definition the shared attitudes of others and she develops a natural social perspective originating in an other-based self-consciousness. In effect, the child is learning to act and respond by anticipating how others will act and respond. The phrase "role-taking" or "taking the role of the other" derives from Mead's teaching about this natural basis for social interaction. As the learning process grows more complicated in the social world, the child first internalizes parental attitudes and then role-taking with generalized others in a process identified as the development of a social self or the basis of social control. However it is characterized, Mead's distinctive view of a self that cannot be divorced from social interaction had a powerful influence on the newly developing behavioral sciences.

Piaget's (1926, 1932, 1970/1983) distinctive contribution to the cognitive developmental paradigm was the concept of developmental stages occurring in invariant sequence. Piaget's stage theory has influenced generations of psychologists seeking to understand how children learn. His initial work had to do with how children acquire physical concepts such as space and causality, but he eventually included social and moral concepts within the same basic conceptual framework. This framework is founded on the notion that humans learn by adaptation, molding themselves to the environment and shaping the environment to their use. This reciprocal relationship to the environment, whether physical or social, is at the heart of the cognitive developmental paradigm. Cognitive structures are representations of the environment that allow the individual to receive and organize information. Cognitive structures thereby form, through on-going interactions, the basis of human adaptation.

There are three processes by which adaptation occurs, according to Piaget (1970/1983), and all three are interactional. In the first two, assimilation and accommodation, existing cognitive structures receive, organize, and use information in such a way that the structures themselves gradually change to reflect the individual's adaptation to the environment. The information is assimilated into the existing structure and the structure acts on the information to accommodate itself to elaborations and variations. This creates structural changes that will in turn assimilate more complex information, and so on. The third process, called equilibration, maintains a balance between the two poles of the interaction, that is, between the cognitive structures within the individual and the various environmental stimuli. The resulting interaction is dynamic because of the on-going and constantly changing nature of the two processes of adaptation and their equilibration.

This brief and oversimplified description of Piagetian theory is intended only to indicate the broad outline of the interactional basis of the cognitive developmental paradigm. Piaget applied these concepts of adaptation to the learning process of children and derived an empirical description of three cognitive stages: the preoperational stage when language appears, the concrete operations stage, and the formal operations stage. Representational thinking becomes increasingly elaborate and less based on direct experience. A child's developing cognitive capacity, in short, moves away from the concrete egocentrism of early interactions with the environment toward symbolic manipulation, but always within the framework of creating and re-creating the balance between the self and the environment. One of the means by which this movement away from concrete egocentrism occurs is taking the role of the other, whereby the individual gradually develops the capacity to free herself from the single perspective on reality.

This interactional framework, which characterized the thinking of both Mead (1932) and Piaget (1970/1983), is fundamental to the cognitive developmental paradigm. Piaget tested it empirically on the process of learning physical concepts (1926) and only later applied it to the development of social perceptions and moral reasoning (1932). When he did investigate social interaction, Piaget was able to identify two basic stages that are consistent with both the learning of physical concepts and interpersonal learning. The first stage, variously termed "moral realism" or "a morality of constraint," is characterized by egocentrism, objective responsibility, and obedience to authority. The second stage is termed "a morality of cooperation," which is characterized by awareness of differing points of view, willingness to consider intentionality, and a belief in equality. The movement from one stage to the next is a shift in social cognition but it parallels the child's move from an egocentric perspective on the external world to a capacity for seeing the world from differing perspectives, a move that is necessary for formal operational thought as well as for taking the role of the other. The child's understanding of the physical world and physical concepts changes radically during this cognitive development, just as her understanding of the social world is changed when she is able to take the viewpoint of others.

While Piaget (1932) was interested in social cognition broadly defined, his two stages have specific implications for legal socialization. In the first place, the egocentric basis of the morality of constraint is not only a function of cognitive immaturity but also of the child's relationship with authority. Adults are perceived as the source of all power and rightness, so the morality of constraint accepts arbitrary punishment and inflexible rules as just. For Piaget, this acceptance is natural and a necessary stage through which all children must pass as they mature. It is also natural that children, in the process of adaptation, begin to take on the perspective of others and thus learn to view authority and rules differently. The extent to which children develop toward the morality of cooperation may be limited because adverse social conditions can deprive them of opportunities for reciprocal social interaction. Learning the rules of children's games is a fundamental experience, however, that provides these opportunities routinely, albeit at fairly low levels of development.

Kohlberg and Moral Development Theory

The legacies of Piaget (1926, 1932, 1970/1983) are the concepts of cognitive structure, stage development, and equilibration, in addition to his belief that social interaction is the basis for cognitive development. Some of his views, especially his claims about the invariant sequence and universality of stage development, have been strongly challenged (Gelman & Baillargeon, 1983). Nonetheless, his influence has been and continues to be wide throughout the behavioral sciences as the primary source of the evolving cognitive developmental paradigm. When we narrow our focus to those aspects of the paradigm that bear on legal socialization, the major work is that of Lawrence Kohlberg (1969, 1976, 1981, 1984, 1986) who turned his attention to social cognition and, even more specifically, moral development. Kohlberg's theory is even harder to summarize intelligently than Piaget's because of its extensive empirical as well as theoretical elaboration. For purposes of understanding the relevance of the cognitive developmental paradigm to legal socialization, however, Kohlberg's distinctive contributions are his emphasis on the moral dimension of social cognition and his extension of the stage and sequence model.

Kohlberg (1969, 1976, 1981, 1984, 1986) begins with fundamental assumptions about human learning drawn from Piaget's (1970/1983) cognitive developmentalism. For example, in his classic statement of the paradigm, "Stage and Sequence: The Cognitive-Developmental Approach to Socialization" (1969), Kohlberg posits cognitive structures that develop through processes of interaction between "the structure of the organism and the structure of the environment" in the direction of an equilibrium or reciprocity (1969, p. 348). Like Piaget, Kohlberg conceives of the person as actively engaged in the process of development, as creating her own opportunities for movement and learning through reciprocal interaction and equilibration. Arguing against associationist social learning theories, he stresses that cognition "is an active, connecting process, not a passive connecting of events through external association and repetition" (1969, p. 349). But this active learner is also constrained by the processes of assimilation, accommodation, and equilibration because together they prevent her from having a direct relationship with the external world. The very cognitive mechanisms that ensure this active, self-generating learning mode also stand between the individual and the environment. Kohlberg's elaborated doctrine of stage and sequence articulates this constraining logic of development and the view of interactional learning that underlies it.

Kohlberg (1969, 1976, 1981, 1984) argues that there are three levels of moral development, encompassing six stages. The three levels are termed preconventional, conventional, and postconventional because each represents a kind of relationship between the individual and the social environment based on the individual's attitude toward society's conventions. The social environment to which he refers explicitly includes rules. The young child, being egocentric in Piaget's sense of the term, can only interpret the social world as external to herself in the same nonreciprocal way she sees the physical world. Authority controls, punishment is "immanent," obedience is good. Stage 2 children are individualistic but aware of others and aware that others have interests as well. Children at this stage are willing to exchange on a principle of equality and are able to see agreements and rules governing agreements in terms of fairness. Both of these stages are preconventional, however, because they exclude conformity to group-based feelings and norms.

Children at the conventional level are open to influence from societal expectations and willing to sacrifice individual interests to group conformity. Conventional children differ in their relative focus on interpersonal relations (Stage 3) or the social system (Stage 4). Shared feelings are powerful at Stage 3, along with group norms and mutual interpersonal expectations. Stage 4 is characterized by a concern for legalistically defined expectations stemming from the social order, its institutional structure, and its rules. The postconventional level is sometimes termed principled because, in Kohlberg's (1969) view, people who are postconventional have interposed ethical principles between their personal judgments and their commitment to a social order. At Stage 5, people are primarily concerned with the moral basis of the social contract and of obligation to law. At Stage 6, universality becomes the perspective and all laws are judged according to their conformity to universal principles of justice.

Because the logic of stage and sequence governs moral development, it is Kohlberg's (1969, 1984) view that individuals pass through these stages in accordance with their cognitive maturity. That is, children necessarily begin in egocentrism with respect to both physical and social concepts. Progress through the stages is by invariant sequence and the capacity for physical concepts is prior to that for social concepts. A child who has not reached the capacity for formal operational thought cannot take advantage of role-taking opportunities that are appropriate for developing conventional moral reasoning. On the other hand, cognitive capacity alone will not ensure that an individual will reach the highest stages of moral development. Stimulation from the social environment, in the form of appropriate role-taking opportunities, is necessary for development. Kohlberg's theory essentially accepts the possibility that the experiences of some individuals, and even the content or repressive character of some cultures, can prevent or seriously inhibit moral development.

This logic of stage and sequence is, therefore, restrictive in two ways. First, the processes of assimilation, accommodation, and equilibration prevent any direct relationship between cognition and the social environment. Second, development proceeds by stages in an invariant sequence so that individuals cannot assimilate information from or reason at any level above their current stage. These two restrictions are, of course, matters of controversy both within cognitive psychology and within the broader world of learning and socialization theory (see Bandura, 1969b; Turiel, 1983, 1989). They are fundamental to the cognitive developmental paradigm, however. Despite much criticism over the years, cognitive developmentalists remain convinced of their position. Cognitive structures are not beliefs about the world, either simple or complex, but rather ways of organizing information about the world. While data show that individuals sometimes reason below their cognitive stage, considerable data (including cross-cultural) indicate that they do not reason above their cognitive stage unless they are clearly in a transitional period.

Legal Development Theory

The cognitive developmental paradigm has been applied to legal socialization, with impressive results. Tapp and Kohlberg (1977) have reported data from two studies, one involving U.S. youth and the other a cross-cultural survey, using a law-oriented variation of Kohlberg's (1969, 1984) moral development model. Tapp and Kohlberg interpreted the preconventional level as representing a "rule-obeying perspective," the conventional level a "rule-maintaining perspective," and the postconventional level a "legislative or rule-making perspective" (p. 92). Adopting the cognitive developmental processes of assimilation, accommodation, and equilibration as their conceptual base, Levine and Tapp (1977) constructed what they called an "interactional cognitive model of legal reasoning." They suggested that legal activities and institutions provide role-taking opportunities in the classic Mead (1934)–Piaget (1932) sense and that learning takes place in a continuing dialectic between cognitive stages. This focus on the effects of specific kinds of role-taking opportunities is both an application of cognitive developmental theory to legal socialization and an extension of the theory's conceptual base to qualitatively specific social interactions.

The levels of legal development identified by this research were described in terms of responses to three kinds of questions (Tapp & Kohlberg, 1977). The first has to do with the value and function of rules and laws. For example, subjects were asked "What if there were no rules?" Preconventional (rule-obeying) respondents, who view the social environment from an egocentric and concrete perspective according to cognitive developmental theory, answered that rules prevent crimes and physical harm. Conventional (rule-maintaining) subjects gave a "law and order" response, referring to the social order and the need to constrain self-indulgent behavior. Postconventional (rule-making) respondents preferred to think that people can control their own behavior by moral principles without the need for rules. When subjects were asked "What is a rule?" preconventionals talked about rules as simple prohibitions, but conventionals could reason about a system of rules that served the purpose of maintaining society and postconventionals discussed principles that lie behind a system of law. All of these responses fit the Kohlbergian (1969, 1984) stage and sequence logic of moral development even though the questions are specifically about rules and the answers are framed in terms of the social context of rules rather than personal morality.

Comparable stage or level responses could be distinguished in response to two other kinds of questions that are important to legal socialization, i.e., reasons for following rules and the possibility of changing rules. Preconventionals were primarily concerned with avoiding punishment and obeying authority, and could not differentiate between the existence of a rule and its purpose. Conventionals were more concerned with social desirability and conformity than with principles. Postconventionals gave principled reasons and were willing to accept or reject rules on the same basis. Overall, these legal reasoning responses conformed strikingly to Kohlberg's (1969, 1984) moral development levels. It is fair to conclude, therefore, that cognitive structural levels of legal development exist and that they coincide with the logical and substantive distinctions predicted by cognitive developmental theory. In short, the cognitive developmental paradigm applies to legal socialization at least to the extent that it suggests a powerful explanation of variations in specific qualitative dimensions of legal reasoning. Whether this theory of legal development explains the relationship between reasoning and the other aspects of legal socialization such as attitudes and behaviors, or even provides the only explanation of variations in reasoning, is a further question.

Levine and Tapp (1977; Levine, 1979) have approached this question of the relevance of cognitive legal development to legal socialization by reformulating a major premise of cognitive developmental theory. They accept the fundamental processes of assimilation, accommodation, and equilibration originally outlined by Piaget (1970/1983). They believe that human development is a matter of adaptation to the environment by reciprocal interaction according to the dynamic inherent in these processes. Adaptation to the legal environment, initially to rules and the exercise of authority by parents and teachers, is a function of cognitive structures assimilating information from the environment and changing by accommodation on the basis of that information in a dynamic process of equilibration. In accordance with this theoretical formulation, there is no direct relationship between the individual and the social environment, but rather "an infinite series of continuous interactions between social variables and natural potentialities" (Levine & Tapp, 1977, p. 164). They also accept Piaget's (1926, 1932, 1970/1983) characterization of cognitive levels, finding clear evidence of egocentrism and concrete operationalism in preconventionals and the capacity to see the social world from other perspectives in conventionals. But they depart from Piaget and Kohlberg (1969, 1984) at a crucial point by postulating a dialectical process of change across the stages of legal reasoning rather than an invariant sequence of stages.

This departure is important, we would argue, because the dialectical model of legal development fits the public world of legal activity better than does the invariant stage model of moral development. There are important differences in the nature of conflict between the two spheres. Both moral development theory (Kohlberg, 1969, 1984; Piaget, 1932, 1970/1983) and legal development theory (Levine & Tapp, 1977; Tapp & Kohlberg, 1977) encompass conflict as a component of the interaction between the individual and the environment. If an individual has attained a level of cognitive development that permits the social perception of role-taking, she is then able to see other perspectives, to understand the thoughts and feelings that underlie them, in short, to take the role of the other. The kind of social context that promotes role-taking is necessarily characterized by diverse perspectives and probably by disagreement. On these points, the moral development model and the legal development model agree. But Piaget and Kohlberg identified reciprocity and cooperation as the key social conditions for moral development. Conflict enters because of the diversity of experiences implied by their concept of reciprocity, in short, because there are other points of view in the world. Consequently, judgments of right or wrong, or of fairness, require taking the role of the other, according to moral development theory. These judgments are personal moral decisions, however, which take into account the perspectives of others but are not made in the arena of conflict. Legal socialization requires the kind of role taking that is essential for moral development, but it also requires interaction with a social environment of conflict.

Tapp and her associates (Levine, 1979; Levine & Tapp, 1977; Tapp et al., 1988; Tapp et al., 1983; Tapp & Kohlberg, 1977) appear to go beyond both Piaget (1926, 1932, 1970/1983) and Kohlberg (1969, 1976,

1981, 1984, 1986) in delineating what "interaction" means in cognitive developmental theory and in making the theory applicable to the actual conditions of legal socialization. Their formulation of how change occurs in the socialization process speaks to the environmental and institutional conditions of conflict underlying legal activity. With the cognitive developmental concept of equilibration as their point of departure, they point out that change occurs during disequilibrium, when the individual's cognitive structures are accommodating to new information that is being assimilated. Levine and Tapp use the notion of dialectical movement to describe how this kind of change fits their interactional model. They suggest that an individual often reasons at different stages at the same time under conditions of conflict, debating between thesis and antithesis, because disequilibrium often occurs in a legal or political context. In such a context, the variety of individual perspectives and conflicting claims are not simply matters for personal decision, but rather are issues that can only be solved by joint action. Dealing with conflicting claims over public issues is at the heart of legal development. Levine and Tapp argue that change in one's level of reasoning under conditions of environmental conflict is not a "function of an ordered, mutually exclusive progression" of stages. Instead, they suggest, "the dialectic of reasoning simultaneously at diverse stages can stimulate stable, integrated cognitive growth in the individual" (1977, p. 166).

In sum, the social context of role-taking opportunities for legal socialization is inherently one of conflict. The dialectical process proposed by Levine and Tapp (1977) acknowledges both the condition of conflict and the need to provide developing individuals with the kinds of role-taking opportunities that optimize the facilitative effects of conflict on legal development. Role-taking opportunities are situations in which individuals are in a position to see the diverse viewpoints of others. In legal socialization, such situations occur whenever questions of justice arise. Asserting and adjudicating rights claims, exercising authority for social control, holding individuals responsible for their actions, deciding whether or not to comply with a rule, and questioning the legitimacy of rules all produce conditions that are ripe for disequilibrium and change. Under such conditions, according to cognitive developmental theory, individuals are in a position to see the viewpoint of others because these are situations of controversy characterized by conflicts in values and diverse claims. Role-taking opportunities like these are rarely the gentle, participatory exercises often envisioned in the moral development literature. An important but unanswered question, however, is whether the challenge of a conflictful social environment always facilitates legal development. More research is necessary in order to understand more fully what "interaction" means in cognitive developmental theory. We agree with Levine and Tapp (1977) that this kind of research is most productively done in naturalistic settings such as the setting for the present study.

Criticism of the Cognitive Developmental Paradigm

The cognitive developmental paradigm is strongly contested by more behaviorally oriented social scientists, as discussed later. Extensive empirical testing of the moral development model has produced an array of controversial results. The greatest controversy centers around the claims of invariant stage sequence and universality and the question of the relationship of cognitive structures to behavior. Kohlberg and his associates have not wavered in their claim that development proceeds by an invariant sequence of stages and the debate often centers around disagreements over measurement issues (Kohlberg, 1984). The debate over the claim of universality focuses on Kohlberg's formulation of the postconventional stages, especially Stage 6, because principled reasoning varies considerably across cultures (Snarey, 1985). Leaving the definitional question aside, cross-cultural studies, including those reported by Tapp and Kohlberg (1977), provide general support for the theoretical claim that stage development is universal. Critics are unwilling to accept these results, on both empirical and philosophical grounds. Although the current study is not an appropriate vehicle for extending this general debate, we offer the following criticisms as a means of delineating the relevance of cognitive developmental stage theory to our own study of legal socialization.

There is a fundamental conceptual problem with both the claim of invariant stage sequence and the claim of universality. Kohlberg (1969, 1976, 1981, 1984, 1986) has created a model of "natural" development based on particular moral preferences, e.g., a preference for stability over disorder, individualism over the claims of community, and abstract reasoning over emotional attachment. Each of these preferences can be argued or criticized on their own merits, but that is quite different from ascribing them to the real world of human development. We may (or may not) prefer a world in which children "progress" from egocentrism to an appreciation for reciprocity and ultimately achieve the capacity to reason and behave according to Kohlberg's Stage 6, but our preferences do not create empirical reality. It is a fundamental conceptual error to define the real world in terms of a model world based on the preferences of the researcher (Brodbeck, 1968). Although he has consistently denied the charge (Kohlberg, 1984), it is clear that Kohlberg confuses prescription and description. Unfortunately, the many exceptions to his model world that have been discovered during empirical investigation (Kohlberg, 1984; Modgil & Modgil, 1986; Snarey, 1985) have not prompted him to redefine the model so that it compares with empirically observable attitudes and reasoning.

This conceptual error is more than a matter of confusing preferences with a description of empirical reality, however. The substance that Kohlberg (1969, 1976, 1981, 1984, 1986) has captured in his scheme are the ideals of liberal democracy. These ideals are the dominant goals of legal and political socialization in this nation, as well as in many other Western societies. Consequently, Kohlberg's model world replicates, for the special purpose of studying legal socialization, a particular empirical reality: the rhetorical and symbolic cues that American institutions put forward in deliberate and self-conscious attempts to socialize American youth toward the ideals of liberal democracy. While Kohlberg's theory does not replicate the socialization cues or the behavioral responses that are characteristic of other societies, it does provide an empirically valid model of legal socialization in a particular legal culture. It does not possess the theoretical power claimed for it—invariant stage development and universal applicability—but it serves another empirical purpose in the study of legal socialization. Kohlberg's model allows us to determine the extent to which American institutions are successful in socializing young American citizens to the ideals of liberal democracy.

One area of cultural content inherent in the Kohlberg (1969, 1976, 1981, 1984, 1986) model merits special comment because of its particular association with legal socialization in liberal democracy. As is already clear from the earlier discussion of role-taking, Kohlberg conceptualized the interaction between reasoning and environment in terms of conflict. Cognitive moral development occurs in the process of coping with the conflicting perspectives of individualistically defined persons. This process, according to Piaget (1932, 1970/1983) and Kohlberg, is an outcome of the maturational shift from egocentrism in all cognitive development. Critics suggest that the focus on conflicting perspectives is a consequence of cultural bias and not a reflection of biological maturation (Broughton, 1986; Gilligan, 1982). It is liberal democracy, and not biology, that insists on individual autonomy and self-interested behavior. The tradition of natural rights theory (see discussion in Chapter 1), which is so closely associated with the historical development of American democractic culture, was and is a pseudo-scientific means of grounding the tenets of liberal democracy in human nature. Kohlberg's attempt is no different, the critics charge, despite his more sophisticated measurement tools. Kohlberg himself cites Rawls (1971) and Kant (1949, 1965) as his philosophical compatriots, and his extensive writings about the concept of justice intermingle philosophical and psychological perspectives.

It is clear that there are numerous problems with the cognitive developmental paradigm as it has been applied to moral and legal socialization. Its moral and cultural biases disqualify it as a general theory of human reasoning. Beyond that level of applicability, however, it remains an open question whether the cognitive developmental search for structures of reasoning fails empirically or is irrelevant to legal socialization. The conceptual problems inherent in Kohlberg's (1969, 1976, 1981, 1984, 1986) work do not imply that reasoning structures are nonexistent or that the concepts of accommodation, assimilation, and equilibration are inaccurate characterizations of the processes by which reasoning is linked to experience. The existence of reasoning structures and their role in legal socialization are empirical questions, and the work of Tapp and Levine (1977) provides ample justification for pursuing them in the current study. The relationship between cognitive structures and behaviors is a particularly important matter for further exploration. In our view this is an essential question for legal socialization. A major purpose of the present study is to explore the relevance of cognitive developmental theory to legal socialization effects, including attitudes and behaviors as well as reasoning. Kohlberg's (1969, 1984) theory and the work of Tapp and Levine (1977) both imply a relationship between reasoning and attitudes and behaviors, but do not specify it beyond discussions of role-taking opportunities. We propose to test this implied relationship empirically.

The Social Learning Paradigm

The social learning paradigm (Akers, 1985; Akers et al., 1979; Aronfreed, 1968, 1969; Bandura, 1969b, 1977) is radically different from the cognitive developmental paradigm (Kohlberg, 1969, 1984; Levine & Tapp, 1977; Piaget, 1932, 1970/1983; Tapp & Kohlberg, 1977). It emphasizes the role of affective learning processes rather than abstract reasoning and it locates the individual in a context of environmental influence. Like any major theory, it has undergone some historical change as new adherents elaborate the fundamental concepts. But the most basic characteristic of the social learning paradigm has remained unchanged over time. That is, the tension between internal and external factors that underlies most theories of human behavior is weighted in the direction of environmental influence, in contrast to the cognitive developmental emphasis on internal factors. Just as the major unresolved issue for cognitive developmentalists is the nature of the interaction between cognitive processes and the social environment, the major unresolved issue for social learning theorists is the extent to which cognitive or other internal factors play a role in a learning process controlled by contingent stimuli.

The Basic Model

For the purposes of understanding legal socialization, the social learning paradigm characterizes the way in which the social environment affects normative behavior. The basic social learning concepts do not easily encompass a complex environment, however. The paradigm has its roots in what is now called "radical behaviorism," which relies on a S → R (or some version thereof) model of human behavior (Gewirtz, 1969). At its most general level, this model does not distinguish between human and animal behavior. The social environment is conceptualized as a variety of stimuli to which the human organism responds. These stimuli are classified as antecedent and consequent, the responses as, respectively, respondent and operant. Operant conditioning is more complex and more appropriate for social behavior than respondent conditioning, largely because it requires an S → R → S sequence to incorporate the consequence into the learning process.

The power of social learning theory (Bandura, 1969b) lies in its parsimonious simplicity. The challenge when applying it is to avoid distorting the complexity of a social environment. The concept that behavior is controlled by its consequences can be demonstrated in laboratory experiments; but when it is applied outside the laboratory, the very simplicity that is its power becomes problematic. For social scientists, the issue is often not the power of the theory in the laboratory, but instead the power of the theory to account for a significant percentage of the variance in a social situation. On the other hand, control of behavior by its consequences is one popularly accepted model of social control. It is not surprising, therefore, that the use of "behavior modification" techniques and other activities of sociopolitical agents of social control is often assumed to be effective in shaping attitudes and behaviors with respect to rules (Bandura, 1969a). What operant conditioning can tell us about the effects of a complex social environment on legal socialization is another question.

Two major variations of the operant conditioning model are particularly relevant to the study of legal socialization. Internalization (Aronfreed, 1968, 1969) is the focus of many students of child development, particularly those interested in the role of discipline and other parental behavior in socializing the child. The other variation is a focus on observational learning (Bandura, 1969b, 1977). The principles of operant conditioning, in both variants, have been prominent in the long debate (White, 1974; White & Straus, 1981) over importing behavioral science techniques into public institutions and programs designed as "treatments" for those who do not conform to the law and other general societal norms. Internalization refers to a learning process whereby a continuing pattern of consequences (S → R → S), usually in a form of nurturance, results in the adoption of the mode of behavior that is being reinforced (Aronfreed). Because the behavior is maintained in the absence of the external controls, it is inferred that an "internal monitor" has been established. Observational learning focuses on modeling as a mechanism for the acquisition of behaviors (Bandura, 1969b, 1977). In modeling, the basic response is imitation followed by some form of reinforcement.

It is difficult to describe briefly either internalization (Aronfreed, 1968, 1969) or observational learning (Bandura, 1969b, 1977) without oversimplifying these well-elaborated theoretical approaches and perhaps misleading the reader. Some brief comments are necessary, however. Internalization has been primarily concerned with affective processes. Because of the prominence of this concept in the literature on early childhood, it has frequently been identified with discussions of the learning effects of punishment. The literature (Aronfreed, 1968, 1969) distinguishes between discipline that sensitizes a child to direct punitive consequences and discipline that induces an internal mechanism in the child for controlling future behavior. Both "sensitization" and "induction" techniques produce anxiety in the child (fear of punishment or feelings of shame or guilt) related to offending behavior. In theory, the anxiety created by sensitization to punishment requires the presence of the punishing agent, whereas the anxiety created by induction depends more on internalized mediating feelings, such as guilt. The popular term "conscience" is often used to refer to induced anxiety (Aronfreed, 1968).

Because it is such a common experience, the discipline setting has been a major social laboratory for those debating the relative merits of internalization (Aronfreed, 1968, 1969) and observational (Bandura, 1969a, 1969b, 1977) approaches to learning. Those who focus on observational learning argue that the primary mechanism in the discipline process is not internalization but modeling. They argue that the child is as likely to imitate good (compliant) behavior as to react with fear or guilt to forms of punishment. Studies have shown that aggressive behavior is imitated (Bandura, 1969a, 1973) and that children of aggressive punishers are themselves more aggressive toward their peers (Becker, Peterson, Luria, Shoemaker, & Helmer, 1962; Eron, Walder, Toigo, & Lefkowitz, 1963). On the other hand, other findings suggest that the child who is punished by largely nonphysical (inductive) means is more likely to develop internalized controls over his offending behavior than is the child who is physically punished (Allinsmith, 1960; Aronfreed, 1968; Sears, Maccoby, & Levin, 1957). Therefore, internalization theory holds that induced controls are motivational and not modeling responses to discipline (Aronfreed, 1968).

The problem with both of these approaches, at least in their early and rather crude form, is their lack of predictive power over time in a complex social environment. The rules or norms that a child learns in the family do transfer beyond that setting, particularly the modeling of different ways of exercising authority and the legitimacy of violence (Owen & Straus, 1975; Straus, Gelles, & Steinmetz, 1980; White, 1972, 1974). But as the social environment enlarges during the child's maturation, the nature and schedule for reinforcement varies. This introduces ambiguities into the process of anticipating and recognizing outcomes. What may be a consistently reinforced pattern of behavior for the small child in the home often becomes an inconsistently reinforced, and therefore nonpersistent, set of behaviors in the larger and more complex world beyond. The original pattern of behavior is a rule or norm for the child, but transferring that rule to other settings inevitably meets ambiguities. Because the basic S → R → S model probably cannot accommodate such ambiguities in rule transference, its applicability to legal socialization is questionable at best (White & Straus, 1981).

Recent Applications

The debate over observational versus internalization approaches to normative learning illustrates different ways to apply a theory of operant conditioning to legal socialization. Both approaches rely on affective rather than cognitive processes to explain how children learn what the social environment expects of them and how they are brought into conformity with these expectations. Two more recent elaborations of social learning theory bring the possibility of application closer to legal socialization. Both are offshoots of the observational model. One is cognitive social learning theory (Bandura, 1986; Mischel & Mischel, 1976) and the other is differential association-reinforcement theory (Akers, 1985; Akers et al., 1979; Burgess & Akers, 1966). Each theory has refined the basic social learning paradigm so that it is more applicable to a complex social environment as well as more tailored to complex human behavior. As will be seen, both theories incorporate some form of cognitive process into the general social learning concept that behavior is controlled by its consequences.

Cognitive social learning theory conceptualizes normative behavior as a process of self-regulation. This process combines the effects of consequences ($S \rightarrow R \rightarrow S$) with the constructive capacity to transform acquired information into new forms of behavior. "There is little doubt that instead of mimicking models or emitting unedited copies of earlier observations, every person constructs (generates) his renditions of 'reality' in a highly selective fashion" (Mischel & Mischel, 1976, p. 86). These "construction competencies" are cognitive in nature and are related to, but distinguishable from, an individual's propensity to perform in a particular way in particular situations. Performance is motivational and depends on incentives, while competency is not. The addition of cognitive factors reflects a recognition that complex human behavior involves more than a simple response to consequences. Thinking or reasoning plays a role in normative behavior, although expressly not the kind of autonomous role accorded to reasoning in cognitive-developmental theory.

The heart of cognitive social learning theory is the concept of self-regulatory behavior, in which cognitive activities play a particular role. Normative behavior is self-regulatory because individuals are governed in large part by their "specific expectancies about the consequences of different behavioral possibilities in that situation" (Mischel & Mischel, 1976, p. 89). These expectancies affect both competence and performance, although it is the latter that is more obviously controlled. Observational learning (information-processing) is not likely to be either inhibited or facilitated by differential consequences such as rewards or punishment but the propensity to perform what one has observed will be affected. Cognitive factors enter the picture through self-reinforcement as well. Through the setting of goals for their own performance, individuals regulate their behavior according to self-imposed "contingency rules." These specify appropriateness, standards, and consequences for different kinds of behaviors and for the particular conditions under which they might occur (Mischel & Mischel, 1976, p. 92). In short, cognitive social learning theory accommodates the problem of a complex social environment by introducing rather common sensical stipulations about cognitive guidance.

An even more cognitively based variant of social learning theory has been developed by Bandura (1986). His "social cognitive theory" joins consequences and cognitive self-regulation, but it also elaborates the cognitive aspect by emphasizing the role of "representational knowledge" in anticipating outcomes and processing external cues from modeled behavior and other positive and negative reinforcers. He is particularly interested in the fact that individuals can model behavior without an initial "trial," contrary to the assumptions of the S → R → S schema, and that their normative behaviors persist well past periodic reinforcement. He concludes, therefore, that representational knowledge has intervened and is controlling future behavior through self-regulation. While he remains committed to the basic mechanism of observational learning, Bandura argues that "contingent experiences create lasting effects mainly by fostering abstract knowledge structures, rather than by forging specific associations" (1986, p. 457). Lest this sound too much like cognitive developmentalism (he derides Kohlberg's view of reasoning as relying on "cognitive perturbations"), Bandura proposes a model of "triadic reciprocality" in which behavior, cognition, personality, and environmental influences all mutually interact (1986, pp. 23–24).

As we have argued earlier, the weakness of the basic operant conditioning model for the study of socialization is its simplicity and resulting lack of predictive power in a complex social environment. The weakness of cognitive social learning theory (or social cognitive theory) appears to be the opposite. Because it encompasses all influences in mutual interaction, the theory seems to have accommodated itself to complexity by becoming equally complex. It is hard to see how it might be falsified because there will always be one more influence to measure or one more variable to add to the mutual interaction. Cognitive social learning theory clearly differs from cognitive developmental theory in two ways: it does not postulate stages of development other than simple maturational changes and it admits a role for abstract reasoning structures only as they relate to self-regulation and the evaluation of consequences. But if it is to have value for the study of legal socialization, a theory should enable one to identify, independently of the relevant cognitive variables, those aspects of the social environment that shape normative judgment and behavior, and then to specify those relationships. Because it insists on including all variables, it is our view that cognitive social learning theory presents an inadequate alternative to cognitive developmental theory.

Differential association-reinforcement theory comes closer to providing a useful version of the social learning paradigm for the purpose of studying legal socialization. This formulation combines the concepts of operant conditioning with the theory of differential association originally developed by the criminologist Edwin H. Sutherland (Sutherland, 1947; Sutherland & Cressey, 1978). The central premises of Sutherland's theory state that deviant behavior is learned, that individuals lean toward compliance or deviance depending on how they have learned to define situations that give rise to occasions for deviance, and that this learning occurs through association with others. These social psychological aspects of this approach were given a sharpened theoretical edge by the introduction of operant conditioning concepts in the work of Burgess and Akers (1966) and later elaboration by Akers and his colleagues (Akers, 1985; Akers et al., 1979). Akers' formulation combines a concern with explaining how a certain kind of social behavior (deviance) is learned with a recognition of the role played by cognitive factors in the learning process. Because deviant behavior is one form of response to legal socialization, differential association-reinforcement theory is the most directly relevant formulation of the social learning paradigm for our purposes.

Akers (1985) defines the social learning variables in terms of their application to deviance. His first two variables are derived from Sutherland (1947). Differential association is defined as differences in interaction with compliers and noncompliers and in "exposure to their perceived norms" (p. 55), with specific reference to forms of deviant behavior. His second variable is definitions: "one's own general, conventional, conforming attitudes and specific definitions favorable or unfavorable toward" (p. 55) a specific form of deviant behavior. His third variable, differential reinforcement, introduces consequent stimuli. It refers to the increase or decrease of behaviors resulting from either reinforcement or punishment. Positive reinforcement includes a variety of possible positive social sanctions, such as social approval or direct rewards that bring about complying behavior; negative reinforcement refers primarily to avoidance behavior in the face of aversive stimuli in the environment. When the S → R → S sequence results in a decrease in a form of behavior, the process is called punishment. Punishment can be either positive, through the use of punishers, or negative, through the removal of approval or rewards. The fourth variable is imitation or modeling, which operates either through vicarious reinforcement (when the model is seen to be rewarded) or through imitation with no external reinforcement.

Akers' (1985) four variables are standard in the social learning lexicon, especially the operant conditioning model. What is significant is his attempt to explain a complex form of human behavior (deviance) in a complex social environment using only these variables. Although applications have been limited and rather crude to date, Akers et al. do report some success (1979). The focus on the learning process, external reinforcers and the role of definitions or articulated norms is directly relevant to our three-stage model of legal socialization. The feedback relationship between external reinforcement contingencies and deviant/nondeviant behavior is partly but not solely dependent on normative meanings that are learned through the same process of exposure and reinforcement. Although it is difficult to measure reinforcement patterns with any precision outside the laboratory, the addition of a cognitive variable that is specific to the normative environment and the specification of normative contingencies puts the social learning paradigm on the same empirical footing as other approaches to legal socialization.

We have argued that both internal and external factors are significant in legal socialization and that the nature of their relationship is a central empirical question. It is clear that the social learning paradigm weights external factors more heavily. Arguing specifically from differential association-reinforcement theory, one can almost say that an individual's legal socialization is an accident of exposure to particular conditions. In a sense, the theory implies the normality of deviance, i.e., whether or not any one individual becomes a complier or noncomplier depends on the interpersonal forces and other aspects of that individual's normative environment over time. Becoming a deviant can happen to anyone, on this account, depending on one's exposure to deviant behaviors and attitudes in others. Even internal factors, such as moral reasoning and rational choice, must be conceptualized as part of the feedback-based learning process—a product of the ongoing relationship between external reinforcement contingencies and self-regulation. They are a function of exposure to "definitions" of complying and noncomplying behavior, to the expression of social approval and disapproval within groups, and to the neutralizing vocabularies (Sykes & Matza, 1957) common among deviant subcultures.

One might argue that differential association-reinforcement theory supplies the behavioral basis for the influence of structural factors such as class or gender. There are, of course, too many levels of analysis for such claims to be testable. In addition, the many layers of the social environment allow considerable variation across individuals and thereby render the theory inapplicable as a general social theory. Its power to identify the consequential influences of the social environment is clear, however. Akers' (1985) description of how discriminative stimuli affect the social behavior of individuals provides an instructive example.

> In addition to the reinforcers, other stimuli are ordinarily present when behavior is reinforced—the physical surroundings, one's own feelings, others' behavior, one's own and others' spoken words, and so on. Those that customarily accompany reinforcement (or punishment) come to be associated with it; they set the stage or provide the cues for the reinforcement. In a sense, discriminative stimuli signal the actor that when they are present he or she can expect reinforcement. In social interaction the place, the people, and what they say all act as cues which allow one

to recognize situations in which certain behavior is appropriate and is apt to be rewarded or is not appropriate and is apt not to be rewarded (1985).

Translated into the particular context of legal socialization, one can see from Akers' (1985) description how questions relating to rule compliance pervade ordinary life. They cannot be relegated to a single compartment of an individual's life, to be confronted only on certain occasions or with specialized cognitive skills. The social learning paradigm directs one's attention to aspects of compliance behavior that are clearly significant to the study of legal socialization, but are not within the purview of cognitive developmental theory. The rule-governed environment is the setting for a range of behaviors and the cues provided by discriminative stimuli within that environment collectively form the engine that drives the social machine. This is not to say that the traditional concerns of legal socialization—for example, how one learns about rules, fairness, and being responsible for one's actions—are entirely reducible to a set of propositions derived from an operant conditioning model of learning. But it is to say that broader formulations of these concerns can lead to important insights about both the nature and the dynamics of legal socialization.

Telling examples abound. The general question: Why do people obey or not obey rules? is informed by understanding the processes by which consequences control behavior. Other relevant questions suggested by social learning theory are provocative in terms that are unrelated to cognitive developmental theory. Why do different conditions within the social environment tend to produce different levels of deviance? Indeed, why are entire cultures, including the affected subgroups, willing to accept and comply with differential treatment in law and custom? What are the patterns of social and political reinforcement in such cultures and how do they differ from reinforcement patterns in more egalitarian cultures? These sorts of questions result from a focus on external factors, on the power of the rule-governed social environment to control individual behavior. If legal socialization is defined as the intersection of rules and behavioral norms, it is clear that the social learning paradigm in general, and the concepts of differential association-reinforcement theory in particular, provide a useful and provocative basis for analysis.

In sum, the social learning paradigm contributes an important dimension to the study of legal socialization. It prompts one to consider the nature of the rule-enforcing environment—not so much the particular norms or enforcement practices as the general effect that legal culture has on how an individual learns to become a member of a society. It is consideration of this general content that demands a comparative test between the two theories we have been discussing. Unlike legal development theory, in which the relationship between cognitive structures and the environment is unspecified, the concept of a rule-enforcing environment is part of the logic of differential association-reinforcement theory.

Conclusion: Comparing Theories

The purpose of this chapter has been to describe two different theoretical approaches to studying legal socialization. The two theories are entirely different conceptually, and yet each has its strong adherents. In terms of our three-stage model, we found that the theories differ significantly with respect to (1) the nature and function of cognitive structures, (2) the role of norms and other situational factors, and (3) the effects of the rule-enforcing environment. Both theories include cognitive structures. Legal development theory suggests little about their relationship to rule-violating behaviors, however, whereas cognitive social learning theory claims that self-regulation encompasses both cognitive structures and behaviors. Legal development theory does not differentiate norms or attitudes from cognitive structures, and in fact does not indicate how reasoning is related to situational factors except by reference to the rather vague concept of role-taking opportunities. Cognitive social learning theory does not acknowledge a difference between reasoning and norms or attitudes. Legal development theory suggests that different kinds of experiences with particular rules and rule violations have an indirect but ultimately limiting effect on the socialization process. Cognitive social learning theory asserts that differential experience with rule-enforcing environments is critical in the shaping of future attitudes and behaviors.

The two theories also provide an intriguing contrast between possible strategies for bringing individuals to moral/legal maturity. For example, the philosopher Rawls (1971) has drawn on each paradigm in discussing how individuals come by a "sense of fairness." In his view, social learning theory suggests that "the aim of moral training is to supply missing motives," whereas for cognitive developmentalism "moral learning is not so much a matter of supplying missing motives as one of the free development of our innate intellectual and emotional capacities according to their natural bent" (1971, pp. 458–459). Both theories assert that the nature of the relationship between the person and situational factors in the rule-enforcing environment is essential. But the theories imply different techniques for socializing individuals into the moral/legal culture. For the social learning approach, the environment impinges on the individual. The task for moral/legal training, therefore, is to manipulate the environment so as to supply the *correct* missing motives. For the cognitive developmental approach, the individual in a period of disequilibrium acts on the environment in a process of testing newly developing competencies. The task for moral/legal training in this approach is to provide appropriate role-taking opportunities that will facilitate, rather than inhibit, that development.

In short, comparing these two theories of legal socialization yields both competing explanations of the process and competing strategies for manipulating it. As we suggested earlier, thinking about the content as well as the process of socialization leads one to consider strategies by which the process can be manipulated or enhanced, and thinking about the strategies leads one to recognize the importance of determining how internal and external factors interact in a context that includes rules, norms, and the exercise of authority. We turn now to operationalizing the theories: the variables, the research design, and the field setting that provided us with the opportunity to test these competing hypotheses.

3

Scope of the Study

We have argued in the first two chapters that legal socialization entails a linkage of factors internal to the individual and factors in the rule-governed environment. That linkage is the focus of this study. Our three-stage model translated the basic argument into specific variables and the discussion of the two leading theories of legal socialization suggested possible relationships among these variables. This chapter describes our research design, delineating the setting, population, key variables, hypotheses, and experimental manipulations.

Setting

In 1980, June Louin Tapp suggested that future research in the law and society field would be most productive if it turned from laboratory and classroom attitudinal surveys to natural settings. Following this suggestion, we chose a university residential community in a small town in which to test our hypotheses about legal socialization. We consider this setting to be a natural laboratory for this purpose because it is a microcosmic legal culture. Residents live in rooms or apartments that they think of as their homes for 9 months of the year. The community of residence halls involves every aspect of student life and is the base for all their social relationships. The rules governing this community include state criminal statutes and local ordinances as well as university residential regulations and rules of conduct. The norms of behavior are primarily peer norms, little influenced by parents or university staff.

Enforcement in this community stems from three sources: town police, often backed up by representatives of the state liquor commission; the university's own public safety officers; and student "residential assistants" (RAs) who live in the dorms. In each residence hall, RAs are supervised by an adult hall director who is a member of the university staff. The activities of these three sets of enforcers overlap somewhat because both the state and the university enforce drinking regulations, which are frequently violated in and around residence halls, and because violations of other criminal laws also occur on campus. The enforcement that is most salient to residents, however, is that carried out through the university's own system. Students seldom receive more than a fine from the criminal court, while they can be evicted from residence halls and suspended or dismissed from the university through the university system. Police officers tend to hand students over to university officials for punishment involving simple assaults, vandalism, stealing, sexual offenses, and alcohol use. Therefore, the university rules governing these and other behaviors are of more immediate concern to the resident population.

The university is located in a small town (population 10,000), which is 10 miles from a small city and 60 miles from a major metropolitan area. Although there is bus service to the more populated areas, students tend to spend most of their time in the university environs. The institutions of social control that most affect the students are concentrated within this small town, whether they are internal to the university or a function of the public authority. These include rules, enforcement, adjudication proceedings, and punishments. Consequently, we are confident that the university residential community comprises an identifiable legal culture. The ways in which questions of justice arise and are dealt with, the formal and informal practices of social control, and the responses of residents to enforcement reveal much about the community's normative structure.

Each fall, new members enter the community and learn what behaviors count as violating the rules, how the rules are enforced, and the norms of behavior and response to enforcement. This initiation represents the process by which a legal culture is transmitted, maintained, and possibly changed over time. Because we were interested in how individuals were socialized into the legal culture, our research design included two longitudinal studies. The first focused on the socialization effects of the legal culture for entering freshman, measured at the beginning and end of the freshman year. The second focused on the socialization effects of two different enforcement practices for the (multiclass) residents of two residence halls, measured at the beginning and end of the same academic year. This longitudinal design enabled us to test hypotheses about legal socialization, as well as to describe the legal culture itself.

Population

Two populations were studied: a random sample of entering freshman and a representative sample of residents who participated in an experimental manipulation involving four residence halls. Both populations were surveyed twice: at the beginning of fall semester during their first weekend in the residence hall and near the end of spring semester during their last few

TABLE 3.1. Demographics for university sample and experimental samples

Variable	University sample	External authority	Peer authority	Two control groups
		Experimental samples		
Gender				
Male	116 (32.9)*	29 (31.5)	23 (44.2)	40 (45.5)
Female	235 (66.6)	62 (67.4)	29 (55.8)	47 (53.4)
Age				
Mean	18.6	19.0	19.1	19.1
Standard deviation	6.86	2.28	1.00	6.72
Father's education				
Completed high school	45 (13.2)	11 (12.0)	10 (19.2)	13 (14.8)
Training school	31 (9.1)	11 (12.0)	9 (17.3)	6 (6.8)
Some College	42 (12.3)	9 (9.8)	5 (9.6)	7 (8.0)
Completed College	109 (32.0)	34 (37.0)	10 (19.2)	31 (35.2)
Graduate Degree	70 (20.5)	18 (19.6)	14 (26.9)	21 (23.9)
Other	45 (13.1)	9 (9.8)	4 (7.7)	10 (11.4)
Mother's education				
Completed high school	104 (30.4)	27 (29.3)	14 (26.9)	27 (30.7)
Training school	69 (20.2)	16 (17.4)	12 (23.1)	10 (11.4)
Some College	45 (13.2)	11 (12.0)	11 (21.2)	10 (11.4)
Completed College	74 (21.6)	21 (22.8)	8 (15.4)	22 (25.0)
Graduate Degree	24 (7.0)	10 (10.9)	4 (7.7)	10 (11.4)
Other	26 (7.6)	7 (7.6)	3 (5.8)	9 (10.2)
Father's occupation				
Professional	180 (53.4)	56 (60.9)	27 (52.9)	52 (59.8)
Prop.	43 (12.8)	15 (16.7)	8 (15.7)	8 (9.2)
Clerical/Sales	28 (8.3)	1 (1.1)	1 (2.0)	8 (9.2)
Skilled	50 (14.8)	9 (10.0)	9 (17.6)	12 (13.8)
Other	41 (12.0)	11 (11.9)	7 (13.5)	8 (9.1)
Mother's occupation				
Professional	91 (26.6)	23 (26.7)	17 (34.0)	30 (34.5)
Clerical/Sales	69 (20.2)	15 (17.4)	15 (30.0)	19 (21.8)
Not outside	114 (33.3)	22 (25.6)	14 (28.0)	24 (27.6)
Other	68 (19.9)	32 (34.8)	6 (11.5)	15 (17.0)
Class				
Freshman	342 (100.0)*	27 (29.3)	12 (23.1)	54 (61.4)
Sophmore		24 (26.1)	21 (40.4)	24 (27.3)
Junior		36 (39.1)	10 (19.2)	3 (3.4)
Senior		5 (5.4)	9 (17.3)	7 (8.0)
Origin				
In state	202 (57.5)	44 (47.8)	28 (53.8)	59 (67.0)
Out of State	144 (41.0)	48 (52.2)	24 (46.2)	28 (31.8)
Residence				
Farm	9 (2.6)	4 (4.3)	2 (3.8)	—
Fringe	13 (3.7)	4 (4.3)	2 (3.8)	1 (1.1)
Up to 2500 population	26 (7.4)	8 (8.7)	4 (7.7)	5 (5.9)
Up to 25,000 population	161 (46.0)	45 (48.9)	21 (40.4)	38 (44.7)
25,000 to 100,000 population	112 (32.0)	25 (27.2)	18 (34.6)	33 (38.8)

TABLE 3.1. *Continued*

Variable	University sample	Experimental samples: External authority	Peer authority	Two control groups
100,000 to 1 million population	26 (7.4)	5 (5.4)	5 (9.6)	7 (8.2)
1 million and high population	3 (0.9)	1 (1.1)	—	1 (1.2)
Religion				
Protestant	120 (34.7)	34 (37.0)	15 (28.8)	24 (27.9)
Catholic	167 (48.3)	41 (44.6)	29 (55.8)	45 (52.3)
Jewish	16 (4.6)	2 (2.2)	2 (3.8)	5 (5.8)
None	20 (5.8)	6 (6.5)	3 (5.8)	4 (4.7)
Other	22 (6.4)	9 (9.8)	3 (5.8)	8 (9.3)

* Valid Percentage

weeks in the residence hall for that year. The demographic profile of the two samples can be found in Table 3.1.

Variables

The primary variables were: legal reasoning, attitudes toward a set of 24 rule-violating behaviors, attitudes toward enforcing rules against those behaviors, and frequency of engaging in those behaviors. We also varied the socializing conditions for a subpopulation of our sample. These experimental conditions, to be described in detail below, included two variants of the rule-enforcing environment: a peer enforcement condition and an external authority condition. Each of the following chapters uses these variables somewhat differently. For the most part, however, legal reasoning and the socializing conditions are the independent variables whereas the attitudinal and behavioral measures are the dependent variables and represent the effects of legal socialization.

In addition, we gathered descriptive data on various other aspects of the rule-enforcing environment in the university residential community throughout the academic year. These included systematic observations by participant observers, including participants in adjudication proceedings; extensive open-ended interviews with peer enforcers and other members of the community; tape recordings of adjudication proceedings; and incident reports and detailed records of enforcement activity from the duty logs of the enforcers in each residence hall. All of these additional measures are discussed in detail in later chapters.

Legal reasoning was measured by legal development level, using the Tapp-Levine Rule-Law Interview (TLRLI) (Levine & Tapp, 1977; Tapp, 1970; Tapp & Levine, 1974). This consists of seven open-ended questions:

"What if there were no rules?"
"What is a rule?"

"What is a law?"
"Why should people follow rules?"
"Why do you follow rules?"
"Can rules be changed?"
"Are there times when it might be right to break a rule?"

Responses to each question of the TLRLI were coded into preconventional (1), conventional (2), and postconventional (3) levels of legal reasoning according to Levine and Tapp's (1977) coding procedures. To compute the LDL, it is necessary to calculate a mean LDL (on a scale from 1 to 3) based on each subject's responses to the questions. The mean LDL for the university sample of freshmen was 2.19 in the fall and 2.14 in the spring.

The attitudinal measures are based on behavioral definitions of norms and rules, as discussed in Chapter 1. Our purpose was to elicit attitudes toward rule-violating behaviors and toward enforcing the rules that prohibit those behaviors. We selected 24 actions that represented a range of rule-violating behaviors. We then asked the respondents whether they approved or disapproved (on a 6-point scale) of each of these rule-violating behaviors. The responses produced a measure of the normative status of the behaviors. We also asked whether they approved or disapproved of enforcing rules against each of those behaviors. These responses produced a measure of the enforcement status of the rules. Both normative status and enforcement status can be reported for each behavior, and by groupings or factors. We would expect these two variables to be highly negatively correlated.

Parallel behavioral measures were constructed by asking the respondents whether they had engaged in each of the 24 behaviors during the previous semester/year. We were thereby able to measure the frequency of rule-violating behavior for each individual. Measures were taken on the opening day of fall semester and in the latter part of spring semester.

These three variables are our measures of the effects of legal socialization. Instead of dealing with 24 individual items for each of the three independent variables, we conducted a varimaxrotated factor analysis on students' ratings of the behavioral measures. Items were rated on a 6-point scale from 0 (never) to 6 (20 times or more). This technique for gaining information about rule-violating behaviors was used by Straus et al. (1980) in their research on violence in the family.

Three major statistical behavioral factors emerging from the factor analysis were labeled "destructive," "disorderly," and "social disturbance" (see Table 3.2). Destructive behaviors (e.g., breaking furniture and other forms of vandalism, fighting) violate university rules, but they also violate state criminal statutes. We assume that norms for these behaviors have been strongly formed prior to entering the university community. These behaviors are likely to be less subject to change as a result of socialization within the residence halls. Disorderly behaviors (e.g., yelling, cursing at

TABLE 3.2. Factor Analysis on the list of rule-violating behaviors

Individual item	1	2	3
Destructive behavior			
Discharging fire extinguishers for fun	0.77	−0.05	0.07
Setting off fire alarms for fun	0.77	−0.03	0.05
Breaking furniture, damaging building	0.69	0.10	0.28
Taking lounge furniture	0.61	0.19	0.18
Physical fighting	0.69	0.10	0.10
Making unwanted sexual advances	0.56	0.08	0.15
Behavior causing social disturbances			
Under-age drinking in dorm room	0.01	0.69	0.24
Under-age drinking in dorm public areas	−0.11	0.70	0.18
Being drunk in dorm	0.05	0.75	0.31
Smoking marijuana in dorm	0.16	0.63	0.05
Loud parties indorm	0.15	0.55	0.32
Disorderly behavior			
Yelling or making noise in corridor	0.04	0.28	0.67
Reckless and endangering behaviors in corridor	0.18	0.20	0.62
Cursing or yelling at others	0.28	0.13	0.58
Making sexual remarks	0.06	0.16	0.52
Percantage variance accounted for	50.40	25.30	9.00
Eigenvalue	6.69	3.35	1.98

staff, reckless and endangering behavior) violate university rules, but they may or may not violate state criminal statutes and are generally not enforced by the state. They represent the kinds of disruption that often plague group living and are especially salient to life in a university community. The norms for disorderly behaviors are probably subject to change through the socialization process at the university. Social disturbance behaviors (e.g., loud and drunken parties, under-age drinking) violate university rules and state criminal statutes and are highly salient to the university community. We expect these behaviors to be subject to change through socialization.

In addition, we formulated four conceptual factors to represent clusters of behaviors that could be expected to affect the socialization process. These behaviors were labeled crime, dishonest, sex-related, and alcohol use. The statistical and conceptual factors were not mutually exclusive. Alcohol use and sex-related behaviors were assumed to be highly salient to the community attitudes toward rules and enforcement; crime and dishonest behaviors were assumed to be less salient to these attitudes. We expect that alcohol use and sex behaviors will be subject to change through socialization processes in the university community. We expect dishonest behaviors to be moderately subject to socialization change. For each factor, we computed the normative status for the behaviors, the enforcement status for the rules, and the frequency of engaging in the behaviors. The items included in these factors can be found in Table 3.3.

TABLE 3.3. Items in the Conceptual Factors

Conceptual factors	Items
Alcohol	Under-age drinking in dorm room Under-age drinking in dorm public areas Being drunk in dorm
Dishonest	Writing a paper for a friend Taking a test for a friend
Crime	Smoking marijuana in dorm Using hard drugs Breaking furniture, damaging building Stealing from others in dorm
Sex-related	Making sexual remarks Making unwanted sexual advances Sexually hassling without force Sexually harassing with force

Experimental Manipulation

As discussed in Chapter 2, the two leading theories of legal socialization provide different explanations of how individuals acquire their beliefs, values, attitudes, and behaviors with respect to rules. Legal development theory (Levine & Tapp, 1977; Tapp & Kohlberg, 1977), drawing on the cognitive developmental paradigm (Kohlberg, 1969, 1976, 1981, 1984, 1986; Piaget, 1926, 1932, 1970/1983), suggests that cognitive structures are formed through invariant stages of development. These cognitive structures provide the capacity for legal reasoning, which is then related to individuals' behaviors and attitudes through their various experiences with role-taking. Differential association-reinforcement theory (Akers, 1985; Akers et al., 1979), a version of social learning theory (Aronfreed, 1968, 1969; Bandura, 1969a, 1969b, 1977), suggests that legal socialization effects are produced by imitation or modeling, exposure to predominantly compliant or noncompliant definitions of normative behavior, and a variety of consequent stimuli. We now state these theoretical positions as competing hypotheses. Legal development theory predicts that differences in legal socialization effects will be based on legal development level and not on the socializing conditions, whereas differential association-reinforcement theory predicts that differences will be based on socializing conditions regardless of legal development level. We were able to test these hypotheses by manipulating a set of conditions critical for legal socialization, namely, the rule enforcement practices in the residence halls.

Four residence halls were chosen for experimental manipulation. Each was medium-sized (150–225 residents) and included a representative distribution by age and gender. We varied the rule-governed environment in two of the halls by creating two distinct kinds of rule enforcement. In one case, the rules were heavily and consistently enforced by residence staff and police. In the other case, the rules were enforced by a participant board of residents selected by the group for that purpose. Both conditions differed from the normal pattern of enforcement, which varied in consistency across residence halls and types of violations. The other two residence halls in the experimental manipulation served as controls. In one we provided information about the university's rules, and in the other no intervention occurred. The manipulated conditions were complicated to implement and maintain in the field setting, and we therefore describe our procedures in detail.

The first variation was the external authority condition. Under this condition, residents had no control over rule enforcement. Rules were strictly enforced by the hall director, with no discretionary flexibility. RAs were instructed to report all rule violations to the hall director, including underage drinking and the ubiquitous "hall sports." This procedure was in contrast to the typical discretionary practice in nonexperimental residence halls in which RAs would "write up" any violations they felt should be pursued but ignored many others or dealt with the offenders by informal means (Cohn & White, 1985). Under the external authority condition, all violations were reported to the hall director, who would then personally "write up" the incident and report it to the Dean of Students' office. First offenses were usually dealt with by a formal warning, unless they were serious violations, such as assault. In any case, once the formal report was made there was no opportunity for discretionary enforcement. The Dean of Students' office then proceeded to bring charges against the offender before the University Judicial Board.

The second variation was the peer community condition. Under this condition, residents operated their own internal hearing board composed entirely of peer members of their residence hall community selected to represent all residents. The RAs and/or the hall director would "write up" any violations that they believed, within their discretion, should be pursued. These "write ups" would then be reported to the internal hearing board, which would hear testimony, decide guilt or innocence, and determine a penalty for anyone who was found guilty. There was no notification of violations to the Dean of Students' office or the police. Although provision was made to call in the town police (not the Dean of Students' office) if a serious incident occurred, no such need arose during the experimental period. This internal hearing board became the primary social control mechanism for the residents of the peer community because the RAs and the hall director had no recourse beyond it.

These two conditions were established in order to test competing hypotheses generated by the two theories of legal socialization. Specifically, we varied the rule-enforcing environment to the maximum possible extent in order to provide different authority conditions and salient consequences for behavior that violated the rules. For the purposes of the experiment, only the relative significance of legal development level and the socializing conditions were at issue, that is, we were interested in whether the normative status of the behaviors, the enforcement status of the rules and rule-violating behaviors were more likely to be related to the environment or to the respondents' level of legal development. The two variations produced two kinds of models for exercising authority and distinctly different consequent stimuli. In the external authority condition, the residents had no control over rule enforcement, i.e., which rules were necessary for the safety and maintenance of the community, and how to enforce them. The existing rules—including those governing drinking, keg parties, noise, and rowdy behavior—were enforced rigidly with no allowance for discretionary judgment. By contrast, control over rule enforcement was shared by residents in the peer community condition, and the internal hearing board followed a selective enforcement policy depending on community norms and individual circumstances.

Implementing and maintaining such rigid procedures required the full commitment of the hall staff, which was not easy to achieve. The year-long experiment was viewed as a test of social control strategies, but practitioners are never as flexible and detached from consequences as are researchers in a field experiment. In order to maintain morale and commitment, as well as to monitor the process, the research team met with the staff of both residence halls each week to debrief and discuss what was happening. No field experiment can match the laboratory for controlled conditions, of course, but we were able to prevent some contamination problems and be fully informed of any difficulties as the year progressed. The reactions of residents in the external authority condition were somewhat volatile, causing discomfort for the hall staff and interesting patterns of compliance/noncompliance over the course of the year. The internal hearing board in the peer community condition was carefully monitored, as was the sometimes defensive reaction of the hall staff when the board did not support them. The weekly meetings allowed us to keep in close touch with reactions within the two experimental communities and to maintain the experimental conditions. All meetings and hearings were taped to provide an objective record of the process.

In sum, the study was designed to provide measures of the variables encompassed in our multiple-stage model from members of a community with its own rule-governed environment. Because this was a study of legal socialization, we focused on new members of a community and measured their responses to the rule-governed environment over time. We introduced controlled experimentation procedures to permit us to test hypotheses drawn from the leading theories of legal socialization. Finally, this was a natural setting in which we could reasonably assume that all members of the community had a shared understanding of the meaning of the various rules, rule-violating behaviors, and enforcement practices.

Part II

Testing Competing Hypotheses

The purpose of this section is to test the hypotheses proposed in the previous section. First, we present the changes in legal socialization that occurred over the course of a year. Second, we test the effects of our cognitive developmental factor (legal development level) versus our social learning factor (residence hall) on the behavioral and attitudinal (the normative status of the rule-violating behaviors and the enforcement status of the rules) measures. Finally, we test the effects of the interaction between the cognitive developmental factor and the social learning factor on the same behavioral and attitudinal measures.

In Chapter 4, we focus on the changes from fall to spring for students living in the different rule-enforcing environments. Specifically, we are interested in whether legal development level increases or decreases, and whether such changes vary depending on the conditions under which the respondents were living. We also are interested in the changes to the behavioral and attitudinal measures. We expect that both the frequency of engaging in rule-violating behavior and the normative status of rule-violating behavior increase from fall to spring, particularly among the freshmen. We also expect that enforcement status of the rules decreases from the fall to the spring. Changes in these measures among those living under the two experimental conditions are of special interest.

In Chapter 5, we empirically test the predictions of legal development theory (Levine & Tapp, 1977; Tapp & Kohlberg, 1977) versus social learning theory (Akers, 1985; Akers et al., 1979; Bandura, 1969b, 1977) directly. We operationalize legal development theory with the legal development level measure (Tapp & Kohlberg, 1977). Our social learning factor, the rule-enforcing environment, focuses on the two experimental residence halls (the peer authority and the external authority residence halls) and the two control halls. We compare the effects of the two variables (legal development level and residence hall) on the behavioral and attitudinal variables.

Finally, in Chapter 6, we are interested in the effects of the interaction between the legal development factor (legal development level) and the social learning factor (residence hall) after controlling for the effects of legal development level and residence hall alone. Our expectation is that the unique combination of both factors will have an effect on the behavioral and attitudinal variables. As in Chapter 5, we confine the analysis to the two experimental (peer authority and external authority) and two control residence halls.

4

Changes in Legal Socialization over Time

Our descriptive model of legal socialization includes three kinds of variables: legal reasoning, attitudinal factors rooted in particular situations, and behaviors. Our first empirical task is to describe these variables within our sample populations and show whether and how they changed during the socializing period. In this chapter we present a descriptive mapping of the socialization process, showing how legal development level, normative status of the behaviors, enforcement status of the rules, and frequency of rule-violating behaviors changed between the beginning and the end of the academic year. Possible relationships among the variables as they change, including our test of the competing hypotheses, are discussed in later chapters. Here we report data from two socialization designs: the first, which reflects natural socialization, follows a sample population of entering freshmen to the end of their first academic year; the second is an experimental design in which we manipulated the rule-enforcing environment for a representative population in four resident halls.

Two Socialization Designs

The two samples will give us two different kinds of information about the socialization process: the effects on entering members of a community of their new socializing environment and the effects of different socializing environments on similar populations. The first, or university, sample was made up entirely of freshmen (330 females and 172 males). These respondents completed the questionnaire at hall meetings during their first day on campus at the beginning of fall semester. This fall measure, then, is uncontaminated by the norms of behavior and rule enforcement in the existing community. These fall respondents are "innocents" with respect to the experiences and attitudes of those in the community, although they may not be innocent in any other respect. They are about to enter a peer community with distinct socializing characteristics: freedom from close scrutiny and control by parental and school authority, norms of behavior and rule enforcement that were shaped by peers under this condition of freedom, and the potential for continual group activities that enhance and promote peer social bonding (Hirschi, 1969). These characteristics combine to produce a lively environment for legal socialization, especially with respect to issues of rules, fairness, and being responsible for one's actions.

The university sample meets two requirements for one kind of information about socialization. First, the respondents are basically similar at entrance in socioeconomic status and age. While they are coming together, for the first time, from middle class homes all along the east coast, their background is sufficiently similar to exclude major effects for background variation. They are also all either 17 or 18 years old and just graduated (liberated) from similar institutions: the American middle-class high school. Developmentalists (Kohlberg, 1969, 1976, 1981; Piaget, 1970/1983) tell us that such individuals are in a crucial transitional state, in terms of social maturation, and probably in a receptive state of psychological "disequilibrium" as well. In short, as fellow innocents, they face the socializing experiences to come on the same basis. During the socializing period, their normative order will be assaulted and perhaps disrupted by the same forces. So these respondents meet another requirement necessary for a study of socialization: they undergo the same socializing experiences for a significant period of time. The second measure of our variables is taken near the end of the first academic year.

The second kind of information about socialization can be derived from our second or experimental sample. This sample (138 females and 92 males) includes all four classes, although it is predominantly freshmen and sophomores. Except for the freshmen, these respondents are not "innocents." The socialization information that this sample yields, therefore, is based on the experimental manipulation of socializing conditions discussed in Chapter 3. Briefly restated, we varied the rule-enforcing environment in two residence halls to provide different authority conditions (peer authority and external authority) and differing salient consequences for behavior that violated the rules. Two other residence halls were used as controls, with no intervention in one and the provision of special information about the rules in the other. Although the respondents were not, except for the freshmen, new members of the community, we varied the socializing conditions to produce different experiences with rules and enforcement for four subsamples. This procedure provided a second kind of information about legal socialization.

The Socialization Variables

Legal Development Level

Legal development level (LDL) was measured at the beginning of fall semester and near the end of spring semester in both the university sample and the experimental sample. Several studies using this measure (Levine, 1979; Levine & Tapp, 1977; Tapp & Kohlberg, 1977) indicate that college students are more likely to use prescriptive (conventional) than proscriptive (preconventional) criteria in legal reasoning, but that some at that age level also use beneficial-rational (postconventional) criteria. Therefore, we expect to find most of our sample at Level 2, with some at Level 3. Because disequilibrium is characteristic of their maturational stage (late adolescence), cognitive developmental theory (Piaget, 1926, 1970/1983) would suggest the possibility of significant change during the socialization period. The direction of change is problematic, however, because studies show that legal development can decline as well as advance (see Levine & Tapp, 1977). Strict cognitive developmentalists would deny that possibility, but legal development theorists (Levine & Tapp, 1977) acknowledge it. As was discussed in Chapter 2, legal development theory does not assume strict unidirectionality. Kohlberg (1984) has admitted some instability, but argues that such minor shifts do not affect the invariant sequence overall.

Both the magnitude and direction of change in legal development level depend in part on the kind of role-taking experiences available to the respondents, according to legal development theory (Levine & Tapp, 1977; Tapp & Kohlberg, 1977). As discussed in Chapter 3, these role-taking experiences provide the basis for interaction between the individual and the environment and therefore the conditions for the cognitive developmental processes of accommodation, assimilation, and equilibration to occur. The only longitudinal study we know of that measures change in legal development level during a relevant role-taking experience was reported by Tapp et al. (1983). Tapp et al. measured legal development level in members of a jury before a trial and again after the jury completed its deliberations. The case involved provocative issues of justice in this country, particularly in terms of diverse perspectives, and the jury process was therefore considered a salient role-taking experience for changes in legal development. The trial raised many questions about the effects of racial discrimination in our society, and especially about whether laws had been enforced even-handedly against Native Americans. Exposure to these diverse perspectives on law enforcement resulted in a significant increase in legal development level among the jurors, according to this study.

The implications for direction of change in legal development level of our two socialization designs, and of the experimental manipulations in socializing environment inherent in the second design, are not clear. For the university sample, the college experience in itself is one of weakened external constraints. There is no basis for predicting how this kind of difference in the life of a late adolescent affects direction of change in legal development, however. One could argue that the weakened external constraints and easy availability of opportunities to violate the rules might produce fear of disorder and therefore a regression toward Tapp and Kohlberg's (1977) Stage 3 law-and-order conventionality. On the other hand, the wider range of role-taking opportunities in such an environment could engender the diverse perspectives that facilitate an increase in legal development level. It is a measure of the limitations of cognitive developmental theory that it does not provide a clear basis for predicting direction of change in the context of legal socialization.

Our second socialization design suggests a clearer basis for predicting change in legal development level. The experimental conditions imply different experiences of authority and different role-taking opportunities. One would expect that the external authority condition places the community member in potential conflict with rule enforcement and induces antiauthoritarian social bonding with peers. It is possible that such individuals would lean toward a prohibitive preconventionality and therefore a decline in legal development level. The peer authority condition changes the authority structure from hierarchical to communitarian, which could have the effect of minimizing conflict with rule enforcement and enhancing egalitarian social bonding with peers. It is possible that these individuals would lean toward a beneficial-rational postconventionality, and therefore an increase in legal development level. These different experiences of authority also imply entirely different role-taking possibilities. In the other-regulated situation, perspectives on rules and norms of behavior may be limited to those of enforcer and enforcee. In the self-regulated situation, these perspectives are as diverse as those in the community. The experience of having cases heard and decided by community members, which is specifically provided for in the peer authority condition, should enhance the possibility that legal development levels would increase.

Attitudinal Variables

The two attitudinal variables, the normative status of the behaviors and the enforcement status of the rules, should change in response to social bonding among peers and experiences in situations in which the rule-violating behaviors occur and situations in which the rules are enforced. The innocents of the university sample are being socialized into a peer community with an existing set of behavioral norms. While we do not assume that the level of approval or disapproval of specific behaviors is the same for each member of this community, pilot studies of norms indicated that there is a normal distribution of responses around the mean with the exception of destructive, sex, crime, and dishonest behaviors, which are all positively skewed with the majority of students reporting that they do not approve of the behavior (i.e., low normative status).

Our first socialization design, using the university sample, looks at the effects of the college experience on innocents. Differential association-reinforcement theory suggests that an "excess of definitions favorable to violation of law" (Sutherland & Cressey, 1978, pp. 75–77) is an important factor in delinquency. A more recent formulation points to "the presence of normative statements, definitions and verbalizations" (Akers, 1985, p. 41) that are favorable to rule violation, in the process of learning deviance. On the basis of this theoretical perspective, entering individuals should tend to follow the direction of the existing norms for those behaviors that are salient to community life. Therefore, we would expect change in the direction of community norms in the normative status of behaviors that violate rules governing "partying," group activities, and sexual behavior, even among those respondents who do not engage in these behaviors frequently. We expect to find less or no movement in the normative status of behaviors that are less salient to community life. Both individual and community change will be measured in order to detect the existence of normative subgroups.

Attitudes toward rule enforcement are normative in two respects. First, our measure is exactly parallel to our measure of the normative status of behaviors in that it asks for respondents' level of approval or disapproval of enforcing the rule against each of the behaviors. Therefore, these attitudes reflect the respondents' evaluation of the particular behavior as well as of the rule. Second, enforcing a rule is an exercise of authority. Therefore, attitudes toward enforcement reflect the legitimacy, or illegitimacy, of that authority in the eyes of the respondents. The addition of this second normative aspect puts the enforcement status of the rule in a different, and less predictable, theoretical category because differential association and reinforcement are not necessarily the major bases for prediction. The enforcement status of a rule is more "legalistic" in that it is an indicator of one's view of the role of general rules in a community and the legitimacy of enforcing them. Although a situational variable, it is closer to legal reasoning than the normative status of a behavior. Nonetheless, we believe that group norms will be as significant for enforcement status as for normative status because of the weakened external constraints that characterize these new socializing conditions. In this natural socialization design, we expect enforcement status to move in the same direction as normative status for behaviors that are salient to the community and to show little change for other behaviors.

The experimental design represents a twofold intervention on this natural setting for legal socialization. By varying the rule-enforcing environment, we introduced different models of authority and different consequent stimuli. Because the purpose of the intervention was to test the relative predictive power of our two theories, we were not primarily concerned with predicting the attitudinal socialization effects associated with each variant. We can speculate about the possible impact of the two kinds of experiences with authority, however. Our theory of social learning directs attention to modeling, differential association, and differential reinforcement. Our setting offers two sources of authority, each of which could be imitated, depending on the attractiveness of the external authority and the strength of group norms. The strong effect of peers in late adolescence points to the possible impact of group norms through differential association. The consequent stimuli provided by peer authority should differ from that provided by external authority depending on the kind of behavior involved, with peer authority reflecting the prevailing behavioral norms in the community and external authority enforcing the rules regardless of community norms. It is not clear whether these consequent stimuli affect attitudes as strongly as they affect behaviors, however.

Rule-Violating Behaviors

We measured the frequency of rule-violating behaviors by self-report. According to our multiple-stage model, the relationship between reasoning and behaviors is problematic, as is the relationship between the attitudinal measures and the behaviors. It is not likely that these relationships will be completely inconsistent, however, so we assume that weakened external constraints and peer approval of certain kinds of behaviors result in an increase in rule violation. Entering freshmen in the natural socialization design will experience strong social bonding around certain kinds of behaviors that are especially salient to the community. Behaviors related to "partying," including illegal drinking (the drinking age is 21), loud stereos, kegs, and permissive sexual behavior, are not only salient to the peer community but also particularly susceptible to group activity. The minimal external constraints provide conditions conducive to an increase in rule-violating behavior.

The focus of enforcement is behaviors, although enforcers in the university setting do attempt to change attitudes as well. Our experimental design varied the source of enforcement: external authority contrasted with peer authority. Both manipulations focused on the actual enforcement of the rules. In a situation of weakened constraints and strong social bonding, we would expect the strict enforcement condition to result in a decrease in rule-violating behaviors over time. We would expect the peer authority condition to result in a self-reported level of rule-violating behaviors that conforms to the norms of the community. There are many confounding possibilities, however, which is why the relationship between reasoning, norms and behaviors is so intriguing. The magnitude and direction of change in behaviors are both dependent on the reinforcement contingencies that developed over a period of time in each of the experimental settings, factors that could not be controlled in detail during a large-scale field experiment.

The Statistical and Conceptual Factors

As described in Chapter 3, we do not report findings for each specific behavior but rather for clusters of behaviors. For the statistical factors, we assume that destructive behaviors will not be affected by socialization processes within the university community, but that disorderly and social disturbance behaviors will be affected. Much of the social life of the university community centers around the activities governed by the rules covering disorderly and social disturbance behaviors. Therefore, they are particularly salient to attitudes toward these behaviors and toward enforcing rules against them. The four conceptual factors also differ with respect to their salience and susceptibility to socialization change. We anticipate that alcohol and sex behaviors are particularly salient to this community, dishonest behaviors less so, and crime behaviors not at all.

Analysis Plan

As explained earlier, two different kinds of procedures were used to determine changes from fall to spring. The first statistical techniques conducted were *t*-tests on the fall and spring measures. These measures (described in Chapter 3) included legal development level, frequency of engaging in three statistical and four conceptual rule-violating behaviors, and the normative status of the behaviors and the enforcement status of the rules for the same seven behavioral factors. The analyses were conducted on the university sample of 387 college freshmen who completed the questionnaires at the beginning of the fall semester and the end of the spring semester. In addition, the analyses were conducted separately on the samples from each of the two experimental dormitories and the combined two control resident halls. The second analyses conducted were the correlations between fall and spring. The chi square test for differences between correlations (Edwards, 1984) was conducted to determine whether the correlations were stronger between the different factors. These analyses were also conducted on both the freshmen sample and the experimental/control samples.

Results

Changes in Legal Measures from Fall to Spring

Paired-sample *t*-tests were conducted to determine the effect of time (fall, spring) on subjects' legal development level, reports of normative status of the behaviors and enforcement status of the rules, and the frequency of rule-violating behaviors. Please remember that normative status refers to the extent to which subjects approved of the rule-violating behaviors and enforcement status refers to the extent to which subjects approve of enforcing rules against these behaviors. The analyses were conducted for both the freshmen university sample and the experimental sample (parti-

TABLE 4.1. Means, standard deviations, and *t* Values for changes from fall to spring for the university sample

Measures	Fall	Spring	*t*	*p*	df
Behavior					
Destructive	3.51 (6.13)	2.60 (8.20)	1.86	ns	339
Social disturbance	36.52 (20.54)	47.19 (24.46)	−9.89	0.001	329
Disorderly	20.24 (15.20)	34.58 (24.66)	−11.15	0.001	330
Alcohol use	44.08 (20.65)	59.79 (26.89)	−12.52	0.001	333
Dishonest	4.46 (8.97)	1.89 (9.40)	4.61	0.001	344
Crime	12.09 (14.17)	9.40 (12.77)	5.23	0.001	334
Sex-related	17.19 (14.51)	15.27 (13.78)	2.23	0.027	326
Normative status					
Destructive	8.74 (10.55)	10.65 (12.49)	−2.70	0.007	334
Social disturbance	48.16 (22.58)	55.59 (20.91)	−6.90	0.001	338
Disorderly	39.16 (17.82)	42.03 (18.96)	−2.69	0.007	334
Alcohol use	57.53 (24.41)	64.95 (21.84)	−6.08	0.001	343
Dishonest	14.74 (17.98)	14.69 (19.33)	0.04	ns	346
Crime	11.87 (13.11)	15.69 (16.12)	−5.10	0.001	338
Sex-related	16.78 (14.66)	18.42 (15.51)	−1.82	ns	331
Enforcement status					
Destructive	81.90 (23.16)	85.29 (16.25)	−2.57	0.011	314
Social disturbance	54.11 (21.47)	48.72 (21.47)	4.25	0.001	327
Disorderly	58.13 (19.92)	57.84 (20.31)	0.23	ns	315
Alcohol use	46.50 (24.53)	39.47 (23.39)	4.89	0.001	333
Dishonest	70.97 (28.58)	75.50 (26.34)	−2.31	0.022	333
Crime	81.57 (21.82)	82.70 (17.44)	−0.86	ns	339
Sex-related	73.97 (23.72)	74.95 (20.04)	−0.67	ns	317
Legal development level (LDL)	2.19 (0.27)	2.14 (0.27)	2.54	0.012	322

cipants who lived in the two experimental and the two combined control residence halls).

University Freshman Sample

The means and standard deviations for the university sample can be found in Table 4.1. What is most striking about these data is that the normative status of the rule-violating behaviors increases from the beginning to the end of the freshmen year (fall to spring) with the exception of dishonest and sex-related behaviors. This means that subjects are more approving or less disapproving of these behaviors in the spring than in the fall. Legal development level decreases from the fall to the spring.

The data are a little more complicated when one considers both enforcement status of the rule-violating behaviors and the actual frequency of the same rule-violating behaviors. The enforcement status of social disturbance and alcohol rules decreases, which is consistent with the increases in the normative status. In contrast, the enforcement status of destructive and dishonest rules increases, and remains the same for disorderly, crime, and sex rules.

The frequency of social disturbance, disorderly, and alcohol behaviors increases from fall to spring. This is consistent with normative status data. In contrast, the frequency of dishonest, crime, and sex-related behaviors decreases and the frequency of destructive behaviors is unchanged.

Experimental Sample

The means and standard deviations can be found in Table 4.2. The first residence hall of interest would be the combined control halls, because one would expect that they would be comparable to the university freshmen sample. The only difference is that the control halls contained sophomores, juniors, and seniors as well as freshmen.

In general, the residents of the control halls show the same significant effects as the university sample, although not as dramatically. The normative status of all the rule-violating behaviors decreases from the fall to the spring with the exception of dishonest behaviors. This is very comparable to the university sample. Legal development level tends to decrease from the fall to the spring ($p < 0.07$) as was the case for the university sample. The decreases in enforcement status of social disturbance and alcohol rules from the fall to the spring are also similar to the university sample. Finally the increases in the frequency of social disturbance, disorderly, and alcohol use behaviors are the same as in the university sample.

The next question is how changes in the control residence halls compare to those in the two experimental residence halls. In contrast to the significant changes in the control halls, the two experimental residence halls show no significant changes from fall to spring. A more fine-grained analysis of the direction of the t values shows that different trends occurred

TABLE 4.2. Means, standard deviations, and *t* Values for changes from fall to spring for the experimental sample

Behavior	Fall	Spring	*t*	*p*	df
External authority					
Destructive	1.85 (5.12)	3.22 (10.84)	−1.14	ns	90
Social disturbance	41.18 (24.22)	39.30 (27.04)	0.82	ns	90
Disorderly	30.78 (23.07)	31.58 (24.39)	−0.35	ns	88
Alcohol use	49.69 (25.83)	47.34 (30.41)	0.81	ns	90
Dishonest	1.92 (5.13)	3.02 (12.58)	−0.78	ns	91
Crime	9.75 (11.77)	9.75 (15.26)	0.00	ns	88
Sex-related	15.00 (13.92)	15.55 (15.19)	−0.36	ns	90
Peer authority					
Destructive	3.07 (5.90)	3.00 (8.39)	0.05	ns	50
Social disturbance	47.40 (27.41)	41.60 (26.21)	1.42	ns	50
Disorderly	31.50 (24.47)	34.92 (24.29)	−0.97	ns	50
Alcohol use	58.44 (30.48)	51.67 (30.64)	1.52	ns	50
Dishonest	2.88 (6.58)	2.56 (8.82)	0.25	ns	52
Crime	8.33 (11.47)	7.48 (13.58)	0.50	ns	49
Sex-related	16.58 (17.81)	15.73 (11.95)	0.33	ns	49
Controls					
Destructive	3.25 (5.12)	1.72 (2.89)	3.26	0.002	85
Social disturbance	38.27 (23.55)	44.48 (24.91)	−3.26	0.002	81
Disorderly	26.47 (21.93)	33.89 (26.55)	−2.74	0.008	82
Alcohol use	47.39 (25.49)	57.36 (28.55)	−4.03	0.000	83
Dishonest	2.01 (4.75)	1.44 (4.79)	0.85	ns	87
Crime	10.04 (11.94)	8.03 (11.40)	−2.03	0.045	83
Sex-related	15.22 (12.91)	13.68 (10.99)	1.14	ns	81

TABLE 4.2. *Continued*

Normative Status	Fall	Spring	t	p	df
External authority					
Destructive	8.07	8.48	−0.24	ns	88
	(12.41)	(13.60)			
Social disturbance	52.75	54.69	−0.92	ns	86
	(22.31)	(21.81)			
Disorderly	39.80	40.05	−0.13	ns	85
	(18.16)	(19.42)			
Alcohol use	59.49	63.23	−1.56	ns	89
	(22.89)	(22.70)			
Honest	12.73	11.99	0.36	ns	91
	(17.32)	(19.53)			
Crime	14.41	15.09	−0.43	ns	87
	(14.43)	(14.28)			
Sex-related	16.42	18.19	−0.93	ns	85
	(13.18)	(16.21)			
Peer authority					
Destructive	10.06	9.73	0.23	ns	51
	(12.03)	(10.17)			
Social disturbance	56.53	52.52	1.23	ns	49
	(24.14)	(18.07)			
Disorderly	40.20	40.03	0.05	ns	51
	(16.79)	(19.54)			
Alcohol use	62.64	59.26	0.80	ns	51
	(25.07)	(21.76)			
Honest	15.03	13.40	0.59	ns	51
	(19.37)	(19.80)			
Crime	15.10	15.10	0.00	ns	48
	(15.51)	(14.42)			
Sex-related	15.75	16.58	−0.28	ns	50
	(18.22)	(12.75)			
Controls					
Destructive	9.05	13.46	−2.85	0.006	81
	(11.51)	(15.31)			
Social disturbance	48.62	56.42	−4.11	0.000	82
	(23.00)	(20.15)			
Disorderly	38.29	44.20	−2.72	0.008	84
	(16.75)	(21.45)			
Alcohol use	57.74	65.74	−3.44	0.001	84
	(25.47)	(20.98)			
Honest	12.35	14.12	−0.72	ns	85
	(16.19)	(20.05)			
Crime	12.35	15.96	−2.25	0.027	83
	(14.38)	(15.20)			
Sex-related	14.89	19.79	−2.63	0.01	80
	(19.79)	(17.86)			

TABLE 4.2. *Continued*

Enforcement status	Fall	Spring	*t*	*p*	df
External authority					
Destructive	87.30 (18.37)	87.26 (18.51)	0.02	ns	84
Social disturbance	50.84 (21.03)	50.00 (22.99)	0.34	ns	87
Disorderly	59.65 (20.09)	59.60 (19.90)	0.02	ns	82
Alcohol use	44.19 (23.54)	42.20 (25.07)	0.73	ns	89
Honest	76.68 (28.10)	71.82 (32.82)	1.25	ns	89
Crime	83.68 (19.17)	82.29 (17.01)	0.63	ns	84
Sex-related	77.78 (17.76)	75.46 (21.55)	1.03	ns	81
Peer authority					
Destructive	86.60 (15.30)	88.50 (15.97)	−0.97	ns	49
Social disturbance	50.78 (21.92)	50.35 (14.48)	0.13	ns	47
Disorderly	58.25 (18.66)	58.33 (21.55)	−0.03	ns	49
Alcohol use	43.98 (24.14)	41.09 (17.52)	0.71	ns	48
Honest	74.83 (30.83)	77.55 (27.39)	−0.52	ns	49
Crime	85.90 (15.96)	84.75 (12.39)	0.53	ns	47
Sex-related	76.19 (22.87)	79.42 (15.60)	−1.05	ns	49
Controls					
Destructive	84.46 (19.99)	83.78 (19.59)	0.26	ns	74
Social disturbance	53.03 (21.48)	45.96 (20.76)	2.73	0.008	76
Disorderly	60.91 (19.40)	57.18 (23.10)	1.35	ns	76
Alcohol use	42.88 (25.16)	36.25 (22.00)	2.21	0.03	78
Honest	73.09 (27.98)	75.00 (28.39)	−0.48	ns	83
Crime	82.63 (19.09)	81.65 (20.10)	0.37	ns	77
Sex-related	78.11 (21.51)	74.78 (22.17)	1.10	ns	75

Legal Development Level	Fall	Spring	*t*	*p*	*n*
External authority	2.20 (0.27)	2.11 (0.31)	0.18	0.86	39
Peer authority	2.10 (0.32)	2.11 (0.32)	−0.12	0.91	49
Controls	2.14 (0.25)	2.06 (0.26)	1.83	0.07	83

in the two experimental halls. In the external authority hall, the normative status of rule-violating behaviors increases, while legal development level and the enforcement status of the rules decrease. In contrast, in the peer authority hall, normative status decreases, while legal development level and enforcement status increase. None of these changes are significant, but they do suggest differences between the two different experimental halls. More evidence comes from analyzing the standard deviations of the normative status of social disturbance, alcohol use, and sex-related behaviors in the two halls. One notices that the standard deviations do not change from fall to spring in the external authority hall, whereas they decrease from fall to spring in the peer authority hall. This suggests that residents of the peer authority hall were becoming more similar in their norms. This did not happen in the external authority hall.

University Sample

The correlations between the fall and spring legal measures were calculated. The correlations can be found in Table 4.3. These correlation

TABLE 4.3. Fall to spring correlations

	Correlation	*p*	*n*
Behavior			
Destructive	0.25	0.001	339
Social disturbance	0.63	0.001	329
Disorderly	0.39	0.001	330
Alcohol use	0.56	0.001	333
Dishonest	0.15	0.003	344
Sex-related	0.40	0.001	326
Crime	0.67	0.001	334
Normative status			
Destructive	0.38	0.001	334
Social disturbance	0.59	0.001	338
Disorderly	0.44	0.001	334
Alcohol use	0.53	0.001	343
Dishonest	0.41	0.001	346
Sex-related	0.42	0.001	331
Crime	0.57	0.001	338
Enforcement status			
Destructive	0.34	0.001	314
Social disturbance	0.43	0.001	327
Disorderly	0.38	0.001	315
Alcohol use	0.40	0.001	333
Dishonest	0.15	0.003	333
Sex-related	0.32	0.001	317
Crime	0.28	0.001	322
Legal development level	0.41	0.001	322

coefficients indicate the relationship between one's fall measure and one's spring measure. The higher the correlation, the more similar the relative position in the fall and spring; the lower the correlation, the less similar the relative position in the fall and spring.

The correlations between the normative status of social disturbance, alcohol use, and crime behaviors in the fall and spring are significantly higher than the correlations between the normative status of the other rule-violating behaviors. The correlation between the enforcement status of social disturbance and alcohol use rules in the fall and spring is significantly higher than the enforcement status of destructive, sex-related, and crime behaviors in the fall and spring. Finally the correlation between the frequency of social disturbance, alcohol use, and crime behaviors in the fall and spring is significantly higher than the correlation between the frequency of destructive, disorderly, and sex-related behaviors.

Although the average normative status and frequency of the behavior may increase while the average enforcement status decreases from the fall to the spring, the relative positions within these distributions do not change from the fall to the spring. In contrast, the lowest correlation is between the frequency of destructive behaviors in the fall and spring. Different people are engaging in the destructive behaviors in the fall and spring. It may be that there is more exposure to social disturbance behaviors than destructive behaviors; therefore the normative status and the frequency of destructive behaviors may be subject to more change.

The correlation between legal development level in the fall and spring is 0.408 ($p < 0.0001$). This is a moderately strong relationship.

Experimental Sample

Comparing the data of the two experimental residence halls and the combined control hall in Table 4.4, one is struck by the similarly relative high correlations between the normative status of the rule-violating behaviors in the fall and spring in the external authority hall and the low correlations between the normative status of disorderly, alcohol use, and sex-related behaviors in the fall and spring in the peer authority hall. The range of correlations in the peer authority hall (from 0.10 to 0.62) is much more dramatic than the changes in either the external authority hall (0.38 to 0.53) or the control halls (0.28 to 0.43).

In terms of changes in legal development level from fall to spring, the two control dorms have the highest and most significant correlation (0.322, $p < 0.003$). The correlation in the external authority residence hall has borderline significance of 0.276 ($p < 0.005$), whereas the correlation in the peer authority residence hall is not significant ($r = 0.164$). This suggests that the most change in relative position in legal development level occurred in the peer authority residence hall.

TABLE 4.4. Fall to spring correlations (all four residence halls)

	External authority			Peer authority			Controls		
Measures	Correlation	*p*	*n*	Correlation	*p*	*n*	Correlation	*p*	*n*
Behavior									
Destructive	0.13	ns	90	0.02	ns	50	0.54	0.001	85
Social disturbance	0.64	0.001	90	0.42	0.001	50	0.75	0.001	81
Disorderly	0.59	0.001	88	0.48	0.001	50	0.50	0.001	82
Alcohol use	0.53	0.001	90	0.47	0.001	50	0.66	0.001	83
Dishonest	0.03	ns	91	0.29	0.018	52	0.12	ns	87
Sex-related	0.49	0.001	90	0.32	0.013	49	0.49	0.001	81
Crime	0.53	0.001	88	0.55	0.001	49	0.70	0.001	83
Normative status									
Destructive	0.20	0.028	88	0.59	0.001	51	0.49	0.001	81
Social disturbance	0.61	0.001	86	0.45	0.001	49	0.69	0.001	82
Disorderly	0.58	0.001	85	0.21	ns	51	0.49	0.001	84
Alcohol use	0.51	0.001	89	0.18	ns	51	0.59	0.001	84
Dishonest	0.46	0.001	91	0.50	0.001	51	0.22	0.019	85
Sex-related	0.31	0.002	85	0.10	ns	50	0.47	0.001	80
Crime	0.49	0.001	87	0.53	0.001	48	0.51	0.001	83
Enforcement status									
Destructive	0.52	0.001	84	0.62	0.001	49	0.38	0.001	74
Social disturbance	0.46	0.001	87	0.33	0.011	47	0.43	0.001	76
Disorderly	0.53	0.001	82	0.50	0.001	49	0.36	0.001	76
Alcohol use	0.43	0.001	89	0.10	ns	48	0.38	0.001	78
Dishonest	0.28	0.004	89	0.21	ns	49	0.19	0.045	83
Sex-related	0.48	0.001	81	0.42	0.001	49	0.28	0.007	75
Crime	0.38	0.001	84	0.46	0.001	47	0.31	0.003	78
Legal development level	0.28	0.005	81	0.16	ns	47	0.32	0.003	78

Discussion

Our two socialization designs have revealed distinct difference between the effects resulting from the natural socialization process and those resulting from our experimental conditions. The university sample shows an increase in the normative status of all the rule-violating behaviors except those in the dishonesty factor. (The increase in sex-related behaviors was not significant.) These findings indicate that the normative structure of the community into which the "innocents" are being socialized has an important impact on new members. New members change their attitudes toward rule-violating behaviors in the direction of community norms. The only exception to this finding, dishonest behaviors, is not central to the social life of the community and may not be relevant to the social bonding process. The weakening of external constraints for youths entering college occurs primarily with respect to social and group behaviors.

The findings that emerge from the experimental manipulation indicate that the legal socialization process is susceptible to differences in rule-enforcing conditions. Unlike the university sample, respondents in our experimental sample show no significant changes in the normative status of any of the rule-violating behaviors or in the enforcement status of the rules. This finding demonstrates that the interventions successfully undermined the natural socialization process or that any changes occurred before the study began (because upperclassmen predominate). A close look at the *t* values and the standard deviations reveals more about the effects of the interventions. The external authority condition produced a trend that was similar to the natural socializing conditions as the normative status of rule-violating behaviors increased. An opposite trend was found among the peer authority respondents, the only group for whom normative status decreased. The standard deviations of some behaviors (social disturbance, alcohol use, and sex-related behaviors) for the two sets of respondents suggest that the peer authority residents were becoming more cohesive through the socialization period, with no such change occurring among the external authority residents. The cohesiveness effect is consistent with the peer-based exercise of authority which was being implemented. We can speculate that the peer authority residents were making judgments about rule-violating behaviors on the basis of their effects on the community rather than personal or group desires to be free of external constraints.

Another significant difference between the two samples arises when we compare the two attitudinal variables. The normative status of the rule-violating behaviors shows a more consistent effect from all the socializing conditions than does the enforcement status of the rules. This appears to be a direct effect of group norms. For the university sample, the enforcement status of social disturbance and alcohol use behaviors decreases, consistent with the increases in normative status for the same behaviors. We would expect that attitudes toward "partying" behavior, which is central to the social life of the community, would reflect the general group norms of approval for the behaviors and disapproval for enforcing rules against them. We have also argued that the enforcement status of the rules reflects a more legalistic attitude in that one's conception of the role of general rules in a community and the legitimacy of authority are invoked. Thus the increase in enforcement status for destructive and dishonest behaviors suggests a different judgment about the impact of these behaviors on the community. The fact that there is no change in the enforcement status of rules governing disorderly, crime, and sex-related behaviors may indicate that the respondents in the university sample are ambivalent about the intrusion of authority in these areas.

Our experimental manipulation of rule-enforcing conditions produced a more consistent pattern of relationships between the normative status of rule-violating behaviors and the enforcement status of the rules. The effects for attitudes toward enforcement were the same as the effects for attitudes toward the rule-violating behaviors. While there were no statistically significant changes from fall to spring, the t values indicate consistent trends: increasing normative status and decreasing enforcement status under the external authority conditions and decreasing normative status and increasing enforcement status under the peer authority conditions. These are the patterns we would expect if the intervention was successful. They also indicate that rule enforcement is more acceptable when carried out under a participatory form of authority, regardless of the kind of behavior being proscribed. This finding further suggests that social bonding under conditions where authority is rejected is very different from social bonding under conditions in which authority is within the control of the community itself.

5

Testing Competing Hypotheses

In the preceding chapter, we found that manipulating the rule-enforcing conditions in two residence halls resulted in significantly different legal socialization effects than were produced through the natural socialization process. In order to better understand these varying effects, we tested competing hypotheses drawn from the two leading theories of legal socialization. According to legal development theory (Levine & Tapp, 1977; Tapp & Kohlberg, 1977; Tapp & Levine, 1970), legal socialization occurs through stage-dependent change in the cognitive structures that produce legal reasoning, which is then reflected in an individual's legal development level. By contrast, social learning theory (Akers, 1985; Akers et al., 1979; Aronfreed, 1968, 1969; Bandura, 1969a, 1969b, 1977) holds that differential association and reinforcement contingencies shape an individual's attitudes and behaviors with respect to rules and the exercise of authority and that these factors therefore control the learning process that is legal socialization.

In this chapter, we restate in brief the basic concepts of each of these theories of legal socialization. We then report the results of our experimental manipulation of rule-enforcing conditions in which we tested hypotheses drawn from the two theories.

The Two Hypotheses

Legal Development Theory

We discussed the two major theories of legal socialization in Chapter 2, with particular attention to the relative weight accorded to internal and external factors. The cognitive developmental paradigm focuses on internal factors, specifically the process by which cognitive structures are created and evolve as the individual's reasoning capacity adapts to incoming information. Legal development theory (Levine & Tapp, 1977; Tapp & Kohlberg, 1977) postulates that the cognitive structures used in legal reasoning are "rules for processing information" that change in a dialectical process according to stages. Each stage "represents a qualitatively different organization of thought, not a set of specific beliefs" (Tapp & Kohlberg, 1977, p. 90). Thus legal socialization, on this account, is a process of social learning that is largely dependent on one's developing capacity for reasoning about rules, fairness and being responsible for one's actions.

There are six stages of legal development (Levine & Tapp, 1977; Tapp & Kohlberg, 1977; Tapp & Levine, 1970, 1974). These can be described in terms of Kohlberg's (1969, 1976, 1981) three levels of moral development because legal development theory is a variant of that basic model. The first level of reasoning (preconventional) can be labeled prohibitive. When asked about the value and function of rules and laws, reasoners at this level think in terms of proscriptions and preventing harm, rather than promotion of a positive social good. Prohibitive reasoners think that people should follow rules in order to avoid punishment and they hold a rigid view of obeying authority. The second level of reasoning (conventional) can be labeled prescriptive. Reasoners at this level think about the value and function of rules and laws in terms of maintaining social order and facilitating a necessary system of constraints. Prescriptive reasoners think that people should follow rules in order to conform to societal expectations and preserve law and order. The third level of reasoning (postconventional) can be labeled self-regulatory. When asked about the value and function of rules and laws, reasoners at this level think in terms of achieving beneficial and rational purposes for the general welfare. Self-regulatory reasoners think that people should follow (or sometimes break) rules in order to conform to principles of justice and thereby benefit society.

Legal development theory (Levine & Tapp, 1977; Tapp & Kohlberg, 1977; Tapp & Levine, 1970) holds that the process of change through these six stages requires a period of disequilibrium in the individual and role-taking opportunities that will facilitate adaptive processing of new information. There is no direct relationship between the environment and legal reasoning on this view, but rather an indirect linkage through the process of equilibration in a context of social interaction. An important factor in legal socialization is role-taking, or experiences that lead one to take the perspective of others. As the child grows into adulthood, the passage through the developmental stages depends in part on the availability of appropriate experiences in which issues about the fair enforcement of rules and holding people responsible for their actions are confronted. Reasoning through such issues, especially under circumstances that require the individual to take the perspective of others, provides a context for change in the level of legal reasoning. It is assumed that change in legal development level is linked to attitudes and behaviors expressed in specific situations, but this linkage is not elaborated in the theory and, in any case, is not direct.

In general, then, legal development theory hypothesizes that legal socialization is a function of legal development, as measured by changes in legal reasoning. Situational variables have no direct impact on these changes. Instead, differences in attitudes and behaviors with respect to rules are linked to variation in legal development level. This theory would predict no difference between residence halls and a high correlation between legal development level and both attitudes and behaviors.

Differential Association-Reinforcement Theory

Our discussion of social learning theory in Chapter 2 described the basic concepts of contingency socialization in detail. We briefly restate them now in terms that are specific to legal socialization and to the rule-enforcing environments of this study. Differential association-reinforcment theory (Akers, 1985; Akers et al., 1979) is a variant of social learning theory that was devised in order to apply the concepts of operant conditioning to a complex social environment. The operant conditioning model of learning focuses on consequent stimuli which, according to the theory, control much of human behavior. A stimulus occurs in an individual's environment (S), the individual responds (R), and that response creates a new stimulus; thus the operant sequence is S → R → S. The contingent stimulus, which follows the response, is controlling. In other words, the learning process requires feedback from the environment, in the form of consequent stimuli, which then controls future behavior. These consequent stimuli reinforce behavior either positively or negatively or punish behavior either positively or negatively. Repeated series of such stimuli produce learned behavior over time.

Legal socialization is the process of learning about behaviors that are proscribed by rules and laws and about the norms of enforcement that are prescribed either by the rule structure itself or by the legal culture. Differential association-reinforcement theory suggests that this learning process depends on various S → R → S sequences in an individual's experiences with rules and rule enforcement. These experiences begin in infancy, but only basic patterns of response survive into adulthood because reinforcing conditions vary considerably as the child moves away from dependency on parental discipline. In the meantime, an individual will encounter various situations in which rules are enforced: from family to school, from teacher to teacher within a school; from school to military, university, or employment; and so on. It is unlikely that these situations will present consistent models of authority or a consistent set of consequent stimuli. Another important variable during this process is shifting peer groups and the possibilities for normative social bonding. Most individuals do not achieve even relative stability within their rule-governed environments until adulthood.

Differential association-reinforcement theory approaches the complex social development of an individual's preadult career by focusing on the relationship between the processes of social bonding and the consequent stimuli that are encountered in experiences with rule enforcement. Differential association, a concept familiar to criminologists through the influential work of Edwin H. Sutherland (Sutherland & Cressey, 1978), suggests that deviance or noncompliance is behavior learned from peer groups. The theory highlights what are called "definitions" favorable to the violation of laws, which are learned through association with others. These shared normative meanings can incline an individual toward compliance or noncompliance depending on their predominant direction. Thus, differential association implies different shared normative meanings of rule-governed behaviors, and therefore different perspectives on compliance. Akers (1985; Akers et al., 1979) added the concept of reinforcement, from the operant model of learning, to differential association and thereby focused attention on experiences with rule enforcement as well. The combination of these concepts expands the theory to include attitudes toward rules and the exercise of authority as shared normative meanings in addition to attitudes toward rule-violating behaviors.

Even this theoretical elaboration does not solve all the problems of applying the operant model of learning to a complex social environment. It does obviate the need to account for every instance of contingency learning associated with an individual's career to adulthood, however, because it focuses attention on major influences such as child-rearing practices and the nature of peer group relationships. For the purposes of understanding legal socialization, that focusing may be sufficient even though the rewards and punishments, both positive and negative, are complex phenomena in themselves. Differential association-reinforcement theory reconceptualizes compliance in terms that are central to legal socialization because it emphasizes the normality of deviance. The theory suggests that deviance is primarily a function of one's experiences with rule enforcement, including incentives and modeling from differential association, the rewards and punishments that constitute differential reinforcement, and observational or imitative learning from different models of authority. The relative weight of internal and external factors in legal socialization is clearly tilted toward external influences, specifically the role of norms that are learned and maintained through peer associations, and the impact of the rule-enforcing environment.

In general, then, differential association-reinforcement theory hypothesizes that legal socialization is a function of the socializing conditions of one's rule-enforcing environment rather than one's capacity to reason about rules, fairness, and being responsible for one's actions. On this account, situational variables related to rule enforcment have a direct impact on the normative status of behaviors, the enforcement status of the rules, and the frequency of rule-violating behavior. This theory would predict large differences between residence halls and little change in legal development level.

The Experimental Manipulation

Our experimental manipulation of the rule-enforcing environment in two residence halls provided different socializing experiences. Under the external authority condition, residents had no control over rule enforcement. The resident assistants (peer enforcers) reported all rule violations to the Hall Director (a university employee), who then applied the rules by "writing up" the offenders to the Dean of Students' office. Police were called in instances of rowdy parties, assaults, and similar offenses. The hall director had no discretionary flexibility. Offenders were required to face the local court or a university hearing board, which decided guilt or innocence and applied penalties. By direct contrast, residents in the peer authority condition had complete control over enforcing the rules, including hearing cases and applying penalties. No police or external hearings were involved. Residents in the two control conditions experienced the rule enforcement that was typical of the natural setting, in which considerable discretion was exercised by the enforcers. Data reported in Chapter 4 indicate that significantly different socialization effects resulted from these interventions than were produced by the natural socialization process.

The two contrasting conditions produced different models for the exercise of authority and different consequent stimuli. In the external authority condition, enforcement was strict, consistent, and inflexible, dependent only on university policy. In the peer authority condition, enforcement was discretionary and varied, depending on the prevailing norms of behavior and enforcement among the residents. Rule enforcement was entirely outside the control of the external authority residents and entirely in the control of the peer authority residents. These conditions were in place throughout the academic year. Measures of legal development level, the normative status of rule-violating behaviors, the enforcement status of the rules, and the frequency of rule-violating behaviors were taken at the beginning of the fall semester and near the end of the spring semester. Therefore, the length of time during which respondents were exposed to differential association and differential reinforcement was sufficient to yield valid legal socialization effects.

The competing hypotheses can now be stated in terms of these specific manipulations of rule-enforcing conditions. Differential association-reinforcement theory predicts differences in attitudes and behaviors with respect to rules and rule enforcement (normative status of rule-violating behaviors, enforcement status of the rules, and frequency of rule-violating behaviors) depending on the socializing conditions. That is, if the differential association-reinforcement hypothesis is correct, we would expect to find systematic differences in these attitudes and behaviors based on the rule-enforcing environment in which the respondents lived, regardless of legal development level (LDL). By contrast, legal development theory predicts differences in these attitudes depending on LDL and not on differences in socializing conditions. That is, if the legal development hypothesis is correct, we would not expect to find these attitudes and behaviors to be different for respondents in the external authority conditions than they are for respondents in the peer authority condition. Rather, we would expect to find such differences based on LDL.

Analysis Plan

The analyses in this chapter focus on the responses of residents in the experimental sample at the end of the spring semester. Residence hall was represented by three orthogonal contrasts, which were entered into the analysis as one term. The zero-order correlations between legal development level and residence hall and each of the behavioral and attitudinal measures were calculated and presented. The correlations between residence hall and the measures were computed by entering the three orthogonal contrasts as the first step in the multiple regression. The resulting correlation was the zero-order correlations. Then the effect of LDL versus residence hall was assessed by means of multiple regression analyses for each of the three statistical factors and each of the four conceptual factors.

Results

The zero-order correlations between LDL and residence hall and each of the behavioral and attitudinal factors are presented in Table 5.1. This table shows that LDL is significantly correlated with the normative status of all seven rule-violating behavioral factors and the enforcement status of all factors but crime- and sex-related rule-violating behaviors. In contrast, residence hall is correlated with the frequency of engaging in all rule-violating behaviors but crime behaviors and the enforcement status of all behaviors but crime and dishonest behaviors. The only significant correlation between residence hall and normative status is for the normative status of destructive behaviors. In summary, LDL is correlated with the normative status and the enforcement status of the rule-violating behaviors; residence hall is correlated with the frequency and enforcement status of the same rule-violating behaviors.

One must be cautioned from putting too much weight and attention on the zero-order correlations because the effects of the other variables have not been partialed out from the relationships. The advantage of the multiple regression technique over the zero-order correlation technique is that is gives the reader an indication of the relationship between the two variables

TABLE 5.1. Zero-order correlations of LDL and residence hall with the legal measures

	Legal development level	*p*	Residence hall	*p*
Behavior				
Destructive	0.076	ns	0.200	0.05
Social disturbance	0.099	ns	0.195	0.05
Disorderly	0.115	ns	0.202	0.05
Alcohol use	0.122	ns	0.211	0.01
Dishonest	0.142	ns	0.167	0.05
Crime	0.044	ns	0.150	ns
Sex-related	0.053	ns	0.200	0.05
Normative Status				
Destructive	0.232	0.01	0.201	0.05
Social disturbance	0.309	0.001	0.113	ns
Disorderly	0.241	0.01	0.146	ns
Alcohol use	0.310	0.001	0.134	ns
Dishonest	0.241	0.01	0.139	ns
Crime	0.176	0.05	0.085	ns
Sex-related	0.168	0.05	0.154	ns
Enforcement Status				
Destructive	0.236	0.01	0.188	0.05
Social disturbance	0.218	0.01	0.211	0.01
Disorderly	0.194	0.05	0.211	0.01
Alcohol use	0.223	0.01	0.210	0.01
Dishonest	0.227	0.01	0.081	ns
Crime	0.102	ns	0.126	ns
Sex-related	0.158	ns	0.230	0.01

when the effects of the other two predictors have been partialed out or controlled.

The stepwise multiple regression analyses were conducted with LDL and residence hall as the predictor or independent variables. The frequency, normative status, and enforcement status of the three statistical and the four conceptual behavioral factors were the predicted factors. The following three orthogonal contrasts were constructed for entering residence hall into the regression analyses: (1) peer authority versus external authority residence hall (two experimental residence halls), (2) control one versus control two residence halls, and (3) the two experimental residence halls versus the two control residence halls.

The results of the multiple regression analyses can be found in Table 5.2. The first set of columns presents the effects of LDL and the second set of columns presents the effects of residence hall. A stepwise procedure was used so that the best predictor (i.e., the one with highest zero-order correlation) was entered on the first step. The second best predictor was entered into the equation, controlling for the other predictor.

TABLE 5.2. Results of multiple regression analysis

	Legal development level				Residence hall			
	R	R^2	df	F	R	R^2	df	F
Behavior								
Destructive	0.213	0.045	4,166	1.97	0.200	0.040	3,167	2.31
Social disturbance	0.205	0.042	4,164	1.81	0.195	0.038	3,165	2.17
Disorderly	0.227	0.052	4,163	2.22	0.202	0.041	3,164	2.33
Alcohol use	0.226	0.051	4,164	2.21	0.211	0.044	3,165	2.56
Dishonest	0.223	0.049	4,165	2.16	0.167	0.028	3,166	1.60
Crime	0.159	0.026	4,164	1.07	0.150	0.023	3,165	1.27
Sex-related	0.205	0.042	4,164	1.80	0.198	0.039	3,165	2.26
Normative Status								
Destructive	0.232	0.054	1,169	9.65**	0.283	0.080	4,166	3.60*
Social disturbance	0.309	0.095	1,167	17.58****	0.314	0.099	4,164	4.49*
Disorderly	0.241	0.058	1,168	10.37**	0.261	0.068	4,165	3.01*
Alcohol use	0.310	0.096	1,168	17.82****	0.321	0.103	4,165	4.73**
Dishonest	0.241	0.058	1,169	10.45**	0.262	0.069	4,166	3.06*
Crime	0.176	0.031	1,168	5.38*	0.187	0.035	4,165	1.50
Sex-related	0.168	0.028	1,167	4.85*	0.207	0.043	4,164	1.84
Enforcement Status								
Destructive	0.237	0.056	1,166	9.84**	0.277	0.077	4,163	3.38*
Social disturbance	0.218	0.048	1,165	8.27**	0.283	0.080	4,162	3.54*
Disorderly	0.264	0.070	4,162	3.03*	0.211	0.044	3,163	2.53
Alcohol use	0.223	0.050	1,166	8.66**	0.285	0.081	4,163	3.60**
Dishonest	0.227	0.052	1,165	8.96**	0.236	0.056	4,162	2.40
Crime	0.152	0.023	4,162	0.96	0.126	0.016	3,163	0.88
Sex-related	0.257	0.066	4,162	2.87*	0.230	0.053	3,163	3.04*

*$p < 0.05$
**$p < 0.01$
***$p < 0.001$
****$p < 0.0001$

There are two ways to interpret the data. First, one can determine which of the two predictors was most important by the results of the stepwise procedure (i.e., which factor was on the first step in the regression analysis). Second, one can determine whether the linear combination of the two predictors were significant predictors.

LDL is the most important predictor, as can be seen in the Table 5.2. LDL was on the first step (i.e., had the highest zero-order correlation) for the normative status of all seven rule-violating behavioral factors and the enforcement status of destructive, social disturbance, alcohol use, and dishonest behavior factors. In contrast, residence hall was only on the first step for the enforcement status of sex-related behavior factors. The frequency of engaging in rule-violating behaviors is not significantly predicted by either LDL or residence hall.

The linear combination of LDL and residence hall was a significant predictor of the normative status of all rule-violating behaviors but crime and sex-related behaviors and the enforcement status of all rule-violating behaviors but disorderly, dishonest, and crime behaviors. As in the case of individual predictors, the linear combination of LDL and residence hall did not predict the frequency of the behaviors.

Discussion

This study was designed to determine the relative influence of legal development and the rule-enforcing environment on legal socialization. For this purpose we tested competing hypotheses drawn from legal development theory (Levine & Tapp, 1977; Tapp & Kohlberg, 1977) and social learning theory (Akers, 1985; Akers et al., 1979; Aronfreed, 1968, 1969; Bandura, 1969a, 1969b, 1977). As is clear from the reported findings, the results indicate that legal development has a greater influence on legal socialization than does the rule-enforcing environment. LDL was a better predictor of normative status of all rule-violating behaviors and enforcement status for the destructive and social disturbance factors. Residence halls, the variable representing the rule-enforcing environment, did not predict the normative status of any of our factors. This means that the normative status of rule-violating behaviors does not vary by residence hall, even though enforcement practices and the exercise of authority differed. Even enforcement status varied by residence hall only with respect to the sex factor. Frequency of rule-violating behaviors was not predicted by either of our predictor variables. In short, this kind of analysis indicates that the rule-enforcing environment appears to be of limited relevance to legal socialization when LDL is taken into account.

These findings hold interesting implications for our multiple stage model of legal socialization. First, they suggest that legal reasoning is a significant factor in the process of socialization to rules. While the data do not speak at all to the cognitive developmental claim that the capacity for moral/legal reasoning proceeds by an invariant sequence of stages, the claim that stage-defined reasoning is related to the socialization process receives strong support. Legal development level is clearly related to situational norms, although not directly to behaviors. This finding suggests, further, that attitudes play a mediating role between reasoning and behaviors. Our measures of the normative status of rule-violating behaviors and the enforcement status of the rules represent the attitudinal dimension of situational norms. It is reasonable to infer that the behavioral dimension of the same situational norms may be indirectly related to reasoning by virtue of the mediating effect of the attitudes. This implication will be explored further in Chapter 7.

Finally, the weakness of the rule-enforcing conditions as a predictor suggests that we should think about the impact of socializing conditions in a different way. The data reported in Chapter 4 indicated that our experimental manipulation resulted in significantly different socialization effects than occurred in the natural setting. Further, differences in the direction of correlational change from fall to spring and in some standard deviations indicate that residents responded differently to peer authority rule enforcement than they did to enforcement by external authority. On the basis of these findings, we are confident that our manipulation resulted in distinctly different and strong interventions. The impact of these socializing conditions may be indirect, however. It may be that there is an interaction between legal development and rule-enforcing conditions that will explain a significant amount of the variance in the legal socialization factors (normative status of the behaviors, enforcement status of the rules and frequency of rule-violating behaviors). This possibility is explored in Chapter 6.

Leaving aside for now what further analyses might show, there are several possible conclusions from this test of competing hypotheses. We could argue that knowledge of legal development level is sufficient to predict attitudinal legal socialization effects. Or we could conclude that variations in rule-enforcing environments are not useful predictors of the normative status of rule-violating behaviors or the enforcement status of the rules. We could also conclude that neither reasoning nor situational conditions is related to frequency of rule-violating behaviors. These conclusions would be consistent with the findings reported in this chapter. But the further analyses discussed earlier suggest other possibilities: that situational norms mediate between reasoning and behaviors and that there is an interaction between legal development and rule-enforcing conditions that can predict legal socialization effects better than either of these two variables alone. We turn first to the question of interaction.

6

Effects of the Interaction

In Chapter 5, we tested competing hypotheses from legal development theory (Levine & Tapp, 1977; Tapp & Kohlberg, 1977) and social learning theory (Akers, 1985; Akers et al., 1979; Aronfreed, 1968, 1969; Bandura, 1969a, 1969b, 1976) in order to determine the relative influence of internal and external factors in legal socialization. We found that one's level of legal reasoning was a better predictor of attitudes toward rules and rule-violating behaviors than was the rule-enforcing environment. In this chapter, we examine the possibility of an interaction between legal development and the socializing conditions. The theoretical basis for this possibility can be found in both legal development theory and social learning theory. We now test the hypothesis that an interaction between legal development level and rule-enforcing conditions explains a significant amount of the variance in legal socialization effects (normative status of rule-violating behaviors, enforcement status of the rules, and frequency of rule-violating behaviors).

Theoretical Implications

The relationship between person and environment is important for both theories of legal socialization. As discussed in Chapter 2, this relationship is also problematic because the primary focus of cognitive developmental theory (Kohlberg, 1969, 1976, 1981, 1984; Levine & Tapp, 1977; Piaget, 1926, 1932, 1970/1983; Tapp & Kohlberg, 1977; Tapp & Levine, 1974) is the person, while environmental influence is the primary focus of social learning theory (Akers, 1985; Akers et al., 1979; Aronfreed, 1968, 1969; Bandura, 1969a, 1969b, 1977). In each case, an interaction is postulated, but its nature remains an unresolved issue. By designing a study in which hypotheses from both theories can be tested, we have opened the possibility of directly comparing how an interaction between person and environment can be interpreted in the two theoretical frameworks. Before we report the findings, we will review the way in which the postulated interaction is conceptualized by each theory.

Cognitive developmentalism (Kohlberg, 1969, 1976, 1981, 1984, 1986; Piaget, 1926, 1932, 1970/1983) takes the view that learning occurs through the processes of assimilation, accommodation, and equilibration, which combine to insulate the learner from the direct influence of the environment. The seat of this learning is cognition rather than affective or physiological response. The result of these processes is change in cognitive structures through an invariant sequence of stages. Yet Kohlberg, who is the most prominent theorist of cognitive developmentalism in its social context, always emphasized the interaction between person and environment even as he distinguished his view from that of associationist and social learning theorists. He argues that cognitive developmental theories ". . . assume that basic mental structure is the product of the patterning of the interaction between the organism and the environment rather than directly reflecting either innate patterns in the organism or patterns of events (stimulus contingencies) in the environment" (1969, p. 350). The process of interaction is ". . . role-taking, i.e., awareness that the other is in some way like the self, and that the other knows or is responsive to the self in a system of complementary expectations" (1969, p. 349).

In Kohlberg's (1969, 1976, 1981, 1984, 1986) view of moral development, then, stage change in the cognitive structures is the result of a kind of Meadian (Mead, 1934) interaction between the person and the social environment, which he calls role-taking. Legal development theory makes much of this concept, expanding it to include "experience-based activity involving conflict resolution, problem solving, participation in decision making, and role-taking" (Tapp & Kohlberg, 1977, p. 1014). Levine and Tapp (1977) go beyond discussion of role-taking in moral development theory to formulate a version that is more compatible with the conditions of conflict that are characteristic of the legal arena. They describe a dialectical process of change in which individuals learn to tolerate the diverse viewpoints of others in situations of conflict, such as occur when there are competing claims and questions of justice arise. The interaction between person and environment that is conducive to legal development occurs when rights claims are asserted and adjudicated, when authority is exercised for social control, when individuals are held responsible for their actions, when one decides whether or not to comply with a rule or questions the legitimacy of a rule.

The learning that is predicted by legal development theory is change in cognitive structures, that is, change in the way individuals organize their concepts of fairness and legitimacy with respect to rule systems. In this sense, legal development theory would hypothesize an interaction between legal reasoning and our variation in rule-enforcing conditions because the interventions were designed to produce different experiences that would affect perceptions of authority and fairness in enforcing the rules. We created two different legal arenas. In the peer authority condition, questions of justice arose when actions by some in the community were seen by others in the community to be harmful to the group or otherwise to affect adversely the rights of individual members. In the external authority condition, questions of justice arose when nonmembers applied rules regardless of community views of the harmfulness of the prohibited conduct or of the claims that such conduct adversely affected the rights of members. Legal development theory suggests that these two arenas should bring about changes in legal reasoning, as defined by developmental stage, which are related to the rule-enforcing experiences that characterized each condition.

Social learning theory (Akers, 1985; Akers et al., 1979; Aronfreed, 1968, 1969; Bandura, 1969b, 1977), at least in the versions most applicable to legal socialization, holds that learning is controlled by consequent stimuli. The process of learning requires feedback from the environment, in the form of consequent stimuli, which then control future behavior. The interaction between person and environment is, therefore, an integral part of the logic of social learning theory. Recent theorists (Bandura, 1986; Mischel & Mischel, 1976) have explicitly included various forms of social cognition and self-guidance in the feedback loop. In cognitive social learning theory, for example, individuals regulate their own behavior through self-imposed contingency rules that specify appropriateness, standards, and consequences for different kinds of behaviors (Mischel & Mischel, 1976, p. 92). Another form of self-regulation can be found in Bandura's social cognitive theory (1986). Bandura emphasizes the extent to which individuals can control the interaction of environmental and personal factors by taking advantage of the reciprocity in the feedback relationship, rather than simply submitting to or being shaped by external forces.

Of the various versions of social learning theory, Akers' (1985; Akers et al., 1979) differential association-reinforcement theory is particularly pertinent to the fundamental issues of legal socialization because it applies the principles of the operant model of consequent learning to the complex social environment surrounding deviant behavior. Reinforcement encompasses different kinds of environmental cues and incentives, both negative and positive, including observational learning from peers and from models of authority. Exposure to, or imitation of, behavioral norms is central to the theory, which specifies favorable or unfavorable "definitions" of law-violating conduct as key variables. The critical relationship between person and environment in this theory is an interaction between the potentially deviant individual and his or her social situation, including what behaviors are prohibited, what rules are enforced and how, and peer attitudes toward the rule-violating behaviors and the enforcement of the rules.

Consequent stimuli can either strengthen (reinforce) or weaken (punish) responses. Reinforcement can be positive (when a reward is received) or negative (when a punishment is avoided); and punishment can be positive (when a punishment is received) or negative (when a reward is removed).

Rewards include social approval and enjoyable physical sensations such as those from alcohol and drugs. It is impossible to catalog all the rewards and punishments that occurred for our respondents during the period of this study, let alone control them for experimentation. The general patterns were clear, however. Consistent, rigorous, authoritarian rule enforcement prevailed in the external authority condition; punishment received and punishment avoided were the most obvious patterns of consequent stimuli. In the peer authority condition, rules were enforced by peers according to the norms of the community; the most obvious pattern of consequent stimuli was the receipt of reward in the form of social approval. This variation in rule-enforcing conditions produced different incentives for compliance. In addition, the experience of authority was different in each community: negative reinforcement dominated the external authority condition, while positive reinforcement dominated the peer authority condition.

The learning that is predicted by social learning theory (Akers, 1985; Akers et al., 1979; Aronfreed, 1968, 1969; Bandura, 1969b, 1977) is change in attitudes and/or behaviors with respect to rules. Social learning theory would hypothesize an interaction between legal reasoning and our variation in rule-enforcing conditions because the interventions produced different models of exercising authority and different conditions for social bonding and for learning the normative meanings of behaviors. These differences clearly involve cognitive processes, whether of abstract reasoning or normative judgment. Reasoning is required to evaluate the nature of authority in each case, especially when the rules are in conflict with the norms of behavior. The external authority condition focuses attention on rule violation and avoiding punishment. A social cognitive theorist such as Bandura (1986) would likely argue that the external authority condition is compatible with a law-and-order orientation to authority and incompatible with self-regulation. By contrast, the peer authority condition is compatible with the development of personal responsibility and therefore with self-regulation. In addition, the peer group, which is so important for differential association-reinforcement theory, is the primary source of normative definitions of behavior. We found in Chapter 4 that the normative status of rule-violating behaviors tended to increase in the external authority condition and decrease in the peer authority condition.

Analysis Plan

The purpose of these analyses was to extend those conducted in Chapter 5 to include the interaction of LDL by residence hall. Again, first the zero-order correlations were examined. Then the multiple regression analyses were conducted to examine the effect of the interaction after both LDL and residence hall were controlled. The same three statistical and four

TABLE 6.1. Zero-order correlations of LDL and residence hall, and the interaction with the legal measures

	LDL	*p*	Residence hall	*p*	Interaction	*p*
Behavior						
Destructive	0.3076	ns	0.200	0.05	0.203	0.05
Social disturbance	0.099	ns	0.195	0.05	0.158	ns
Disorderly	0.115	ns	0.202	0.05	0.243	0.01
Alcohol use	0.122	ns	0.211	0.01	0.215	0.01
Dishonest	0.142	ns	0.167	0.05	0.145	ns
Crime	0.044	ns	0.150	ns	0.145	ns
Sex-related	0.053	ns	0.200	0.05	0.183	0.05
Normative Status						
Destructive	0.232	0.01	0.201	0.05	0.210	0.01
Social disturbance	0.309	0.001	0.113	ns	0.126	ns
Disorderly	0.241	0.01	0.146	ns	0.153	ns
Alcohol use	0.310	0.001	0.134	ns	0.169	0.05
Dishonest	0.241	0.01	0.139	ns	0.143	ns
Crime	0.176	0.05	0.085	ns	0.090	ns
Sex-related	0.168	0.05	0.154	ns	0.148	ns
Enforcement Status						
Destructive	0.236	0.01	0.188	0.05	0.216	0.01
Social disturbance	0.218	0.01	0.211	0.01	0.209	0.05
Disorderly	0.194	0.05	0.211	0.01	0.218	0.01
Alcohol use	0.223	0.01	0.210	0.01	0.226	0.01
Dishonest	0.227	0.01	0.081	ns	0.084	ns
Crime	0.102	ns	0.126	ns	0.126	ns
Sex-related	0.158	ns	0.230	0.01	0.216	0.01

conceptual behavioral factors were used in the analysis as predicted or dependent variables. The predictor or independent variables included LDL, residence hall, and the interaction of LDL by residence hall.

Results

First the zero-order correlations were calculated (see Table 6.1). The results for LDL and residence hall were presented and discussed in Chapter 5. The interaction was significantly related to the frequency of all rule-violating behaviors but social disturbance, dishonest, and crime behaviors. Also the interaction was significantly correlated with the normative status of destructive and alcohol use behaviors and the enforcement status of all rule-violating behaviors but dishonest and crime behaviors.

As mentioned in Chapter 5, one cannot put too much emphasis on the results of the zero-order correlation analysis, because the effects of other variables have not been considered. What is more important to focus on is the effect of the interaction when the effects of both LDL and residence hall have been controlled.

TABLE 6.2. Results of regression analysis

	Legal development level				Residence hall			
	R	R^2	df	F	R	R^2	df	F
Behavior								
Destructive	0.068	0.005	1,157	0.727	0.214	0.046	4,154	1.85
Social disturbance	0.110	0.012	1,155	1.89	0.172	0.029	4,152	1.16
Disorderly	0.111	0.012	1,154	1.93	0.262	0.069	4,151	2.79[a]
Alcohol use	0.122	0.015	1,167	2.54	0.226	0.051	4,164	2.21
Dishonest	0.142	0.020	1,168	3.46	0.223	0.050	4,165	2.16
Crime	0.044	0.002	1,167	0.32	0.160	0.025	4,164	1.07
Sex-related	0.060	0.004	1,155	0.57	0.189	0.036	4,152	1.40
Normative Status								
Destructive	0.227	0.052	1,157	8.56[b]	0.289	0.084	4,154	3.51[b]
Social disturbance	0.336	0.113	1,155	19.75[d]	0.341	0.117	4,152	5.02[c]
Disorderly	0.251	0.063	1,156	10.47[b]	0.273	0.074	4,153	3.08[a]
Alcohol use	0.335	0.112	1,156	19.69[d]	0.350	0.123	4,153	5.35[c]
Dishonest	0.241	0.058	1,169	10.45[b]	0.262	0.069	4,166	3.06[a]
Crime	0.176	0.031	1,168	5.38[a]	0.187	0.035	4,165	1.50
Sex-related	0.168	0.028	1,167	4.85[a]	0.207	0.043	4,164	1.84
Enforcement Status								
Destructive	0.229	0.052	1,155	8.55[b]	0.301	0.091	4,152	3.79[b]
Social disturbance	0.243	0.059	1,153	9.57[b]	0.291	0.085	4,150	2.42[b]
Disorderly	0.205	0.042	1,153	6.71[a]	0.281	0.079	4,150	3.21[a]
Alcohol use	0.223	0.049	1,166	8.66[b]	0.285	0.081	4,150	3.60[b]
Dishonest	0.227	0.051	1,165	8.96[b]	0.236	0.056	4,162	2.40
Crime	0.102	0.010	4,165	1.74	0.126	0.016	3,163	0.96
Sex-related	0.158	0.025	4,165	4.22[a]	0.230	0.053	3,163	2.87[a]

[a] $p < 0.05$
[b] $p < 0.01$
[c] $p < 0.001$
[d] $p < 0.0001$

A stepwise multiple regression analysis was conducted with LDL on the first step, residence hall on the second step, and the interaction of LDL by residence hall on the third step. The following three orthogonal contrasts were constructed for entering residence hall into the regression analyses: (1) peer authority versus external authority residence hall (two experimental residence halls), (2) control one versus control two residence halls, and (3) the two experimental residence halls versus the two control residence halls. The interactions entered in the regression analyses consisted of the three dorm contrasts multiplied by LDL.

The results of the multiple regression analyses can be found in Table 6.2. The first set of columns presents the effects of LDL, the second set of columns presents the effects of residence hall (controlling for LDL), and the third set of columns presents the effects of the interaction of LDL by residence hall (controlling for LDL and residence hall). The interaction has a significant effect ($p \leq 0.05$) on the frequency of the alcohol use and dishonest behavior factors. Also the interaction had a significant effect on the normative status of all rule-violating behaviors (but dishonest, crime and sex-related behaviors) and the enforcement status of all rule-violating behaviors (but dishonest and crime behaviors).

Discussion

Our findings indicate that there is an interaction between legal development level and the rule-enforcing conditions. It is important to see that the interaction does not predict the frequency of any of the behaviors that are included in our three statistical factors. It does, however, have a significant relationship to the normative status of these rule-violating behaviors and a significant effect on the enforcement status of these rules. The absence of a linkage with behaviors is intriguing because the conditions of enforcement suggest that a direct impact on behaviors is likely. According to social learning theory, variations in the incentives for compliance should affect behaviors. We have now confirmed the absence of such a linkage not only for legal development level and rule-enforcing conditions directly but also for the interaction. This finding suggests that our mediation model may be the most useful way to conceptualize a possible relationship between reasoning and behaviors. The mediation model is the subject of Chapter 7.

The significant relationship between the interaction and normative status of the rule-violating behaviors and the enforcement status of the rules clearly indicates that both legal development and social learning are relevant to legal socialization. Before exploring the interaction with further analyses, it is interesting to identify what patterns exist in our data that help to explain its relationship to legal socialization effects. In Chapter 4, we found a general pattern in the direction of change for respondents in the experimental conditions. In the external authority condition, normative status increased for all the rule-violating behaviors (statistical factors) while the enforcement status of the rules decreased. The opposite pattern occurred in the peer authority condition. In other words, those who lived under authoritarian rule-enforcing conditions became more approving of the rule-violating behaviors and less approving of enforcing the rules against them. But those who lived in a participatory environment became less approving of the same rule-violating behaviors and more approving of rule enforcement.

This general pattern is consistent with an interaction between legal reasoning and rule-enforcing conditions. It supports the importance of differential association (Akers, 1985; Akers et al., 1979) in legal socialization because it indicates that learning normative definitions of behavior is an effect of social bonding within a group, and that it can work either by increasing or decreasing approval of rule-violating behaviors. It also supports the social learning position (Bandura, 1969b, 1977) that observational learning, specifically the modeling of authority in this case, is a significant contributor to the legal socialization process. In the participatory environment, respondents could model or imitate peers who were deemed to be responsible for their actions. By giving them the authority to decide what rules should be enforced and how, the university acknowledged that the student residents were capable of responsible behavior. External constraints were doubly weakened for these residents, and they reacted by becoming less approving of rule violations and more willing to enforce the rules. We can speculate that they began to feel a sense of community and become sensitive to the kinds of behaviors that might be harmful to their fellow residents. Because the opposite pattern occurred in the external authority condition, we have reason to believe that the participatory conditions contributed to the development of more civilized attitudes. Chapter 9 further discusses these possibilities on the basis of qualitative data.

Another clue to the meaning of the interaction gets us closer to the significance of legal reasoning in these patterns. The correlations between fall and spring attitudes reported in Table 4.3 show that residents in the peer authority condition changed their positions more than did the residents in the external authority condition, the control conditions, or the university sample. One can interpret the lack of consistency between fall and spring attitudes as a sign that these respondents were changing their minds because they were doing more thinking about rule violation and enforcement. The fact that their legal development level increased as well is another indication of extensive legal reasoning by the residents of the peer authority condition. These three factors—the group effect for learning normative definitions, the modeling of peer authority toward community values, and indications of extensive legal reasoning in the peer authority condition—suggest that the interaction of legal development level and rule-enforcing conditions had important effects. These were especially striking in the participatory community in which the directional trends for legal socialization effects in the other samples were reversed.

These differences between the two communities, which resulted from our experimental manipulation of the rule-enforcing conditions, indicate not only differences in socialization but also that one pattern runs counter to the intent of the rule system while the other conforms to it. The rules represent university policies. Their enforcement is intended to create an environment that minimizes harm and disruption to others within the residential community. This intent was largely realized in the peer authority condition but was thwarted in the external authority condition. Our findings showed that attitudes toward rule-violating behaviors and enforcing the rules tended to conform to university policies in the first case and depart from them in the second case. While our independent variables did not predict the frequency of rule-violating behaviors, incident reports for the year show that the rate of rule violation was significantly greater in the external authority condition than in the peer authority condition. One might even want to use the phrase "successful socialization" in referring to the peer authority respondents.

"Successful socialization" is a term that is often used in the literature (Renshon, 1974, 1977; Schwartz & Schwartz, 1975) to criticize theories of socialization and political theories that are oriented toward stability and the maintenance of a society or polity. The implication is that such theories support repressive policies, or at the least say nothing about enhancing individual potential for change and personal development. It is assumed that the goal of stability necessarily requires policies that force conformity. Any study of legal socialization must be at the center of this debate. Our finding that the interaction between legal development level and rule-enforcing conditions can produce both conforming and nonconforming patterns is interesting in this context. Even more interesting is the fact that the conforming pattern, the successful socialization, is in no way repressive. Indeed, the conforming community was participatory rather than authoritarian, and it changed toward respect for others and toward enforcing rules that protected both individuals and the community from disruption. In the next three chapters, we report further analyses in order to explore the nature of this interaction.

Part III

Exploring the Interaction

In the last section, we tested competing hypotheses from legal development theory (Levine & Tapp, 1977; Tapp & Kohlberg, 1977) and social learning theory (Akers, 1985; Akers et al., 1979; Bandura, 1969a, 1969b, 1977) to determine which is the better predictor of legal socialization effects. We also tested the hypothesis that an interaction between legal reasoning and rule-enforcing conditions would predict legal socialization effects. We found that legal development level was a better predictor than rule-enforcing conditions and that the interaction explained a significant amount of the variance in attitudes toward rules and rule-violation but not the rule-violating behaviors themselves. The next three chapters focus on the interaction in order to explore the nature of this relationship between legal reasoning and the environment of rule enforcement and its import for understanding legal socialization.

In Chapter 7 we investigate the linkages among our three person variables: legal reasoning, situational attitudes (the normative status of the rule-violating behaviors and the enforcement status of the rules), and the frequency of engaging in rule-violating behaviors. We test the hypothesis, advanced in Chapter 1, that attitudinal variables mediate between reasoning and behaviors. This mediating model suggests that situational factors provide the basis for a linkage between legal reasoning and rule following or rule violation. On the other hand, our previous analyses found that neither legal development level nor the rule-enforcing conditions have successfully predicted the frequency of engaging in rule-violating behaviors. Because both legal development theory and the cognitive versions of social learning theory argue that there is a relationship between some form of reasoning and socialized behaviors, we think it is important to investigate whether the mediating model holds for our variables. Using path analysis, we distinguish between rule-violating and rule-following behaviors and then test the validity of direct versus mediating models and cognitive versus behavioral models (representing cognitive developmental theory and social learning theory, respectively) for each.

Chapter 8 takes a different analytical tack in exploring the interaction.

Here we look at individual differences among our subjects in their propensity toward rule following or rule violation. We investigate whether individuals' offense status is related to their legal development level, to their attitudes toward rules and rule-violating behaviors, to the rule-enforcing conditions in which they lived during the socialization period, and to the kind of behavior being controlled. Both rule-following and rule-violating modes of behavior are explored. Successful legal socialization may be largely a function of legal development or of rule-enforcing conditions or of situational norms—or, more likely, of some combination of these factors. Deviation may be the mirror image of these relationships or it may reflect a different pattern of interaction altogether.

Chapter 9 describes the experiences of residents in the external authority condition with authoritarian rule enforcement and the experiences of residents in the peer authority condition with their internal hearing board. These experiences, treated as a series of case studies, reveal how the rule-enforcing conditions in each experimental condition affected social interactions in the residence halls. The qualitative data from interviews, participant observation and tape recordings illustrate how residents reacted to various kinds of rule-enforcement problems. Each community developed its own enforcement norms and its own pattern of rule violation. We pay particular attention to the legal socialization effects of the internal hearing board and to the kind of learning that took place when the residents were confronted with responsibility for their own community.

7

Legal Reasoning and Behaviors: The Mediating Model

In Chapter 6, we found, that an interaction between legal development level and rule-enforcing conditions explains a significant amount of the variance in legal socialization attitudes (normative status of the rule-violating behaviors and enforcement status of the rules). Cognitive developmental theory (Levine & Tapp, 1977; Tapp & Kohlberg, 1977) and social learning theory (Akers, 1985; Akers et al., 1979; Bandura, 1969a, 1969b, 1977) offer different accounts of the nature of this interaction. Cognitive developmental theory implies that reasoning justifies future action and therefore is prior to behaviors, while social learning theory implies that reasoning is a rationalization and therefore follows behaviors. One approach to assessing the adequacy of these accounts for the purpose of explaining legal socialization is to test cognitive versus behavioral path models of the possible relationships among the central variables: legal reasoning, as measured by legal development level; attitudes toward rule enforcement (enforcement status) and rule-violating behaviors (normative status); and the frequency of engaging in rule-governed behaviors. One purpose of this chapter is to determine which model, cognitive or behavioral, best explains the relationship between legal development level and rule-following or rule-violating behaviors. Another aim is to determine whether the relationship is direct or mediated.

Linkages among Legal Socialization Variables

Legal socialization is the acquisition of values and norms concerning rules or laws and their enforcement. We have argued that there are three person-based components of legal socialization: legal reasoning, attitudes toward rule-violating behaviors and rule enforcement (normative and enforcement status), and behaviors that violate the rules. We include legal reasoning because the resolution of legal and political issues typically entails generalized prescriptive thinking about the appropriate uses of law to constrain behavior. Reasoning about the role of law in defining a community invokes issues of freedom and individual liberty and leads to ways of conceptualizing authority. Attitudes toward rule-violating behaviors and enforcement are included because they bear on more specific situational factors such as prevailing norms, the kinds of behaviors that are proscribed, and enforcement style. Behaviors are included in legal socialization because the views that citizens hold, whether general or specific, are irrelevant if their actions are unrelated to their reasoning and attitudes (Blasi, 1980).

A way to conceptualize the interaction between legal development level and rule-enforcing conditions is to consider how the three person-based components of legal socialization are related to each other. The meaning of the interaction may be forged by experiences with rule enforcement and lie in linkages between reasoning, situational attitudes, and the propensity to engage in rule-violating behaviors. But we must acknowledge the classic stumbling block discussed in Chapter 1, i.e., that the existence of such linkages, especially between reasoning and behaviors, is difficult to substantiate. On the one hand, if legal development theory is correct, reasoning is a necessary factor in the legal socialization process. Our finding that legal reasoning level predicts situational legal socialization effects provides strong support for that claim. On the other hand, our analysis also found that legal reasoning did not predict the frequency of engaging in rule-violating behaviors. These findings suggest that further analysis is called for before we can proceed to formulate hypotheses about linkages among the components of legal socialization.

Cognitive Development versus Social Learning Approaches

Our first step is to examine why our two theories of legal socialization offer two different models of how cognitive factors are related to the social environment.* Legal development theory (Levine & Tapp, 1977; Tapp &

* The regression analysis reported in Chapter 5 represents one means of examining the linkages among components of legal socialization. Path analysis, another means, offers an interesting opportunity to explore these linkages, but it also poses a logical complication. In studying socialization, we are concerned with the role played by the reasoning-behavior connection in the learning process. Legal development theory holds that reasoning is dominant in that process, even though it may not be possible to predict particular behaviors on the basis of reasoning level. For legal development, action or behavior is a product of rules or general criteria that suggest a generative model of the reasoning-behavior connection. Social learning theory treats reasoning as one factor in a feedback loop that suggests a circular rather than a causal model of these relationships. By contrast, the logic of path analysis is causal, i.e., if a statistically significant relationship between reasoning and behaviors is found, a direction is postulated such that one is seen as causing the other. In addition, the situational factors that will be hypothesized as

Kohlberg, 1977; Tapp & Levine, 1974) is straightforwardly developmental in its conceptualization of relationships among the several variables associated with legal socialization (see Chapter 2). It relies primarily on Piaget's (1926, 1932, 1970/1983) theory of learning for its fundamental concepts. Piaget delineated two cognitive processes, assimilation and accommodation, that shape the reception of new information. A third process, equilibration, maintains a balance between the cognitive structures that are undergoing adaptation and the influence of the environment. Role-taking equilibration is the dynamic of interaction for legal development theory. It is not strictly causal in the sense that environmental influences directly "cause" changes in cognitive structures or that cognitive structures "cause" behaviors. Rather, its central process is an ongoing equilibration between an individual's cognitive capacities and role-taking experiences. Cognitive structures generate a way of understanding these experiences that affects how one then behaves, and the new experiences in turn relate back through the adaptive processes to modify the cognitive structures. Encountering "discrepanicies" or conflict between "expectancies" and experience (i.e., disequilibrium) drives the equilibration process (Kohlberg, 1969).

Social learning theory, by contrast, is causal in its approach, even when one considers the feedback concept of normative self-regulation that characterizes Bandura's (1986) social cognitive theory. At least it is causal in the sense that one expects to find relationships between independent and dependent variables and between predictor and predicted variables. From the social learning perspective, the linkages among the components of legal socialization should reflect the direct impact of reinforcement through normative approval and disapproval and punishment. This direct impact of the social environment for social learning theory is in contrast to the indirect influence postulated by legal development theory. On the other hand, situational factors play a role for both theories. For example, if one were to construct path models representing how the two theories would predict the linkages among the components of legal socialization, both models would include situational attitudes as mediating variables. That is, the normative status of the rule-violating behaviors and the enforcement status of the rules will mediate between reasoning and the frequency of engaging in the behaviors for both theories.

The differences in how the two theories account for the interaction do not mean that either theory disregards situational factors, but rather that

mediators must be conceptualized as part of this causal path. This implies a sort of linear causation that does not fit either the legal development or the social learning conception of interaction. We think that path analysis is a valid statistical tool for exploring the linkages among components of the legal socialization process but we caution that the implied linear causal path is a logical construction and should not be taken literally.

cognitive factors play different roles for each. Cognitive structures control the influence from the social environment according to legal development theory. In social learning theory, reasoning has no generative role but is instead just one of the factors in the feedback loop. Since this is a study of socialization processes, as opposed to an attempt to predict compliance behavior, we are primarily interested in how reasoning is related to experiential influences from the social environment. In our view, the differences in how the two theories conceptualize the linkage between reasoning and experience will produce two different path models: the path model for legal development theory begins with reasoning in the fall and leads through situational attitudes to spring behaviors; the path model for social learning theory begins with fall behaviors and leads through situational attitudes toward spring reasoning. Role-taking equilibration may or may not result in a relationship between reasoning and behaviors, but any such relationship that occurs will depend on the processes of assimilation and accommodation. Therefore, reasoning is prior to behavior for legal development theory. For social learning theory, reasoning may or may not be linked to behavior. If there is a linkage, it is more likely that behaviors are prior to reasoning because the role of reasoning is to elicit guidelines for self-regulation from one's experiences.

Thus, we can postulate two path models: a cognitive model in which legal reasoning "causes" rule-violating behaviors and a behavioral model in which the frequency of engaging in rule-violating behaviors "causes" legal reasoning. In both cases situational factors, the normative status of the rule-violating behaviors and the enforcement status of the rules may play a mediating role between legal reasoning and the frequency of engaging in rule-violating behaviors.

Linkages between Reasoning and Behaviors

Before considering empirical linkages, it is instructive to examine the conceptual meaning of a relationship between legal reasoning and rule-following or rule-violating behavior. We might start with Blasi's comment about the connection between moral reasoning and moral action: "Few would disagree that morality ultimately lies in action and that the study of moral development should use action as the final criterion" (1980, p. 1). This nice conceptual point about morality has a legal parallel in Gerstein's concept of "fidelity to law" (Gerstein, 1972). For Blasi, one cannot be thought of as "moral" if one's actions contradict one's moral principles. For Gerstein, violations of law contradict the basis of legal and political obligation, i.e., "a society in which each person governs his own conduct by applying to himself the rules which have been laid down by society for everyone" (1972, p. 35). This is especially the case for conduct that causes harm to others or is a violation of the sense of community implied by general rules. The point for both Blasi and Gerstein is not that one has to act in a certain way in order to prove that one is moral or a good citizen, but rather that the concepts of morality and of law (Hart, 1961, 1968) imply a logical connection between principles and actions.

In the context of understanding legal socialization, we take the implication one step further. If there is no empirical connection between legal reasoning and rule-governed behaviors, one can infer that nothing has happened in the real world to engage the reasoning with the normative meaning of the behaviors. The obvious question becomes: what causes reasoning and behaviors to engage? The clear implication of both the Blasi (1980, 1983) and Gerstein (1972) positions is that a conceptual connection exists between moral or legal reasoning and moral behavior or compliance. That is, the rational force of moral or legal obligation compels a connection between reasoning and behavior, and that connection implies rule following. But this formulation begs important empirical questions. Does the engagement between legal reasoning and rule-governed behaviors occur only for followers? Or do violators also experience a connection? If so, is there any qualitative difference between the rule-following and the rule-violating connection?

Legal development theory suggests a way to sort out and analyze these empirical questions. According to legal development theory, conflict causes a creative disequilibrium in an individual, thereby inducing developmental growth and change (Levine & Tapp, 1977; Tapp & Kohlberg, 1977; Tapp & Levine, 1974). As we discussed in Chapter 2, role-taking experiences involve diverse points of view and produce a context of conflict. This suggests that we should ask whether and in what form conflict leads to engagement between legal reasoning and rule-violating behaviors. For example, we can ask whether engagement is more likely to occur when one disagrees with a rule. Or is agreement with a rule as likely to foster engagement? By the same token, we should ask whether engagement is more likely to occur when one violates a rule or when one follows a rule. Conflict might also effect engagement through the enforcement process. Since authoritarian enforcement is liable to be more conflictful than participatory enforcement, we can ask whether engagement is more likely to occur under authoritarian or participatory enforcement. These questions are addressed in the following sections.

Agreement Versus Disagreement With the Rule

First there may be variation for both violating and following behaviors, depending on whether or not one agrees with the rule. Our analysis has already revealed that there is norm/rule congruence for some rule-governed behaviors, but that for others the norm and the rule disagree. Violation of a rule with which one disagrees may be a quite different experience from violation of a rule with which one agrees. Although violating may seem to be more removed from reasoning than rule following, it does not make sense to assume that all rule violation is simply mindless behavior. Those who approve of behaviors that are prohibited often consider the prohibition to be unjust and its enforcement unfair. Regardless of the merits of such a claim, it would be unwarranted to exclude thinking about a law as unjust or its enforcement as unfair from the realm of legal reasoning. Similarly, the issue of norm/rule congruence poses empirical questions about the nature of rule following. Disapproval of prohibited behaviors implies a normative attachment to the rule. Such an attachment could have its basis in reasoned consideration, implying a connection between reasoning and behaviors, or it could simply reflect an affective propensity to obey rules. In light of these varied questions, we would argue that the empirical engagement between legal reasoning and rule-governed behavior is more complex than the purely conceptual connections suggested by Blasi (1980, 1983) and Gerstein (1972).

Rule Following versus Rule Violating

The linkage between legal reasoning and rule-violating behaviors may also depend on whether one is following or violating the rule. The measure of legal reasoning used in this study (as discussed on pp. 53–54) suggests a basis for a possible empirical connection between reasoning and both rule-violating and rule-following behaviors. The scale used by Tapp and Levine (1974; Levine & Tapp, 1977; Tapp, 1970) to establish their legal levels typology consists of seven questions designed to gauge individuals' reasoning about several aspects of legal reasoning: the value of rules and laws ("What if there were no rules?"), the function of rules and laws ("What is a rule?" "What is a law?"), the dynamics of legal compliance ("Why should people follow rules?" "Why do you follow rules?"), the changeability of rules and laws ("Can rules be changed?"), and the breakability of rules and laws ("Are there times when it might be right to break a rule?"). Responses are coded in terms of a (Kohlbergian) developmental levels typology: preconventional responses reflecting a fear of sanctions, conventional responses oriented to conformity, and postconventional responses based on principles that are independent of any legal system. Since the responses are open-ended, the resulting LDL score reflects a series of acts of reasoning about rules rather than reactions to preestablished terms and categories. Therefore, whatever our data show about any connections between legal reasoning and rule-governed behaviors, the measures provide ample opportunity for either or both kinds of engagement to be revealed.

The question "what if there were no rules?" evokes references to specific harms that could occur and to general social disorder, implying that rules deter or prevent harmful behaviors. Some respondents take the opposite tack, mentioning the possibility that individuals can control their own harmful behavior. All three responses could underlie compliance behavior, and the third response could provide a justification for violating a rule as well. Similar responses are made to the questions about the function of rules and laws. The questions about the dynamics of legal compliance ("Why should people follow rules?" "Why do you follow rules?") probe more deeply into the basis for compliance by underscoring that there is a choice between following and violating. Even so, the questions are biased toward rule following, as responses range from references to punishment and authority to social conformity and the maintenance of order to the requirements of principles of justice.

The question "Can rules be changed?" indirectly raises the issue of the relative validity of rules and it evokes answers ranging from assertions that rules are absolute to admissions that rules can be judged to be good or bad on the basis of other standards. The notion that rules are not themselves the source of right and wrong again raises the prospect that the existence of a rule does not ensure that it merits compliance. The final question, "Are there times when it might be right to break a rule?," explicitly assumes that violation is not only a possibility but perhaps an acceptable possibility. In short, our measure of legal reasoning, while somewhat biased toward rule following, does not preclude responses that contemplate the violation of rules that might be considered unjust. It invites the respondent to speculate about grounds for both following and violating rules.

Of course, the existence of plausible reasons, or reasoning, to justify or explain both rule-violating and rule-following behaviors does not mean that empirical linkages between reasoning and the behaviors obtain in fact. As we have pointed out previously, the social science literature on connections between reasoning and behaviors has produced few unambiguously positive findings. It is also possible that the engagement that we hypothesize is not straightforwardly a reasoned justification for a particular behavior. For example, Kohlberg (1969, 1976, 1981, 1984, 1986) and his moral development associates (e.g., see Modgil & Modgil, 1986) have always argued that preconventional reasoning (fear of punishment) is related to misbehavior. Blasi's (1980) review of the literature on connections between moral reasoning and actions found studies indicating that those who reason in terms of fear of punishment are more likely to engage in juvenile delinquency. This implies that some legal reasoning may have nothing to do with justifying particular actions even when there is a statistical relationship between legal development level and rule-governed behaviors.

A different kind of example can be found in the literature on philosophy of law in which the concept of legal/political obligation is founded on acceptance of the logic of general rules (Hart, 1961, 1968; Morris, 1976). The logic of general rules implies that obeying rules, including those with which one disagrees, is necessary for the survival of the system of rules and is therefore to the advantage of everyone. On this argument, legal/political obligation is a kind of logically based and self-interested reciprocity. Both

Kohlberg (1969, 1986) and Levine and Tapp (1977) find reciprocity in this sense to be the basis for Stage 4 and Stage 5 reasoning. It is clear that this concept of obligation requires neither a normative attachment to each rule one obeys nor agreement with its prescription. In short, it is possible that connections between legal reasoning and behaviors may be more circuitous and complex than is found in direct justifications.

It is important to remember, also, that this is not a study of compliance but of socialization. We are not trying to predict which kind or level of reasoner is compliant and which is not. Rather, we are trying to determine whether or not reasoning is a factor in the legal socialization process. We have postulated that some form of engagement between reasoning and behaviors does occur and that it may or may not reflect a direct justification. Blasi (1980) goes further and suggests that moral connections, at least, have to do with the exercise of "judgments that express general criteria" (p. 7). To Blasi, judgment is not a matter of "causation" but is rather a "product of rules." He suggests that the terms "determination" or "generation" replace the causal conceptualization that has characterized most social science approaches to understanding the relationship between reasoning and behaviors (1980, p. 4). Otherwise, he argues, moral reasoning is "essentially irrational" (p. 3).

Situational Context and Conditions

The situational context and conditions under which a rule is enforced may also affect the linkage between legal reasoning and rule-violating behaviors. Our mediating model may not fully answer Blasi's (1980) challenge to the causal orientation of traditional social science literature, but it does provide a basis for constructing path models using situational attitudes as well as cognitive developmental measures of reasoning. As we seek to discover the role played by reasoning in legal socialization, we can assume some kind of engagement between legal reasoning and behaviors mediated by situational attitudes as part of the learning process. We further assume that engagement occurs in a legal context, that is, there must be opportunities for legal reasoning. A legal context provides such opportunities through variations in the content of rules and in the conditions for enforcing the rules.

The content of a rule refers to the type of behavior the rule proscribes. Variations in rule content can be of two basic kinds, each indicating a different congruence between the rule and the prevailing behavioral and enforcement norms. Where the norm and rule disagree, the legal context is unstable and we would expect engagement between legal reasoning and rule-governed behaviors because of conflict over the rule and/or its enforcement. This is consistent with the argument of legal development theory (Levine & Tapp, 1977; Tapp & Kohlberg, 1977) that cognitive development is enhanced in a situation of conflict. On the other hand, a stable legal context, where the norm and rule agree, does not produce conflict. It could be argued, however, that a stable legal context can offer opportunities for legal reasoning because it presents a fertile ground for developing a sense of community and a concept of legal/political obligation. In fact, pure cases of norm/rule agreement or disagreement across the various rules in a society are unlikely. Certainly our data indicate a range of norm/rule congruence across the set of rules in the residential community. We conclude that the mix of norm/rule agreement and disagreement offers provocative opportunities for legal reasoning in a relatively unstable legal context.

The legal context is further defined by the rule-enforcing conditions. These can provide opportunities and incentives to engage in legal reasoning. Variations in rule-enforcing conditions indicate differences in the degree of coercion being applied from one setting to another or from one type of rule to another (Black, 1976). The experimental manipulation of these conditions is an important part of our research design because the subjects were not only placed in a legal context involving their agreement or disagreement with the rules, but were also put to the real-world test of responding to different ways of enforcing them. The role-taking opportunities provided by the internal judicial board in the peer authority hall suggest one kind of incentive to legal reasoning. The coercive atmosphere of the external authority hall, on the other hand, could be either provocative or stifling. In sum, the possibility of engagement between legal reasoning and rule-governed behaviors may depend on both rule content and rule-enforcing conditions, each a situational factor that presents varying opportunities for legal reasoning.

This discussion suggests that three variables define conflict in the legal socialization process: (1) whether people agree or disagree with the rule, (2) whether people follow or violate the rule, and (3) the conditions under which the rule is enforced. Each of these variables can be seen as a way in which the experience of conflicting points of view engages legal reasoning with rule-governed behaviors. Legal development theory argues that such experiences stimulate cognitive growth (Levine & Tapp, 1977; Tapp & Kohlberg, 1977; Tapp & Levine, 1974). According to cognitive developmentalism, "mismatches" in value orientations and "discrepancies between the child's...expectancies and the experienced events" (Kohlberg, 1969) produce a stimulating disequilibrium. In this light, our three variables offer three different ways to operationalize how conflict of this sort might stimulate a connection between legal reasoning and rule-governed behaviors.

The Models

Direct Model

Our discussion so far has assumed that situational factors will mediate between legal reasoning and rule-governed behaviors. This assumption is based on the failure to find a direct relationship between reasoning and behaviors in many studies (see the discussion of this problem in Chapter 1; Blasi, 1980). It is possible, however, that we will find direct relationships between reasoning and behaviors, that is, relationships that are sufficiently strong to bypass the mediators under certain conditions. In such a case, we hypothesize that the path model will also exhibit a significant mediating path through situational factors. It is our view that the situational factors are necessary to the legal socialization process not only because of their mediating function but also because learning about rules and fairness requires experiences, either direct or vicarious, with rule enforcement.

Mediating Model

Our finding of an interaction between legal reasoning and rule-enforcing conditions strongly suggests the existence of mediating factors. Specifically, the interaction suggests that situational factors—in this case, the normative status of the behaviors and the enforcement status of the rules—provide the necessary linkages between reasoning and behaviors. These factors come into play as a result of experiences with rule enforcement. The preceding discussion has reviewed possible explanations for such linkages. It remains to state hypotheses that can be tested by our data.

We first hypothesize that legal reasoning and rule-violating behaviors are directly related. Based on findings from a wide range of literature (e.g., Blasi, 1980), we expect this hypothesis to be disconfirmed. Our most general hypothesis is that legal reasoning and rule-violating behaviors are related, but the relationship holds or does not hold depending on variations in situational factors. More specifically, we expect to find relationships between legal reasoning and rule-violating behaviors in the university and control samples, especially in the behavior categories that are highly salient to the university experience. This expectation is based on the assumption that the residents are thinking about those rules that are being enforced. In fact, social disturbance and alcohol rules were being heavily enforced throughout the residence system, although the enforcement of disorderly behavior rules was less consistent. The residents in the two experimental conditions faced somewhat different situations because of variation in style of enforcement. We expect to find the same salience effect as in the other samples, however. We also expect to find that the role-taking opportunities provided in the peer authority condition increases the likelihood of linkages between legal reasoning and rule-governed behaviors.

We also expect to find differences associated with the alternative explanations, as we have argued earlier. Legal development theory (Levine & Tapp, 1977; Tapp & Kohlberg, 1977) suggests that reasoning precedes behavior, providing the justification for future actions. If there are mediating effects of situational attitudes, they would work through the cognitive processes of assimilation and accommodation. Social learning theory (Akers, 1985; Akers et al., 1979; Bandura, 1969b, 1977) suggests that reasoning follows behaviors because the role of reasoning is to rationalize one's prior experiences. Therefore, we will test our mediating model in two ways in order to determine whether the hypothesized causal path begins with legal reasoning or with rule-violating behaviors.

Analysis Plan

The purpose of the analysis was to determine the model that best describes the relationship between legal reasoning and behavior. Our plan was to compare a direct model, postulating a direct relationship between these variables, to a mediating model, in which the normative status of the behavior and the enforcement status of the rule mediate between the frequency of rule-violating behaviors and legal reasoning level. Both the direct and the mediating models have behavioral and cognitive versions representing the social learning and legal development approaches respectively.

The two direct models are found in Figure 7.1. In the behavioral model, the frequency of rule-violating behaviors, a cumulative measure, is related to the spring legal development level. In the cognitive model, the fall legal development level is related to the spring frequency of rule-violating behaviors. These data were analyzed by calculating separate zero-order correlations between legal development level and the following rule-violating behaviors for the university sample and the three experimental samples (control halls, peer authority hall, external authority hall): destructive, social disturbance, disorderly, alcohol, dishonest, crime, and sex-related. Due to the correlational nature of the model, we cannot determine if legal development level causes the behavioral variable or vice versa.

There are several specific versions of the mediating model, but the two general versions can be found in Figure 7.2. As you can see, the two versions vary in the direction of causality. In the behavioral model, the spring frequency of rule-violating behaviors causes the mediating attitu-

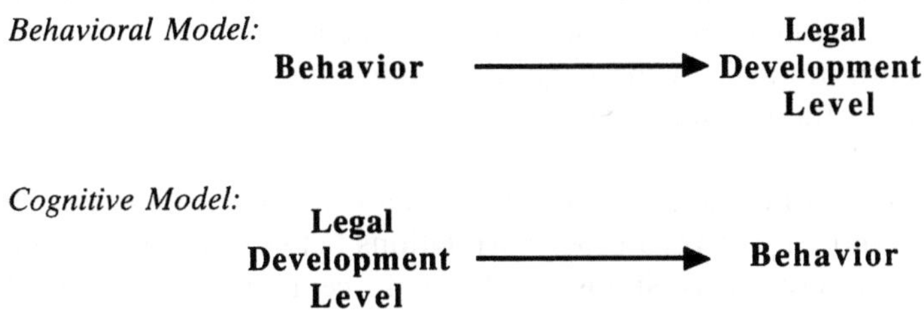

FIGURE 7.1. Direct models.

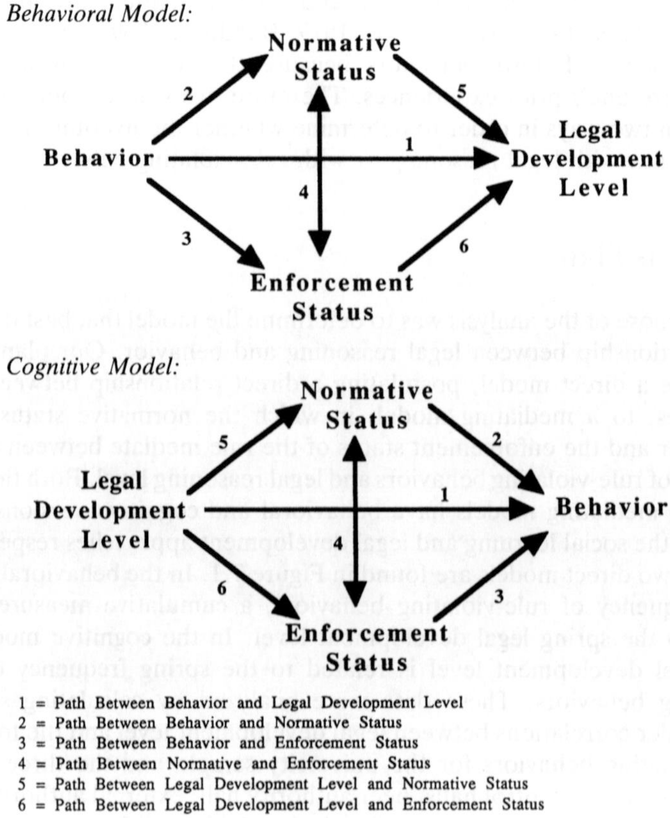

FIGURE 7.2. Mediating models.

dinal factors (normative status of the behaviors and enforcement status of the rules), which cause the spring legal development level. Our rationale for this procedure is that the behavioral measure, while taken in the spring, represents an accumulation of rule violations from the fall. The legal development measure represents the respondents' level of legal reasoning in the spring. Because frequency of engaging in behaviors for the period in question is a cumulative measure, and legal development level a time-slice measure, we believe that our procedure fits the logic of causal analysis required by path models. In the cognitive model, the fall legal development level causes the mediating factors that cause the spring frequency of rule-violating behaviors.

The data for both mediating models were analyzed by path analysis. In the behavioral model, the zero-order correlations between the behavioral measures and the normative status and the enforcement status were calculated. Then the partial regression coefficients between normative status and enforcement status were calculated controlling for the behavioral measure. The partial regression coefficients were calculated between behavior and legal development level, normative status, and enforcement status controlling for all other variables. In the cognitive model, the zero-order correlations between fall legal development level and spring normative status and enforcement status were calculated. Then the partial regression coefficients between normative status and enforcement status controlling for legal development level were calculated. Finally the partial regression coefficients between legal development level and behavior, normative status, and enforcement status were calculated. These path analyses were conducted separately for the university sample, the peer authority sample, the external authority sample, and two control hall samples. This allows one to compare the differences between the three residence hall samples.

We also wanted to compare the path analytical models separately for rule followers and rule violators. We calculated the number of rule violators for each of the seven behaviors for the university sample, the peer authority sample, the external authority sample, and the two control samples. Then we conducted the same path analyses separately for rule followers and rule violators (when the number of subjects permitted). For some behaviors, such as destructive behavior, there were not enough subjects who violated the rules. For other behaviors, such as social disturbance behaviors, there were not enough subjects who followed the rules.

Results

Comparison of Models

Direct Model between Legal Development Level and Frequency of Rule-Violating Behaviors

University Sample

The partial regression coefficients can be found in Table 7.1. As can be seen in the table, only the partial regressions between spring legal development level and spring social disturbance behavior ($B = 0.150$) and dishonest behavior ($B = 0.143$) are significant. Although statistically significant (due to the large sample size), these standardized regression coefficients are very weak because they only account for two percent of the variance. In the experimental samples (with smaller samples), these regressions would not reach statistical significance. Therefore for comparability reasons, we will use 0.200 as our criterion for a significant regression coefficient. In line with this reasoning, we will argue that the direct models do not describe the data from the university sample.

TABLE 7.1. Cognitive and behavioral models of standardized regression coefficients between legal development and rule-violating behaviors for the university sample

	Behavioral	Cognitive
Destructive	0.005	0.016
Social disturbance	0.150**	0.021
Disorderly	0.082	−0.037
Alcohol use	0.085	−0.079
Dishonesty	0.143*	0.024
Crime	0.121	0.027
Sex-related	0.121	0.100

* $p \leqslant 0.05$
** $p \leqslant 0.01$

TABLE 7.2. Cognitive and behavioral models of standardized regression coefficients between legal development and rule-violating behaviors for the experimental samples

	Behavioral	*Cognitive*
External authority		
Destructive	−0.094	−0.102
Social disturbance	0.063	−0.168
Disorderly	0.108	−0.217*
Alcohol use	0.022	−0.154
Dishonesty	−0.060	−0.047
Crime	0.121	−0.221*
Sex-related	0.016	−0.107
Peer authority		
Destructive	0.134	−0.320*
Social disturbance	0.335*	0.110
Disorderly	0.092	0.072
Alcohol use	0.223	0.054
Dishonesty	−0.279*	−0.082
Crime	0.438**	0.164
Sex-related	0.078	0.362**
Controls		
Destructive	−0.030	0.080
Social disturbance	0.129	0.050
Disorderly	0.178	0.053
Alcohol use	0.042	−0.034
Dishonesty	0.084	0.125
Crime	0.273*	0.165
Sex-related	−0.149	−0.040

* $p < 0.05$
** $p < 0.01$
*** $p < 0.001$

Experimental Samples

The partial regression coefficients can be found in Table 7.2. The only regression coefficient that was significant for the residents in the two control halls was the behavioral model between the frequency of engaging in crime behaviors in the fall and legal development level in the spring ($B = 0.273$). In contrast, the direct model did show more significant regressions for the peer authority and the external authority resident halls in the spring. In the peer authority hall, the behavioral model was supported with the significant regression between the frequency of engaging in social disturbance, alcohol, dishonest, and crime behaviors and legal development level. The cognitive model was only supported with the correlation between the frequency of destructive and sex-related behaviors and legal development level. In the external authority hall, only the cognitive model was supported with the significant regression between legal development level and the frequency of engaging in disorderly and crime behaviors.

Mediating Models: Behavioral versus Cognitive

As mentioned earlier, the behavioral model assumes that the frequency of engaging in rule-violating behavior causes the two mediating variables of normative status and enforcement status, which are highly correlated and cause legal development level. The cognitive model assumes that legal development level causes the two mediating variables of normative status and enforcement status, which are highly correlated and cause the frequency of engaging in rule-violating behaviors.

University Sample

The significant path models are indicated in Table 7.3; the betas for the paths are shown in Table 7.4. What is clear from these path models is that the cognitive model does not apply to this sample. The behavioral model

TABLE 7.3. Path analytic models based on the mediating model for the university sample

	Model	
	Behavioral	Cognitive
Destructive		
Social disturbance	X	
Disorderly	X	
Alcohol use	X	
Dishonesty		
Crime		
Sex-related		

TABLE 7.4. Standardized regression coefficients for the path analytical models in the university sample

	Paths					
	1	2	3	4	5	6
Behavioral Model						
Destructive	−0.57***	0.56***	−0.34***	0.01	0.03	0.16
Social disturbance	−0.72***	0.65***	−0.55***	0.15	−0.31**	0.03
Disorderly	−0.71***	0.57***	−0.44***	−0.03	−0.23	0.01
Alcohol use	−0.66***	0.60***	−0.52***	0.09	−0.28**	0.03
Honest	−0.50***	0.18***	−0.09	0.14	−0.10	0.03
Crime	−0.69***	0.66***	−0.49***	0.05	−0.11	0.10
Sex-related	−0.58***	0.43***	−0.27**	0.09	−0.06	0.10
Cognitive Model						
Destructive	0.02	0.47***	−0.03	−0.54***	0.03	0.03
Social disturbance	0.02	0.48***	−0.13	−0.78***	−0.03	0.04
Disorderly	−0.04	0.53***	−0.002	−0.77***	−0.07	0.02
Alcohol use	−0.08	0.28***	−0.22**	−0.73***	−0.04	0.02
Honest	0.02	0.15**	−0.05	−0.48***	0.03	0.06
Crime	0.03	0.53***	−0.10	−0.69***	0.02	0.02
Sex-related	0.10	0.22**	−0.05	−0.56***	−0.01	0.03

1 = path between behavior and legal development level.
2 = path between behavior and normative status.
3 = path between behavior and enforcement status.
4 = path between normative and enforcement status.
5 = path between legal development level and normative status.
6 = path between legal development level and enforcement status.

works for all the rule-violating behaviors except for destructive, crime, and sex-related behaviors.

We can analyze the specifics of the models. As we mentioned earlier, we set 0.20 as the minimum significant regression weight to compare the University sample with so many subjects to the smaller experimental samples. All of the mediating models appear to be a modification of the overall model. The frequency of engaging in fall rule-violating behaviors leads to both the normative and enforcement status of these behaviors (which are highly interrelated); only the normative status of these behaviors directly causes spring legal development.

Experimental Samples

The models that supported the behavioral or cognitive model for the control halls, the peer authority hall, and the external authority hall are indicated in Table 7.5; the betas for the paths are shown in Table 7.6.

In the control halls, one can see that both the behavioral and cognitive models received support. Both models worked for social disturbance, disorderly, crime, and sex-related behaviors. In addition, the behavioral

TABLE 7.5. Path analytical models based on the mediating model for the experimental samples

	Behavioral	Cognitive
External Authority		
Destructive		
Social disturbance	X	
Disorderly	X	
Alcohol use	X	
Dishonest		
Crime	X	
Sex-related		
Peer authority		
Destructive	X	
Social disturbance	X	
Disorderly		X
Alcohol use	X	
Dishonest	X	X
Crime		X
Sex-related	X	
Controls		
Destructive		
Social disturbance	X	X
Disorderly	X	X
Alcohol use		X
Dishonest	X	
Crime	X	
Sex-related	X	

TABLE 7.6. Standardized regression coefficients for the path analytical models for the experimental samples

	Paths					
	1	2	3	4	5	6
Behavioral Model						
External authority						
Destructive	−0.66***	0.79***	−0.56***	−0.09	−0.17	−0.03
Social disturbance	−0.70***	0.66***	−0.61***	0.06	−0.51***	−0.16
Disorderly	−0.52***	0.66***	−0.37***	0.11	−0.4**	−0.08
Alcohol use	−0.71***	0.55***	−0.51***	0.02	−0.43**	−0.03
Honest	−0.46***	0.55***	−0.23*	−0.06	−0.14	0.11
Crime	−0.63***	0.79***	−0.55***	0.12	−0.27**	−0.05
Sex-related	−0.76***	0.62***	−0.3*	0.02	−0.17	−0.10
Peer authority						
Destructive	−0.54***	0.44**	−0.25	0.13	−0.22	0.17
Social disturbance	−0.54***	0.37**	−0.55***	0.33*	0.33*	0.04
Disorderly	−0.65***	0.72***	−0.66***	0.09	−0.09	0.05
Alcohol use	−0.56***	0.19	−0.39**	0.22	−0.39**	−0.11
Honest	−0.57***	0.48**	−0.08	−0.28	0.06	0.39**
Crime	−0.59***	0.53***	−0.55***	0.44**	−0.08	0.15
Sex-related	−0.55***	0.51***	−0.53***	0.08	−0.36**	−0.20

TABLE 7.6. *Continued*

	Paths					
	1	2	3	4	5	6
Controls						
Destructive	−0.69***	0.65***	−0.48***	−0.03	−0.06	0.20
Social disturbance	−0.64***	0.57***	−0.55***	0.13	−0.30**	0.21
Disorderly	−0.71***	0.70***	−0.62***	0.18	−0.23*	0.23*
Alcohol use	−0.66***	0.55***	−0.53***	0.04	−0.15	0.19
Honest	−0.68***	0.24*	−0.13	0.08	−0.33**	−0.08
Crime	−0.56***	0.66***	−0.50***	0.27*	−0.39**	0.14
Sex-related	−0.70***	0.51***	−0.23*	0.15	0.06	0.32**
Cognitive Model						
External authority						
Destructive	−0.10	0.60***	0.03	−0.51***	−0.17	0.02
Social disturbance	−0.17	0.14	−0.50***	−0.80***	−0.02	0.01
Disorderly	−0.22*	0.66***	0.11	−0.69***	−0.19	0.08
Alcohol use	−0.15	0.18	−0.40	−0.77***	−0.07	0.04
Honest	0.05	0.38**	0.05	−0.59***	−0.08	0.17
Crime	0.22	0.73***	−0.04	−0.63***	0.15	−0.07
Sex-related	−0.11	0.31**	−0.02	−0.63***	−0.13	0.02
Peer authority						
Destructive	0.32*	0.26	−0.22	−0.53***	0.12	0.01
Social disturbance	0.11	0.16	−0.18	−0.62***	0.10	−0.14
Disorderly	0.07	0.56**	−0.21	−0.76***	0.21	−0.14
Alcohol use	0.05	0.16	−0.03	−0.62***	0.07	−0.18
Honest	−0.08	0.22	0.07	−0.59***	0.26	−0.05
Crime	0.16	0.08	−0.58***	−0.55***	−0.07	0.23
Sex-related	0.36**	−0.21	−0.53**	−0.69***	0.07	0.09
Controls						
Destructive	0.08	0.53***	−0.01	−0.62***	0.07	−0.13
Social disturbance	0.05	0.64***	0.06	−0.75***	−0.30	0.16
Disorderly	0.05	0.42***	−0.23*	−0.82***	−0.22*	0.06
Alcohol use	−0.03	0.42***	0.02	−0.75***	−0.28*	0.07
Honest	0.12	0.09*	0.01	−0.67***	−0.14	0.05
Crime	0.16	0.63***	−0.10	−0.60***	−0.18	−0.02
Sex-related	−0.04	0.34**	0.12	−0.49***	−0.19	0.10

1 = path between behavior and legal development level.
2 = path between behavior and normative status.
3 = path between behavior and enforcement status.
4 = path between normative and enforcement status.
5 = path between legal development level and normative status.
6 = path between legal development level and enforcement status.

* $p < 0.05$
** $p < 0.01$
*** $p < 0.061$

model was appropriate for dishonest rule-violating behaviors. The cognitive model was appropriate for alcohol behaviors.

For the behavioral models, the whole model in Figure 7.2 was found for social disturbance and disorderly behaviors. For dishonest behaviors, enforcement status was only directly related to normative status; it was not directly related to either the behavior or legal development level. For crime behavior, enforcement status was not related to legal development level. For sex-related behavior, normative status was not directly related to legal development level.

In the cognitive models, the whole model in Figure 7.2 did not describe any of the rule-violating behaviors. For social disturbance, alcohol, and sex-related behaviors, enforcement status was not related to engaging in the behavior. For disorderly behavior, enforcement status was not related to legal development level. For crime behavior, normative status was not related to legal development level and enforcement status was not related to engaging in rule-violating behavior.

In the peer authority hall, only the behavioral mediating models explained the data for all the rule-violating behaviors except disorderly and crime behaviors. The complete model in Figure 7.2 only explains sex-related behaviors. For destructive and social disturbance behaviors, enforcement status is not related to legal development level. For alcohol behaviors, normative status is not related to the behavior and enforcement status is not related to legal development level. In contrast, for dishonest behaviors, enforcement status is not related to the behavior and normative status is not related to legal development level.

Finally for the external authority hall, the cognitive model only worked for dishonest behaviors, while the behavioral model described social disturbance, disorderly, and alcohol behaviors. For the cognitive model, dishonest behavior was different from the whole model in Figure 7.2; enforcement status was only directly related to normative status for dishonest behaviors. For the three behavioral models, enforcement status was not related to legal development level.

Comparison of Direct versus Mediating and Behavioral Versus Cognitive Models

In conclusion, it is helpful to compare the direct versus mediating models and the behavioral versus cognitive models for the four samples: university freshmen, control halls residents, the peer authority residents, and the external authority residents. The results are in Table 7.7. What is obvious from the table is that the mediating models explain the data more successfully than the direct models. With the exception of the control residence halls, the behavioral model is more successful than the cognitive model.

Frequency of Rule Following and Rule Violating

The number of participants who report engaging in rule-violating behaviors (rule violators) and those who report not engaging in rule-violating behaviors (rule followers) are presented in the frequency distributions in

TABLE 7.7. Path analytic models based on the direct and mediating behavioral and cognitive models

	Direct		Mediating	
	Behavioral	Cognitive	Behavioral	Cognitive
University				
Destructive				
Social disturbance	X		X	
Disorderly			X	
Alcohol use			X	
Dishonest	X			
Crime				
Sex-related				
External authority				
Destructive				
Social disturbance			X	
Disorderly		X	X	
Alcohol use			X	
Dishonest				
Crime		X	X	
Sex-related				
Peer authority				
Destructive		X	X	
Social disturbance	X		X	
Disorderly				X
Alcohol use	X		X	
Dishonest	X		X	X
Crime	X			X
Sex-related		X	X	
Controls				
Destructive				
Social disturbance			X	X
Disorderly			X	X
Alcohol use				X
Dishonest			X	
Crime	X		X	
Sex-related			X	

Tables 7.8 and 7.9 for both the university sample and the experimental samples in the fall and spring.

University Sample

As can be seen in Table 7.8, more people follow rather than violate rules regarding destructive and dishonest behaviors. In contrast, more people violate rather than follow rules regarding social disturbance, disorderly, alcohol, and sex-related behaviors. The majority of participants violate rules against crime behaviors in the fall and follow rules regarding these behaviors in the spring. The number of rule followers increase and the

TABLE 7.8. Frequency distribution of rule followers and rule violators in the fall and spring for the university sample

	Time period	
Kind of behavior	Fall	Spring
Destructive		
Rule follower	212	239
Rule violator	132	107
Social disturbance		
Rule follower	17	7
Rule violator	326	331
Disorderly		
Rule follower	44	24
Rule violator	294	319
Alcohol use		
Rule follower	21	8
Rule violator	322	334
Dishonest		
Rule follower	247	309
Rule violator	100	40
Crime		
Rule follower	141	177
Rule violator	202	165
Sex-related		
Rule follower	65	90
Rule violator	272	250

number of rule violators decrease from the fall to spring for destructive, dishonest, sex-related, and crime-related behaviors. In contrast, the frequency of rule following decreases and of rule violating increases for social disturbance, disorderly, and alcohol behaviors. One possible explanation for the different directions of the change may be due to the label of the majority of participants—rule followers or rule violators. For example, almost twice as many people follow rules than violate rules for destructive behaviors. This behavior changes in the direction of increasing rule followers and decreasing rule violators. The only exceptions to this explanation are sex-related and crime behaviors.

Experimental Samples

The frequencies are found in Table 7.9. The same kinds of trends are found as in the university sample. More people follow than violate rules regarding destructive and dishonest behaviors; the frequency of rule following increases and rule violating decreases for these behaviors. In contrast, more people violate than follow rules regarding social disturbance, dis-

TABLE 7.9. Frequency distribution of rule followers and rule violators in the fall and spring for the experimental samples

	Experimental samples					
	Peer authority		External authority		Controls	
Behaviors	Fall	Spring	Fall	Spring	Fall	Spring
Destructive						
Rule follower	31	40	70	75	50	58
Rule violator	19	12	21	16	36	29
Social disturbance						
Rule follower	4	3	5	4	4	2
Rule violator	46	48	85	88	78	82
Disorderly						
Rule follower	6	7	10	9	10	10
Rule violator	45	44	81	80	74	76
Alcohol use						
Rule follower	5	3	5	6	5	3
Rule violator	45	48	85	86	79	81
Dishonest						
Rule follower	41	46	78	82	72	79
Rule violator	11	6	13	10	16	8
Crime						
Rule follower	24	26	42	42	39	47
Rule violator	26	25	47	49	47	38
Sex related						
Rule follower	12	10	25	25	20	23
Rule violator	38	41	67	65	63	33

orderly, alcohol, and sex-related behaviors. The changes from fall to spring for these behaviors are too small to draw any conclusions. Almost as many people follow as violate rules against crime-related behaviors. There were no noticeable differences between the different samples.

Path Models of the Relationship between Normative Status, Enforcement Status, and Legal Development Level for Rule Followers and Rule Violators

Based on the findings for the general path model, we focused on the behavioral model for rule followers and rule violators. Therefore both normative status and enforcement status were used as predictors of legal development level. Due to the small numbers of rule violators and rule followers for some of the rule-violating behaviors, we were only able to investigate the path analyses for rule followers for destructive and dis-

TABLE 7.10. Path analytical models for rule followers and rule violators in the university sample

	Behavior		Cognitive	
	Follower	Violator	Follower	Violator
Destructive		X		
Social disturbance	[1]	X	[1]	
Disorderly				
Alcohol use	[1]	X	[1]	
Dishonest				X
Crime				
Sex-related				

[1] Too few subjects for the analysis.

honest behaviors and rule violators for such behaviors as social disturbance, disorderly, alcohol, and sex-related behaviors. The path between normative status and enforcement status is the zero-order correlation. The other paths (between normative status and legal development level and between enforcement status and legal development level) were calculated by a multiple regression, which yielded two partial regression coefficients that each controlled for the other variable in the equation.

University Sample

The models that worked are indicated in Table 7.10; the values of the standardized regression coefficients (betas) are shown in Table 7.11. For

TABLE 7.11. Standardized regression coefficients for path models in the university sample

	Paths between		
	Normative status and enforcement status	Normative status and LDL	Enforcement status and LDL
Behavioral Model			
Destructive			
Rule Follower	−0.51***	−0.13	0.06
Rule Violator	−0.60***	0.17	0.21**
Social disturbance			
Rule Follower	[1]	[1]	[1]
Rule Violator	−0.76***	−0.22**	0.01
Disorderly			
Rule Follower	−0.37*	0.10	0.09
Rule Violator	−0.74***	−0.20**	0.01
Alcohol use			
Rule Follower	[1]	[1]	[1]
Rule Violator	−0.71***	−0.23**	−0.05

TABLE 7.11. *Continued*

	Paths between		
	Normative status and enforcement status	Normative status and LDL	Enforcement status and LDL
Dishonest			
Rule Follower	−0.47***	−0.11	0.03
Rule Violator	−0.55***	0.09	0.05
Crime			
Rule Follower	−0.55***	−0.16	0.01
Rule Violator	−0.71***	0.10	0.15
Sex-related			
Rule Follower	−0.35**	0.09	0.20
Rule Violator	−0.65***	−0.07	0.05
Cognitive Model			
Destructive			
Rule Follower	−0.52***	−0.5	0.01
Rule Violator	−0.53***	0.09	0.12
Social disturbance			
Rule Follower	[1]	[1]	[1]
Rule Violator	−0.76***	−0.02	0.02
Disorderly			
Rule Follower	−0.56***	0.11	−0.06
Rule Violator	−0.77***	−0.07	0.01
Alcohol use			
Rule Follower	[1]	[1]	[1]
Rule Violator	−0.71***	−0.03	−0.01
Dishonest			
Rule Follower	−0.48***	0.06	0.07
Rule Violator	−0.41*	−0.27	0.01
Crime			
Rule Follower	−0.58***	−0.08	0.07
Rule Violator	−0.64***	0.04	0.01
Sex-related			
Rule Follower	−0.45***	−0.06	0.11
Rule Violator	−0.58***	0.04	−0.05

* $p < 0.05$
** $p < 0.01$
*** $p < 0.001$
[1] Too few subjects for the analysis.

rule followers, the model did not work. For rule violators, the model worked only for social disturbance and alcohol behaviors. For these two models, normative status was related to enforcement status and legal development level.

TABLE 7.12. Path analytical mediating models for rule followers and rule violators in the experimental samples

	Behavior Model		Cognitive Model	
	Follower	Violator	Follower	Violator
External Authority				
Destructive		1		
Social disturbance	1	X		
Disorderly	1	X		
Alcohol use	1	X		
Dishonest	X	1		
Crime	X			
Sex-related	1			
Peer Authority				
Destructive	X	1		
Social disturbance	1	X		
Disorderly	1	X		
Alcohol use	1	X		
Dishonest		1		
Crime	X	X		
Sex-related	1			
Control Dorms				
Destructive	X	1		
Social disturbance	1	X		
Disorderly	1	X		
Alcohol use	1			
Dishonest	X	1		
Crime	X			
Sex-related	1	X		

Experimental Samples

The same path analyses were conducted for the control halls, the peer authority hall, and the external authority hall. The significant models are indicated in Table 7.12 and the standardized regression weights are shown in Table 7.13.

For the control halls, the model worked for rule followers for destructive, dishonest, and crime behaviors. Enforcement status was related to normative status, which was related to legal development level. For rule violators, the model worked for social disturbance, disorderly, and sex-related behaviors (it did not work for alcohol or crime violators). For social disturbance violators, enforcement status was related to normative status, which was related to legal development level. For disorderly and sex-related behaviors, normative status was related to enforcement status, which was related to legal development level.

For the peer authority hall, the model worked for rule followers for destructive, dishonest, and crime behaviors. Normative status was related

TABLE 7.13. Standardized regression coefficients for path models in the experimental sample

	Paths between		
	Normative status and enforecement status	Normative status and LDL	Enforcement status and LDL
External Authority			
Behavioral Model			
Destructive			
Rule Follower	−0.45***	−0.17	−0.03
Rule Violator	1	1	1
Social disturbance			
Rule Follower	1	1	1
Rule Violator	−0.78***	−0.46*	−0.15
Disorderly			
Rule Follower	1	1	1
Rule Violator	−0.55***	−0.33*	−0.06
Alcohol use			
Rule Follower	1	1	1
Rule Violator	−0.75***	−0.46**	0.06
Dishonest			
Rule Follower	−0.39***	−0.21	0.08
Rule Violator	1	1	1
Crime			
Rule Follower	−0.59***	−0.45	−0.09
Rule Violator	−0.60***	0.05	−0.13
Sex-related			
Rule Follower	−0.30	−0.30	0.09
Rule Violator	−0.80***	−0.07	−0.17
Cognitive Model			
Destructive			
Rule Follower	−0.40**	−0.10	0.03
Rule Violator	1	1	1
Social disturbance			
Rule Follower	1	1	1
Rule Violator	0.77***	0.05	−0.07
Disorderly			
Rule Follower	1	1	1
Rule Violator	−0.78***	−0.04	0.01
Alcohol use			
Rule Follower	1	1	1
Rule Violator	−0.74***	−0.02	−0.02
Dishonest			
Rule Follower	−0.54**	−0.10	0.19
Rule Violator	1	1	1
Crime			
Rule Follower	−0.58***	−0.01	−0.01
Rule Violator	−0.42*	0.48*	−0.29

TABLE 7.13. *Continued*

	Paths between		
	Normative status and enforecement status	Normative status and LDL	Enforcement status and LDL
Sex-related			
Rule Follower	−0.13	−0.51*	0.26
Rule Violator	−0.86***	0.06	−0.15
Peer Authority			
Behavioral Model			
Destructive			
Rule Follower	−0.81***	−0.1	0.28
Rule Violator	[1]	[1]	[1]
Social disturbance			
Rule Follower	[1]	[1]	[1]
Rule Violator	−0.66***	−0.38	−0.18
Disorderly			
Rule Follower	[1]	[1]	[1]
Rule Violator	−0.74***	−0.23	−0.06
Alcohol use			
Rule Follower	[1]	[1]	[1]
Rule Violator	−0.63***	−0.46*	−0.26
Dishonest			
Rule Follower	−0.53***	−0.08*	0.44
Rule Violator	[1]	[1]	[1]
Crime			
Rule Follower	−0.68***	0.71	0.49
Rule Violator	−0.62***	−0.44	−0.23
Sex-related			
Rule Follower	−0.87***	−1.64*	−1.40*
Rule Violator	−0.52***	−0.13	−0.01
Cognitive Model			
Destructive			
Rule Follower	−0.83***	−0.18	0.11
Rule Violator	−0.35	0.47	0.27
Social disturbance			
Rule Follower	[1]	[1]	[1]
Rule Violator	−0.60***	0.11	−0.15
Disorderly			
Rule Follower	[1]	[1]	[1]
Rule Violator	−0.17***	0.02	0.39
Alcohol use			
Rule Follower	[1]	[1]	[1]
Rule Violator	−0.63***	0.08	−0.18
Dishonest			
Rule Follower	−0.54***	0.29*	−0.5
Rule Violater	[1]	[1]	[1]

TABLE 7.13. *Continued*

	Paths between		
	Normative status and enforecement status	Normative status and LDL	Enforcement status and LDL
Crime			
Rule Follower	−0.61**	−0.07	0.22
Rule Violator	−0.37	−0.19	0.40
Sex-related			
Rule Follower	−0.81*	−0.50	0.50
Rule Violator	−0.53**	0.24	−0.12
Control Dorms			
Behavioral Model			
Destructive			
Rule Follower	−0.48***	−0.24	0.18
Rule Violater	1	1	1
Social disturbance			
Rule Follower	1	1	1
Rule Violator	−0.74***	−0.25	0.18
Disorderly			
Rule Follower	1	1	1
Rule Violator	−0.74***	−0.07	0.28
Alcohol use			
Rule Follower	1	1	1
Rule Violator	−0.74***	−0.15	−0.20
Dishonest			
Rule Follower	−0.65***	−0.35	−0.09
Rule Violator	1	1	1
Crime			
Rule Follower	−0.45***	−0.42	0.19
Rule Violator	−0.75***	−0.07	−0.05
Sex-related			
Rule Follower	1	1	1
Rule Violator	−0.85***	0.07	0.36
Cognitive Model			
Destructive			
Rule Follower	−0.39*	−0.30*	−0.01
Rule Violator	0.75***	0.57**	−0.36
Social disturbance			
Rule Follower	1	1	1
Rule Violator	−0.70***	−0.30*	0.16
Disorderly			
Rule Follower	1	1	1
Rule Violator	−0.74***	−0.08	−0.14
Alcohol use			
Rule Follower	1	1	1
Rule Violator	−0.71***	−0.27*	0.07

TABLE 7.13. *Continued*

	Paths between		
	Normative status and enforecement status	Normative status and LDL	Enforcement status and LDL
Dishonest			
Rule Follower	−0.65***	−0.13	0.03
Rule Violator	[1]	[1]	[1]
Crime			
Rule Follower	−0.34*	−0.49**	0.01
Rule Violator	−0.70***	0.09	−0.13
Sex-related			
Rule Follower	−0.19	−0.53*	0.03
Rule Violator	−0.71***	−0.07	0.14

* $p < 0.05$
** $p < 0.01$
*** $p < 0.001$
[1] To few subjects for the analysis.

to enforcement status, which was related to legal development level. For rule violators, the model worked for social disturbance, disorderly, alcohol, and crime behaviors (it did not work for sex-related violators). For social disturbance and disorderly behaviors, enforcement status was related to normative status, which was related to legal development level. For alcohol and crime behaviors, normative status and enforcement status were related to each other as well as to legal development level.

Finally, for the external authority hall, the model worked for rule followers for dishonest and crime behaviors (it did not work for destructive behaviors). Enforcement status was related to normative status, which was related to legal development level. For rule violators, the model worked for social disturbance, disorderly, and alcohol behaviors (it did not work for sex-related or crime behaviors). Enforcement status was related to normative status, which was related to legal development level.

Discussion

Earlier chapters have reported finding that an interaction between legal development level and rule-enforcing conditions explains a significant amount of the variance in legal socialization effects. This finding is particularly intriguing because both legal development theory and social learning theory imply such an interaction without explaining how it occurs or specifying the relationships among the variables. The purpose of this chapter was to explore that interaction by examining the possible relationships among the central variables that comprise the effects of legal socialization.

The Reasoning/Behavior Connection

We argued at the outset of this chapter that an adequate account of legal socialization requires some kind of connection between legal reasoning and rule-governed behaviors. We are not referring to compliance behavior *per se*—whether obeying or violating—because one can explain obedience without including the particular values and norms of community obligation that characterize legal socialization. Instead, we are concerned with the role legal reasoning plays in the process of acquiring these values and norms and the effect it has on behavior. To that end, we constructed path models of the connections that developed over the socialization period among legal reasoning (LDL), attitudes toward rule enforcement and rule-violating behaviors, and the tendency to follow or violate these rules. The path analyses have answered some important questions about the relationship between legal reasoning and rule-governed behaviors, particularly the validity of the mediating model, but have also produced some surprising results.

The path analysis allowed us to explore three broad dimensions of the reasoning/behavior connection: (1) whether it is direct or mediating, (2) whether it follows a cognitive or behavioral path, and (3) whether it holds for both rule violators and rule followers. The number of significant betas clearly supports a mediating model. The few direct relationships occur primarily in the peer authority hall, suggesting that the variation in rule-enforcing conditions had a significant effect on the reasoning/behavior connection. The peer authority treatment produced particularly strong relationships between legal reasoning and rule-governed behaviors, which supports the argument of legal development theory that role-taking opportunities are a critical factor in legal socialization.

The results were somewhat more mixed for the comparison of cognitive and behavioral models, although the predominance of the behavioral model supports the social learning premise that behavior is prior to reasoning. This finding suggests that the role of reasoning is more reactive than generative. It may be that the creative disequilibrium discussed by cognitive developmentalists is rooted in experiences as much as in cognitive discord. When such disequilibrating experiences are processed cognitively, they may become mediating factors themselves. While we cannot resolve such questions on the basis of our data, the findings do suggest that behavior is not simply a product of reasoning. In fact, the relative success of the behavioral model may indicate that the relationship between reasoning and behavior in legal socialization involves a process other than what is conventionally described by cognitive developmentalists.

Finally, it is clear that the reasoning/behavior connection holds for following as well as violating behaviors. Even though the methodology of path analysis is less predictive than descriptive when applied to the behavior-based samples, we believe we can conclude with confidence that the acquisition of values and norms of community obligation occurs in the context of both positive and negative responses to rules. But, as we will discuss later, this may not hold true for one's experiences when a rule is being enforced. It is important to draw a distinction between whether one follows or violates a rule, on the one hand, and how the rule is enforced, on the other. As a general matter, however, both rule followers and rule violators evince connections between legal reasoning and behavior.

These findings strongly suggest that the reasoning/behavior connection is an important factor in the interaction between legal reasoning and rule-enforcing conditions. But several aspects of this connection raise questions for further consideration. These are: (1) the specific role of the situational attitudes, (2) the nature of the "conflict" postulated as the basis for engagement between legal reasoning and rule-governed behaviors, and (3) the striking success of the reasoning/behavior connection in the peer authority condition.

The Role of the Situational Attitudes

First, there is no clear pattern in the situational attitudes (normative status of the behaviors and enforcement status of the rules) that mediate between legal reasoning and behaviors. Although the two attitudinal measures are highly correlated, they do not always play the same role in the path models. Both normative and enforcement status appear as mediators in the models, but normative status mediates more frequently than enforcement status. Every possible pattern of mediation is represented, and no one pattern dominates. This somewhat ambiguous finding suggests, on the one hand, that both the norm of behavior and the attitude toward enforcing a rule against it are important situational mediators in legal socialization. On the other hand, the finding does not allow us to specify when each will play this mediating role.

The attitudinal data are important for another reason, however. The fact that enforcement status is a somewhat weaker mediator than normative status demonstrates a significant feature of our mediating model. The attitudinal measure of enforcement status is distinctly different from the measure of legal reasoning, even though both ask specifically about rules. Not only is enforcement status situational ("do you approve or disapprove of enforcing a rule against under-age drinking?") as opposed to abstract ("what is a rule?"), but it also taps an attitudinal dimension of response to rule enforcement that is different from the way one reasons about rules in general. In other words, our situational measure of attitudes toward rules is independent of our cognitive measure of reasoning about rules (legal development level). We can conclude, therefore, that our situational and cognitive variables are measuring different aspects of legal socialization. This underscores the strength of our finding that legal reasoning is related to rule-governed behaviors through attitudinal mediators.

The Concept of Conflict in the Socialization Process

The findings also significantly clarify the role of conflict in the legal socialization process. Legal development theory (Levine & Tapp, 1977; Tapp & Kohlberg, 1977; Tapp & Levine, 1974) argues that experiences involving conflicting points of view stimulate cognitive development. On this basis, we suggested that conflict over the content of rules, including the conditions of enforcement, would produce opportunities and incentives for legal reasoning. Because conflict over rules requires residents to decide to obey or disobey the rule, we argued that the resulting legal context would produce engagement between legal reasoning and behavior. We operationalized this context of conflict in three ways: (1) whether the rule was enforced by external authority or peer authority, (2) whether one agreed or disagreed with a rule, and (3) whether one followed or violated a rule. Each of these operationalizations implies a different connection between legal reasoning and behavior and a different understanding of how the concept of conflict in legal development theory applies to the interaction between legal reasoning and rule-enforcing conditions.

The data provide strong support for the first operationalization, indicating that conflict affects the connection between reasoning and behavior through the impact of rule-enforcing conditions. All of the path models fit the data from the peer authority condition best, followed by the control condition, the external authority condition, and finally the natural socialization setting. Two differences stand out. First, the university sample, in the natural socialization setting, is composed entirely of freshmen, while the other three samples all included some freshmen and some upperclassmen. One can infer a longer-term socialization effect from the fact that more successful path models can be found in the samples with some upperclassmen than in the freshmen sample. Whether this is an effect simply of time spent or of maturation or of experience with conflict is not clear, however.

The other difference is more striking. Significantly more successful (significant beta weights) path models occur in the peer authority condition than in the external authority condition, with the controls in the middle. This indicates that the experience of conflicting viewpoints enhances the connection between legal reasoning and rule-governed behaviors under one set of conditions and not others. The peer authority condition had two key characteristics: it precluded external authority from enforcing the rules and it provided the residents with efficacious role-taking opportunities in which conflicting points of view were raised and resolved by the residents themselves. The external authority condition provided no role-taking opportunities at all, although conflicting points of view were common. The fact that the control condition evinced more successful path models than the external authority condition indicates further that the authoritarian style of rule enforcement had the effect of decreasing connections between reasoning and behaviors.

The data do not, however, support the second operationalization of the role of conflict in legal socialization. We hypothesized that engagement would occur between legal reasoning and behavior depending on whether respondents agree or disagree with the rule. As we reported in Chapter 4, there is considerable variation in both normative and enforcement status across the different clusters of rule-violating behaviors. For example, most respondents agreed with rules against destructive, crime, and dishonest behaviors and disagreed with rules against alcohol use behaviors; they were more middling about rules against social disturbance and disorderly behaviors, although tending to disagree. Given this amount of variation, the data provide a good test of the first operationalization. Is a connection between legal reasoning and behaviors more likely to occur when one agrees with the rule or when one disagrees with the rule? The answer is that both agreement and disagreement can result in a connection between legal reasoning and behaviors. The data indicate that engagement occurs regardless of rule content. While it is clear that the mediating model is more successful than the direct model, and the behavioral more successful than the cognitive, there is no evidence that agreeing or disagreeing with a rule affects the connection between legal reasoning and rule-governed behaviors.

The data further indicate that engagement occurs for both followers and violators, thereby providing no support for the third operationalization of the concept of conflict. This third version of the concept implied that violators would be more likely to feel conflict between points of view than followers, and therefore would be more likely to see issues of justice or fairness when the rule was enforced. Once again no clear pattern emerges from the data, however. Followers are as likely as violators to evidence a connection between legal reasoning and behavior. In short, the context of conflict, when defined in terms of whether a person agrees or disagrees with the rule or whether a person is a follower or a violator seems to be irrelevant to the connection between reasoning and behavior in the process of legal socialization.

We can conclude, therefore, that the concept of conflict in legal development theory means experiencing conflicting viewpoints through role-taking opportunities. This finding confirms the long-standing arguments of Kohlberg (1969, 1976, 1981, 1984, 1986), Tapp and Kohlberg (1977), and Levine and Tapp (1977). It also suggests that the differences between the two rule-enforcing conditions can tell a great deal about the process of legal socialization. To the extent that connections between legal reasoning and rule-governed behaviors are necessary to legal socialization, it is clear that experiencing conflicting viewpoints through role-taking opportunities contributes positively to that learning process while experiencing authoritarian rule enforcement actually undermines such connections. It is important to note that these conclusions are not dependent on any particular kind of response. That is, they hold whether the respondents agree or disagree with the rule and for both rule-following and rule-violating behaviors.

The Importance of the Peer Authority Condition

The power of the peer authority condition in the socialization process raises other questions as well. So far, this study has focused on individual responses to the various socializing conditions. But the actions of participants in the study were social in nature. Taking the roles offered by the internal judicial board and experiencing conflicting points of view through these roles are necessarily part of a process of social exchange. How do individual responses reflect the group experiences that generated them? What does it mean to obey or not obey in a community? These questions can only be answered by analyzing social behavior. We need to examine the operation of the internal judicial board and investigate what part it played in creating the normative structure of that residential community. Were the role-taking opportunities alone sufficient to engage reasoning and behaviors? Or did they produce spin-off effects which drew the attention of a broad range of residents and focused it on the conflicting points of view? The nature of the group process is a necessary part of understanding not only the individual responses we have been analyzing but also the treatment that created the peer authority condition itself.

Most importantly, we must find a way to identify the social and moral meanings of both following and violating behaviors. We know from individual responses how often the respondents violated the rules, whether they approved or disapproved of the violating behaviors, and whether or not they wanted the rules enforced. We also know how these attitudes and behaviors changed through the socializing period. What we do not know is whether and how community definitions of these behaviors affected the individual responses. Since the treatments that produced two different patterns of individual responses were community-wide, it is logical to assume that the process of normative definition was embedded in community perceptions and experiences. The social meanings of the following and violating behaviors are products of group experience. Their moral meanings grow out of the community's need to define what is acceptable and what is unacceptable behavior. Acquiring these moral meanings and participating in the process of normative definition comprise a large part of what we mean by legal socialization.

We do not assume consensus because it is seldom that all individual responses reflect the normative ordering of the community. There are dominant norms, however, and we recognize the necessity of going beyond individual responses to analyze the social process they share. Therefore, the questions provoked by the power of the peer authority condition become the basis for further exploration of the interaction between legal development and rule-enforcing conditions. To this end, we will conduct a qualitative analysis and comparison of the two experimental conditions in Chapter 9.

The Interaction

We began this chapter with the goal of exploring the interaction, found in Chapter 6, between legal development level and rule-enforcing conditions. We have now identified four factors that bear on the interaction. First, path analysis shows that legal reasoning is related to rule-governed behaviors, even though the behaviors were not predicted in the multiple regression analysis of Chapters 5 and 6. As hypothesized, this relationship is mediated by situational attitudes representing norms of behavior and norms of rule enforcement. The success of this mediating model indicates that behaviors, or more likely the experiences that accompany the behaviors, play an essential part in legal socialization. Both legal development theory and moral development theory have been strongly criticized for focusing solely on cognitive processes (Bandura, 1986; Broughton, 1986; Emler, 1983; Emler & Hogan, 1981; Hogan, 1976; Mischel & Mischel, 1976). Bandura has simply dismissed cognitive developmentalism because it focuses on "cognitive perturbations" (1986, p. 486). These criticisms ignore the frequent references to experience by the cognitive developmentalists, but correctly point out that little empirical analysis has been done to show connections between reasoning and behavior. In light of this debate, our analysis begins to fill a large empirical gap.

Second, we have also shown, in terms of the logic of path analysis, that behaviors predict reasoning (through mediation of attitudes) better than reasoning predicts behavior. This finding needs further exploration, but it does suggest that the account of information processing given by the cognitive developmentalists could be at least partially incorrect. If behaviors are prior to reasoning, legal development theory must expand its conceptualization of the socializing process to include, and not simply imply, linkages between legal reasoning and experiences. Tapp and Levine (1977) have already expressly rejected Kohlberg's insistence on the invariant sequence of developmental stages (p. 166), but in other respects they adhere to the cognitive developmental account. Consequently, the legal development approach continues to be confined to the study of developmental change in legal reasoning alone, with only passing reference to variations in experiential contexts such as the conditions under which rules are enforced. Our findings suggest that a shift in focus is warranted.

Third, the stronger relation between reasoning/behavior under the peer authority condition directs attention to the importance of certain kinds of role-taking opportunities. We can reasonably conclude that the interaction between legal development level and rule-enforcing conditions is primarily a function of the kind of role-taking made possible in that setting by our experimental manipulation. The peer authority condition stands out in comparison with other sources of conflict, such as whether the residents agreed or disagreed with the rules and whether they were followers or violators. It is equally notable when compared with the external authority condition, which offered no role-taking opportunities and tended to isolate residents against the exercise of authority rather than encouraging social interaction. We can conclude that legal development theory has correctly focused attention on role-taking opportunities. Certainly, the characteristics of those role-taking opportunities provided in the peer authority condition merit further empirical study.

Finally, our findings clearly indicate that the study of legal socialization should focus more on social processes than has been encouraged by legal development theory. Both moral and legal development theory tend to be individualistic in theory and method. The highest stages of legal development require the most individualized judgment. Principled reasoning (Stage 6) is almost a caricature of Kant's (1949, 1965) "moral man," whose judgments of legal obligation are independent of social convention and even of the rule of law itself. The methodology of cognitive developmentalism treats respondents as if they were isolated commentators on social processes. Our findings strongly suggest that these very social processes are critical to legal socialization and should be examined more closely. We will take the opportunity to do that in Chapter 9.

Conclusion

In exploring the interaction between legal development level and rule-enforcing conditions, two areas of investigation remain open. First, we have yet to examine differences among individuals in background characteristics and personality. It is possible that these individual variables will show significant distinctions among our respondents and thereby provide an alternative explanation for our findings. This possibility will be explored in Chapter 8. Second, as we have suggested earlier, we should examine closely the social processes that characterized each of the experimental conditions. In Chapter 9, we present a qualitative analysis of how these processes affect legal socialization under the peer authority and external authority conditions.

8

Offender Status

Chapter 8 explores another possible explanation for the interaction between legal development level and rule-enforcing conditions in predicting legal socialization effects. In this chapter, we separate our subjects according to their propensity toward rule following or rule violation. We then relate legal development level to their attitudes toward rules and rule-violating behaviors to the rule-enforcing conditions in which they lived during the socialization period and to the kinds of behaviors being controlled. We also consider personality, attitudinal, and demographic measures. Our purpose is to determine whether individual differences account for legal socialization effects.

Differences between Rule Followers and Rule Violators

It is possible that significant differences exist between rule followers and rule violators that must be taken into account by any explanation of legal socialization. One kind of difference between followers and violators is experiential. For example, the experience of violation itself or of one type of enforcement could produce significantly different socialization effects for followers and for violators. Personal characteristics comprise another kind of factor that could differentiate between rule violators and rule followers. These characteristics include legal development level, personality, and demographics such as gender and class background. It is possible that legal development level is high for followers and low for violators. Followers and violators could have different personality characteristics. Violation could be a male activity and following rules could be related to class background.

The path models of Chapter 7 suggest that followers and violators evidence similar legal socialization effects. On the basis of the social psychological literature (e.g., Asch, 1955, 1956; Milgram, 1974), however, we would expect to find some differences between these groups. The findings of Chapter 7 are somewhat tentative because of the low number of violators for some offenses and followers for other offenses. It is also possible that individual differences have been masked by the interaction between legal development level and rule-enforcing conditions. A further analysis is important because some conclusions concerning the process of legal socialization would be valid for only a portion of the population if differences between followers and violators do exist. Furthermore, each of these possibilities, if found to be true, could provide an alternative explanation for legal socialization. It is necessary to explore these possibilities to identify or exclude any alternative explanations.

Experiential Differences

One factor that could differentiate between followers and violators is their respective experiences with violation and enforcement. We can hypothesize that engaging in rule-violating behaviors affects legal socialization. Rule violation can involve a number of striking experiential factors (Katz, 1988), including a desire to engage in the forbidden behavior, the experience of the behavior itself, a decision to violate a rule, the experience of violation, and the experience of "getting away with it" or "getting caught." It is possible that some or all of these factors act to forge a relationship between legal reasoning and rule-violating behaviors, and thereby significantly affect the legal socialization process. This would imply that legal socialization is a different matter for followers and violators, not only because they have had different experiences, but because their reasoning about acts of violation and even the social and moral meaning of such acts would be different for the two groups.

Data from Chapter 7 (see Tables 7.7 and 7.8) indicate that this intriguing hypothesis is not confirmed, however. In Chapter 7, we investigated the relationship between legal reasoning and behaviors, both direct and mediated by situational attitudes. We argued that this relationship is a necessary part of the legal socialization process. The successful path models in Chapter 7 indicate that legal reasoning is often related to behaviors. But these relationships did not hold only, or even primarily, for those who frequently engage in behaviors that violate the rules. Rather, the connection between legal reasoning and behaviors is evidenced by both violators and followers. Our data do not permit a conclusive answer on this point because of small sample sizes for some behaviors. The data suggest, however, that the experience of violation does not differentiate the legal socialization of rule violators from that of rule followers.

Another experiential factor, which has already been shown to play an important part in legal socialization, may outweigh any differences between rule violators and rule followers. Strong situational effects on legal socialization can be seen in the different path models between the freshmen, the peer authority residents, and the external authority residents. The compliance studies of Asch (1955, 1956) and Milgram (1963, 1974; see recent review by Miller, 1986) give situational explanations for why people conform to a majority or obey an authority figure. Asch found that individuals would give incorrect answers about the length of lines in order to conform to incorrect responses given by confederates. In a series of studies, Asch found that group pressure leads to individual conformity. Milgram, a student of Asch's, focused on the conformity pressure of an authority figure on individual behavior. In his classic work, Milgram had a subject play the role of a teacher who had to shock the learner-confederate for incorrect responses. In the original version of the study, 65% of the subjects administered the highest level of shock to the confederate. One could argue that residents in the peer authority residence hall were similar to subjects in Asch's study. Students knew that they were running their own judicial board. There were pressures to conform to the majority who were the leaders in the dorm. In contrast, one could argue that the subjects in the external authority residence hall were more like subjects in the Milgram study, because there was strong pressure to conform to the authority.

In addition to the path analytic models from Chapter 7, there is already evidence in earlier chapters that the strong differences between the two experimental residence halls may have outweighed the differences between rule followers and rule violators. But before concluding that situational factors have prevented these differences from playing a role in legal socialization, we should investigate the possible effects of personal characteristics. One criticism of both Asch (1955, 1956) and Milgram's (1963, 1974) work is that they failed to consider individual differences as a factor affecting compliance and noncompliance with the group or with authorities. For example, all 21 studies in Milgram's research program ignore personality factors. In 1971, Carlson asked "Where is the person in personality research?" We now turn to the relevance of personal characteristics in our own study.

Personal Characteristics

Clearly the person is critical in our cognitive measure of legal development level. The substantive meaning of each level—preconventional, conventional, and postconventional—suggests one's level of legal development could be related to one's propensity to engage in certain kinds of rule-violating behaviors. It is also possible that one's propensity to engage in rule violation at all is related to legal development. As discussed several times earlier, preconventionals tend to reason in terms of fear of punishment rather than thinking about the harmfulness of their acts or the societal need for order. Conventionals are inclined to think in terms of social conformity and order. Postconventionals tend to reason in terms of moral self-regulation and principles that are independent of social order.

Some literature suggests that delinquents tend to be preconventional in their legal and moral reasoning (Blasi, 1980). Kohlberg has asserted (Kohlberg 1969, 1976, 1984) that immoral behavior, and perhaps rule violation, tends to decrease as one's reasoning level increases. Levine and Tapp (1977) assert that conventionals believe strongly in maintaining law and order in their community. These possibilities suggest that there could be a different relationship between legal reasoning and rule-violating behaviors for followers than for violators.

Moving beyond cognitive considerations, it is also possible that specific personality factors play a role in leading some people to violate rules and others to follow rules. It may be that certain personality types are more drawn to rule violation than others or that personality characteristics predispose some people to compliance. Although personality measures vary widely, one scale that seems particularly relevant to the question of rule violation is the Just World Scale (Lerner & Miller, 1980; Rubin & Peplau, 1975); the scale was devised to measure the range of beliefs surrounding the notion that the world is a just place. A just world is one in which "people get what they deserve. The judgment of 'deserving' is based on the outcome that someone is entitled to receive" (Lerner, 1980, p. 11).

Although much of the work on belief in a just world centers on attribution of responsibility (Hamilton, 1978; Heider, 1958), especially the derogation of victims (Lerner, 1980), studies have also shown that the scale is correlated with such personality factors as personal efficacy, internal locus of control, religiosity, and authoritarianism (Rubin & Peplau, 1975). The need to rely on external constraints and beliefs about the role of authority is especially relevant to a belief in a just world. It is possible, therefore, that rule followers and rule violators will tend to score differently on the Just World Scale. If so, such beliefs or personality predispositions may be the most powerful factor in the process of legal socialization, rather than either legal development or experiences.

In his book about the belief in a just world, Lerner (1980) asks the question whether this belief is a personality variable by its relationship to other personality variables. In addition to the variables already found correlated to the belief in a just world (Rubin & Peplau, 1975), Lerner discussed the importance of the Protestant ethic, which views hard work and suffering as the path to righteousness. He conducted a study in 1978 in which he administered a number of personality scales including the Just World Scale to undergraduates. Then he conducted a factor analysis to determine whether the Protestant ethic, the F scale, locus of control, and a set of other personality variables were part of the same factor that included the belief in a just world score. He found that the just world score loaded on the same factor as the Protestant ethic scale, the internal locus of control, and satisfaction and optimism. Variables such as the F scale and the social desirability scale loaded on other factors.

There are also behavioral differences in the belief in a just world scale.

Jurors who scored high on the just world scale were more likely to give stricter sentences to defendants who have been convicted of a crime (Gerbasi & Zuckerman, 1975; R. Izzett, Personal Communication, 1974). It is important to see whether rule followers and rule violators differ in their belief in a just world. On the basis of this literature, we would predict that rule followers would report a higher belief in a just world than rule violators.

Demographic factors should be considered in order to determine whether we can distinguish between rule followers and rule violators on the basis of background characteristics. There are four characteristics that could affect one's tendency to follow or violate rules. First, it is generally the case in studies of crime and delinquency that males are more inclined to engage in criminal or delinquent acts than females. Therefore, gender could not only distinguish between rule followers and rule violators in our population but could also create different legal socialization processes for the two groups (Sutherland & Cressy, 1978). A second possibility is that religion may inhibit the propensity to violate rules and therefore create two different groups and two different processes of legal socialization. Class background is a third possible influence on one's propensity to violate or follow rules. Growing up in lowerclass, middle class, or upperclass surroundings can affect one's view of authority and provide different experiences with rule enforcement (White, 1972, 1974).

Finally we consider our two attitudinal variables—normative status of the rule-violating behaviors and enforcement status of the rules. One would assume that people who follow rules would report low normative status and high enforcement status. In contrast, people who violate rules would report high normative status and low enforcement status. This may not hold for all kinds of behaviors. It may be that rule followers may also be conformists. Therefore they would be affected by the norms in the community. This would lead one to expect stronger differences between rule followers and rule violators when the behavior is one that very few people in the community do (e.g., destructive behavior or crime behaviors).

As pointed out in the preceding paragraph, it is important to remember, however, that our analysis requires more than a simple distinction between rule followers and rule violators. We have information on three major and four secondary kinds of rule violation: destructive, social disturbance, and disorderly behaviors; and alcohol use, dishonest, crime, and sex-related behaviors. We anticipate finding a distinction between followers and violators on the basis of individual differences for some but not all of these kinds of rule violation. Further refinements include the variation in rule-enforcing conditions and whether or not the community norms agree or disagree with the rule. The analysis that follows takes into account all of these permutations amd allows us to determine how each factor affects offense status under varying conditions.

Analysis Plan

Two different analyses were conducted to explore the differences between rule followers and rule violators. We conducted discriminant analyses to determine if we could distinguish between rule followers and rule violators on the basis of legal development level, just world score (Lerner, 1980; Rubin & Peplau, 1975), normative status, and enforcement status. Then we conducted chi square analyses to determine if rule followers and rule violators differed on the following demographic variables: father's education, mother's education, father's occupation, mother's occupation, religion, and gender.

Results

Discriminant Analyses of the Differences between Rule Followers and Rule Violators

In this analysis, we were interested in determining the factors that differ between rule followers and rule violators. To determine these factors, we conducted discriminant analyses with offender status (rule follower or rule violator) as the grouping variable. The dependent variables were legal development level, the just world score, and the normative status and enforcement status of rule-violating behaviors as attitude measures. The analyses were conducted for each rule-violating behavior separately for the freshman sample and the three experimental samples in the spring.

University Sample

The results of the discriminant analyses can be found in Table 8.1. The means and standard deviations are in Table 8.2. At the multivariate level, the differences between rule followers and rule violators were significant for all rule-violating behaviors. At the univariate level, offender status was related to the just world score only for sex-related behaviors. Those who violated rules against sex-related behaviors scored significantly higher on the just world scale than rule followers. Offender status also was related to the normative status and enforcement status of all rule-violating behaviors. Rule violators reported higher normative status and lower enforcement status than rule followers.

Experimental Samples

The results of the discriminant analyses can be found in Tables 8.3 and 8.4. It should be mentioned that the numbers of subjects are so small in some of the categories that it is not possible to conduct the analyses. In the control halls, the multivariate effects that were significant were disorderly, crime,

TABLE 8.1. Summary of significant multivariate Fs for discriminant analysis between rule followers and rule violators for the university sample

		Univariate F			
Behavior	Multivatiate F	LDL	JWS	Normative status	Enforcement status
Destructive	11.54***	0.01	1.03	46.33***	17.14***
Social disturbance[1]					
Disorderly	7.57***	0.22	0.10	28.79***	23.85***
Alcohol use[1]					
Dishonest	2.80*	0.92	0.43	7.04**	7.40***
Crime	25.42***	1.54	1.98	101.81***	46.75***
Sex-related	10.32***	0.10	4.79*	36.22***	18.14***

LDL = Legal development score
JWS = Just world score
* $p < 0.05$
** $p < 0.01$
*** $p < 0.001$
[1] Too few subjects for the analysis.

TABLE 8.2. Means and standard deviations between rule followers and rule violators for personal characteristics of the university sample

	Personal characteristics			
Behavior	LDL	JWS	Normative status	Enforcement status
Destructive				
Rule follower	2.12 (0.27)	61.75 (11.15)	6.57 (7.51)	88.84 (14.46)
Rule violator	2.13 (0.30)	60.13 (11.11)	16.04 (13.66)	80.05 (15.66)
Social disturbance[1]				
Disorderly				
Rule follower	2.15 (0.28)	60.61 (8.75)	21.30 (16.78)	79.40 (19.88)
Rule violator	2.12 (0.28)	61.48 (11.44)	43.44 (16.83)	57.00 (18.60)
Alcohol use[1]				
Dishonest				
Rule follower	2.12 (0.28)	61.70 (11.17)	13.01 (18.33)	78.35 (25.75)
Rule violator	2.18 (0.19)	60.00 (12.44)	24.21 (19.70)	62.30 (26.30)
Crime				
Rule follower	2.14 (0.29)	62.62 (10.88)	7.15 (9.54)	89.83 (14.74)
Rule violator	2.10 (0.26)	60.55 (11.66)	24.61 (16.27)	75.18 (18.05)
Sex-related				
Rule follower	2.13 (0.30)	63.89 (10.15)	8.93 (12.63)	84.06 (17.61)
Rule violater	2.12 (0.27)	60.30 (11.45)	20.13 (12.62)	71.95 (19.86)

LDL = Legal development score
JWS = Just world score
[1] Too few subjects for the analysis.

TABLE 8.3. Summary of significant multivariate Fs for discriminant analysis between rule followers and rule violators for the university sample

		Univariate F			
Behavior	Multivatiate F	LDL	JWS	Normative status	Enforcement status
External Authority					
Destructive	0.74	0.42	1.14	1.78	0.60
Social disturbance[1]					
Disorderly	2.27	0.19	0.06	6.23*	5.73*
Alcohol use[1]					
Dishonest	1.69	0.70	0.26	4.07*	4.95*
Crime	6.01***	0.09	0.73	16.99**	11.11***
Sex-related	3.29*	0.21	0.07	11.26***	1.89
Peer Authority					
Destructive	1.98	0.44	2.90	1.78	5.19
Social disturbance[1]					
Disorderly	4.23*	1.15	0.01	13.43***	7.54**
Alcohol use[1]					
Dishonest	1.35	1.58	0.04	4.74*	1.68
Crime	7.00***	8.58**	1.55	7.85**	9.78**
Sex-related	1.04	0.23	0.38	3.03	2.58
Controls					
Destructive	7.29***	2.51	0.92	29.17	9.30
Social disturbance[1]					
Disorderly	4.84**	0.82	0.25	13.75***	19.72***
Alcohol use[1]					
Dishonest	0.59	0.90	0.76	0.38	0.54
Crime	7.15***	0.64	5.25*	25.50**	3.81
Sex-related	0.72	0.12	0.24	13.18***	0.61

LDL = Legal development score
JWS = Just world score
[1] Too few rule followers to conduct the analysis.

*$p < 0.05$
**$p < 0.01$
***$p < 0.001$

and sex-related behaviors. At the univariate level, people who violated rules against crime and sex-related behaviors reported higher normative status than those who followed those rules. In addition, people who violated rules against destructive and disorderly behaviors reported higher normative status than those who followed those rules. Finally people who violated rules against destructive and disorderly behaviors reported lower enforcement status than those who followed those rules.

In the peer authority hall, the multivariate effects were significant for disorderly and crime behaviors. There was a significant univariate effect for the difference between people who follow and violate rules against crime behavior and for legal development level. People who followed rules in our crime category reported significantly higher legal development level than those who violated those rules. In addition, there were univariate effects for the normative status of disorderly, dishonest, and crime

TABLE 8.4. Means and standard deviations between rule followers and rule violators for personal characteristics of the experimental sample

Behavior	LDL	JWS	Normative status	Enforcement status
	Personal characteristics			
External Authority				
Destructive				
Rule follower	2.18 (0.32)	63.48 (11.87)	6.49 (8.35)	92.06 (9.76)
Rule violator	2.10 (0.27)	57.67 (20.74)	11.11 (4.04)	88.89 (6.21)
Social disturbance[1]				
Disorderly				
Rule follower	2.11 (0.24)	61.80 (10.13)	21.67 (20.71)	80.83 (17.33)
Rule violator	2.18 (0.33)	63.31 (13.20)	41.82 (17.01)	62.58 (16.25)
Alcohol use[1]				
Dishonest				
Rule follower	2.18 (0.33)	62.67 (12.65)	8.18 (14.48)	82.58 (26.75)
Rule violator	2.06 (0.24)	65.80 (17.71)	23.33 (30.28)	53.33 (42.74)
Crime				
Rule follower	2.19 (0.33)	61.66 (11.65)	8.33 (7.85)	91.02 (10.59)
Rule violator	2.16 (0.31)	64.48 (14.17)	19.40 (12.76)	79.74 (15.58)
Sex-related				
Rule follower	2.21 (0.34)	62.44 (10.73)	9.12 (12.56)	83.85 (16.02)
Rule violator	2.16 (0.32)	63.46 (13.72)	20.55 (11.35)	77.84 (14.62)
Peer Authority				
Destructive				
Rule follower	2.18 (0.33)	62.30 (10.52)	7.41 (8.98)	92.96 (7.59)
Rule violator	2.08 (0.32)	54.71 (10.44)	12.38 (7.87)	86.19 (3.56)
Social disturbance[1]				
Disorderly				
Rule follower	2.00 (0.42)	60.75 (10.53)	8.33 (6.80)	85.42 (16.84)
Rule violator	2.19 (0.32)	61.41 (10.55)	41.52 (17.73)	57.76 (19.09)
Alcohol use[1]				
Dishonest				
Rule follower	2.18 (0.32)	60.87 (11.35)	7.78 (14.17)	81.39 (27.57)
Rule violator	1.96 (0.38)	59.75 (6.13)	25.00 (20.41)	62.50 (25.91)
Crime				
Rule follower	2.02 (0.27)	62.89 (12.58)	8.10 (9.53)	90.97 (10.43)
Rule violator	2.31 (0.32)	58.31 (8.10)	20.31 (15.51)	78.39 (13.02)
Sex-related				
Rule follower	2.10 (0.45)	63.00 (11.27)	9.52 (18.43)	86.91 (22.49)
Rule violator	2.17 (0.30)	60.15 (10.82)	18.98 (11.10)	77.32 (11.28)
Controls				
Destructive				
Rule follower	2.08 (0.30)	62.59 (9.49)	6.46 (9.31)	88.96 (19.85)
Rule violator	1.94 (0.25)	59.78 (10.80)	23.33 (12.63)	72.96 (13.28)

TABLE 8.4. *Continued*

	Personal characteristics			
Behavior	LDL	JWS	Normative status	Enforcement status
Social disturbance[1]				
Disorderly				
Rule follower	2.14 (0.39)	59.40 (3.85)	16.67 (11.02)	88.33 (9.03)
Rule violator	2.02 (0.28)	61.77 (10.54)	48.30 (18.60)	50.66 (18.59)
Alcohol use[1]				
Dishonest				
Rule follower	2.01 (0.30)	61.95 (9.01)	13.95 (21.11)	75.78 (31.17)
Rule violator	2.14 (0.18)	57.80 (17.85)	20.00 (15.14)	65.00 (30.28)
Crime				
Rule follower	2.07 (0.32)	64.67 (9.34)	5.95 (7.97)	86.51 (23.53)
Rule violator	2.00 (0.27)	58.41 (9.41)	22.07 (12.81)	75.46 (15.61)
Sex-related				
Rule follower	2.06 (0.33)	60.20 (7.36)	5.83 (7.91)	78.33 (33.38)
Rule violator	2.02 (0.28)	61.93 (10.57)	22.60 (13.99)	71.98 (19.93)

[1] Too few subjects for the analysis.

behaviors. People who followed the rules against these behaviors reported significantly lower normative status than those who violated them. There were also univariate effects for the enforcement status of disorderly and crime behaviors. Rule followers reported higher enforcement status than rule violators.

Finally in the external authority hall, the significant multivariate effects were in crime and sex-related behaviors. At the univariate level, people who engaged in all rule-violating behaviors reported higher normative status and lower enforcement status than people who followed those rules (with the exception of the normative and enforcement status of destructive behaviors and the enforcement status of sex-related behaviors).

Demographic Differences between Rule Followers and Rule Violators

For the freshman sample and the experimental samples, analysis of variance and chi square analyses were conducted that compared rule followers versus rule violators for each rule-violating behavior by the following demographic variables: socioeconomic status, religion, gender, father's occupation, mother's occupation, father's education, and mother's education. Socioeconomic status was calculated by adapting a technique described by Straus (1980). The index was computed by converting both mother's and father's education and occupation into percentiles and then

TABLE 8.5. Summary of significant crosstabs between demographics and spring behaviors for the university sample

	Demographics						
Behavior	1	2	3	4	5	6	7
Destructive	X***						
Social disturbance							
Disorderly	X*						
Alcohol use							
Dishonest							
Crime							
Sex-related	X**						

1 = Gender.
2 = Religion.
3 = Father's education.
4 = Mother's education.
5 = Father's occupation.
6 = Mother's occupation.
7 = Size of home town.

adding the four measures together and dividing by four. This leads to a measure from 0 to 100. An analysis of variance was used to determine the effect of rule follower versus rule violator on SES. Then chi square analyses were conducted with the remaining variables.

University Sample

There were no significant differences between rule followers and rule violators on socioeconomic status. The overall mean was 51.434 (s.d. = 20.913) on a scale from 0 to 100.

The overall findings for the chi square analyses are in Table 8.5. The tables for the significant chi squares are in Table 8.6. Overall, there are only two significant demographic effects. Offender status (rule follower, rule violator) for destructive and sex-related behaviors is related to gender. For destructive behaviors, women are twice as likely to be followers as violators and men are almost equally likely to be violators as followers. For sex-related behaviors, men are over four times as likely to be violators as followers and women are twice as likely to be violators as followers.

Experimental Samples

There were no significant relationships of offender status with socioeconomic status for any of the residence halls. The mean socioeconomic status for the control, peer authority, and external authority halls were 55.36 (s.d. = 21.20), 54.03 (s.d. = 21.06), and 54.18 (s.d. = 20.26), respectively.

As in the case of the university sample, there were very few relationships between offender status and demographic variables. A summary of the

TABLE 8.6. Tables of the frequencies of offender status by demographic characteristics for significant chi-square analysis for the university sample

	Gender	
Behavior	Male	Female
Destructive		
Rule follower	65	171
Rule violator	49	58
x^2 (1) = 11.05, $p < 0.0008$		
Disorderly		
Rule follower	3	21
Rule violator	111	205
x^2 (1) = 5.12, $p < 0.023$		
Sex-related		
Rule follower	20	70
Rule violator	93	154
x^2 (1) = 7.05, $p < 0.008$		

overall chi square effects can be found in Table 8.7. The tables for the significant chi square analyses can be found in Table 8.8.

In the control halls, there were five significant relationships. Offender status for destructive behaviors was related to gender and religion. Rule violators are six times more likely to be men, while rule followers are equally likely to be men and women. Rule followers are most likely to be Catholic; rule violators do not show a religious preference. Offender status for social disturbance behavior is related to father's education. Rule followers had fathers who only completed high school; rule violators had fathers who completed college. Offender status for alcohol behavior is related to mother's education. Mothers of rule followers tended to be employed at home; mothers of rule violators tended to be professionals or managers. Offender status for dishonest behavior is related to religion. Rule followers tended to be Catholics; rule violators are equally divided among the religions.

In the peer authority hall, offender status for sex-related behaviors was related to gender. Men were 18 times more likely to be violators as followers; women were one-and-a-half times more likely to be violators as followers.

In the external authority hall, offender status for destructive, dishonest, and crime behaviors was related to religion. Rule followers for all three behaviors are more likely to be Catholics; rule violators are equally divided except for crime-related behaviors. For crime behaviors, violators are either Catholics or Protestants.

It should be noted that the sample size for rule followers in the social-

TABLE 8.7. Summary of significant crosstabs between offender status and spring behaviors for the experimental samples

	Demographics						
Behavior	1	2	3	4	5	6	7
External Authority							
Destructive		X**					
Social disturbance							
Disorderly							
Alcohol use							
Dishonest	X*	X*					
Crime							
Sex-related							
Peer Authority							
Destructive							
Social disturbance			X*				
Disorderly							
Alcohol use			X*				
Dishonest							
Crime		X*				X**	
Sex-related	X*						
Controls							
Destructive	X*						
Social disturbance			X*				X*
Disorderly					X*		
Alcohol use						X*	X*
Dishonest		X**					
Crime							
Sex-related							

1 = Gender.
2 = Religion.
3 = Father's education.
4 = Mother's education.
5 = Father's occupation.
6 = Mother's occupation.
7 = Size of hometown.

TABLE 8.8. Tables of frequencies of offender status by demographic characteristics for significant chi-square analysis in the experimental samples

	Demographic variable	
Behavior	Origin	
External Authority		
Dishonest	Gender	
Rule follower	23	58
Rule violator	6	4
x^2 (1) = 4.09 $p < 0.43$		

TABLE 8.8. *Continued*

	Religion		
	Protestant	Catholic	Other
Destructive			
Rule follower	29	37	6
Rule violator	4	4	5
x^2 (2) = 8.95, $p < 0.011$			
Dishonest			
Rule follower	29	40	8
Rule violator	5	1	3
x^2 (2) = 6.79, $p < 0.034$			

	Father's education		
	Up to high school	College	Graduate school
Peer Authority			
Social disturbance			
Rule follower	0	0	3
Rule violator	11	24	13
x^2 (2) = 6.97, $p < 0.031$			
Alcohol			
Rule follower	0	0	3
Rule violator	11	24	13
x^2 (2) = 6.97, $p < 0.031$			

	Demographic variable Gender	
	Male	Female
Sex-related		
Rule follower	1	9
Rule violator	21	20
x^2 (1) = 5.57, $p < 0.018$		

	Mother's occupation			
	Not out	Semi/skill	Clerical	Prop/prof
Crime				
Rule follower	8	2	11	5
Rule violator	6	0	4	14
x^2 (3) = 9.75, $p < 0.021$				

	Religion		
	Protestant	Catholic	Other
Crime			
Rule follower	12	12	1
Rule violator	3	17	4
x^2 (2) = 8.05, $p < 0.018$			

TABLE 8.8. *Continued*

	Demographic variable Gender	
	Male	Female
Controls		
Destructive		
Rule follower	22	35
Rule violator	18	11
x^2 (1) = 4.26, $p < 0.039$		

	Religion		
	Protestant	Catholic	Other
Dishonest			
Rule follower	23	43	9
Rule violator	1	2	3
x^2 (2) = 6.36, $p < 0.041$			

	Father's education		
	Completed high school	Completed college	Graduate degree
Social disturbance			
Rule follower	2	0	0
Rule violator	16	43	23
x^2 (2) = 7.51, $p < 0.023$			

	Mother's occupation			
	Not out	Semi/skill	Clerical	Prop/prof
Alcohol use				
Rule follower	3	0	0	0
Rule violator	20	14	18	28
x^2 (3) = 8.12, $p < 0.044$				

	Father's occupation			
	Not out	Semi/skill	Clerical	Prop/prof
Disorderly				
Rule follower	1	0	0	8
Rule violator	0	15	7	51
x^2 (3) = 11.96, $p < 0.011$				

	Residence		
	≤2,500	25,000	≤Million
Social disturbance			
Rule follower	1	1	0
Rule violator	5	35	39
x^2 (2) = 6.02, $p < 0.05$			
Alcohol use			
Rule follower	1	1	0
Rule violator	5	35	39
x^2 (2) = 6.02, $p < 0.05$			

disturbance, disorderly, and alcohol use behavior groups is very small, even from the large group of freshmen. With so few subjects in these categories, the results of the data analyses tend to be unstable.

Discussion

The purpose of this chapter was to determine whether individual differences account for legal socialization effects. In particular, we were concerned with investigating whether significant differences exist between rule followers and rule violators. Although this is not a study of compliance, we have argued that legal socialization includes not only legal reasoning but also situational attitudes and rule-governed behaviors. If significant differences are found between followers and violators, therefore, they would have to be taken into account by any explanation of legal socialization.

Our findings suggest that personal characteristics do not differentiate between followers and violators in any systematic way. If there is any pattern, it is one of randomness: a gender effect here, a religion effect there, and a few scattered SES effects. As discussed earlier, the Just World Scale (Lerner, 1980; Lerner & Miller, 1980; Rubin & Peplau, 1975) has distinguished between people in terms of locus of control, the Protestant ethic, satisfaction, and optimism in previous studies. We thought it was reasonable to expect that it would detect any personality differences between followers and violators. No such differences appeared. Demographic background fared no better as a basis for distinguishing followers and violators. Even gender failed to distinguish followers and violators in most cases.

The findings for two variables deserve special comment. Legal development level, our measure of legal reasoning, has been part of significant legal socialization relationships in analyses presented in prior chapters. This, however, was the first attempt to determine whether violators have lower LDLs than followers. Kohlberg (1969, 1976, 1984) has often suggested such a relationship and Blasi's review (1980) reported several findings to the effect that delinquent behavior is related to low LDL. On the basis of this literature, we had reason to expect that LDL would be related to offender status. No relationship was found, however. We believe this finding is significant because it tends to undercut the developmental import of legal development theory. We know from earlier chapters that legal reasoning, as measured by legal development level, is related to both situational attitudes and rule-governed behaviors. The current analysis suggests that this relationship is not because people at "lower" levels of reasoning are more inclined to violate rules than people at "higher" levels of reasoning.

The findings about the normative status of the behaviors and the enforcement status of the rules also deserve comment. These are situational attitudes rather than personality or background characteristics. Although we often think of attitudes as an attribute of the individual person, they are a product of social processes of normative definition. As such they play a bridging role between individual characteristics and the social environment in which individuals find themselves. It is striking, therefore, that the situational attitudes are the only personal characteristics in this analysis to reach the level of significance in a systematic way. Not only do they mediate between legal reasoning and rule-governed behaviors, as we found in Chapter 7, they also differentiate strongly between rule followers and rule violators. We can conclude, therefore, that offender status is more a function of the social environment than it is of individual propensities.

The lack of significant relationships between personal characteristics and offender status leads to another conclusion. Experiential explanations of legal socialization appears to be more powerful than explanations that rest on individual differences. It is possible, of course, that we have simply used the wrong measures. Perhaps we need to consider some other personality traits that may distinguish between rule followers and violators. Since none of the measures of personal characteristics are related to offender status, we are inclined to doubt that our findings are the result of a measurement problem. We are tempted to speculate about a social process explanation such as was offered by Asch (1955, 1956) and Milgram (1963, 1974). As discussed earlier, it is possible that the powerful experience of living in the peer authority or external authority hall explains the similarity between rule followers and rule violators.

In conclusion, one would have to support the experiential argument, given the lack of systematic significant findings for the personal characteristic factors. This suggests that one can best understand the interaction between legal development level and rule-enforcing conditions by focusing on the diverse experiences of residents in the two experimental residence halls—the peer authority residence hall and the external authority residence hall. In the next chapter, we describe the differences between the two residence halls using qualitative data and we analyze the underlying social processes.

9

A Comparison of Two Rule-Enforcing Experiences

In Chapter 8 we examined individual differences among our subjects in their propensity to follow or violate rules. We found that offense status is related to the rule-enforcing environment and norms of behavior and enforcement but is not related to legal reasoning level or personality. It seems plausible, therefore, that the interaction between legal reasoning and the rule-enforcing environment is more a product of group socialization than of individual propensities. We turn now to an analysis of the nature of that group experience in the two different rule-enforcing environments established by our experimental manipulation.

The Interaction and Group Experience

The design of this research assumed that variations in rule-enforcing conditions could produce different legal socialization patterns and that individuals who are subject to these variations would thereby learn different values, attitude and behaviors with respect to rules. This social learning explanation (Akers, 1985; Akers et al., 1979; Bandura, 1969b, 1977) was tested against the cognitive developmental argument (Levine & Tapp, 1977; Tapp & Kohlberg, 1977; Tapp & Levine, 1974) that differences in what is learned are a function of one's legal development level rather than a direct product of one's environment. Legal development level turned out to be the better predictor than the rule-enforcing conditions, although neither variable directly predicted behaviors. The finding of an interaction between the two predictor variables, however, led us to explore how legal reasoning and the rule-enforcing environment might be related in the socialization process. In Chapter 7 we found that behaviors that are the specific target of rule enforcement are related in a causal path to legal reasoning through attitudinal mediators. Chapter 8 again demonstrated the connection between rule-enforcing conditions and behaviors. We now turn to a qualitative analysis of the group experience under each of the rule-enforcing conditions, which will allow us to examine the complex interplay of all of these factors.

We begin with a brief review of the two theoretical positions as they apply to our experimental manipulation. The two conditions were differentiated by the extent and kind of rule enforcement that prevailed in each setting. This was done in order to test the social learning hypothesis (Akers, 1985; Akers et al., 1979; Bandura, 1969b, 1977) that the legal socialization process is one of control by consequences. The direct consequences for rule-violating behavior were enforcement of the rule and punishment applied to the offender. According to social learning theory, these direct consequences would have a controlling effect on both the offender and observers. The products of this kind of learning would include attitudes, such as norms of behavior and norms of enforcement, and reasoning about rules and enforcement as well as behaviors (Bandura, 1986). One experimental condition featured strict and rigid enforcement of the rules, with violators "written up" to the Dean of Students and required to appear before the university's judicial board for a hearing and (in almost all cases) punishment. The other experimental condition put enforcement in the hands of the residents through their own internal judicial board. In the first instance, rules were applied regardless of residents' own norms of behavior and enforcement. In the second condition, residents' norms determined how the rules were interpreted and applied.

While social learning theory (Akers, 1985; Akers et al., 1979; Bandura, 1969b, 1977) focuses on control by consequences, cognitive developmental theory (Levine & Tapp, 1977; Tapp & Kohlberg, 1977) is concerned with the effect of role-taking opportunities on normative reasoning. Such opportunities put learners in situations where they must deal with diverse viewpoints. Following Mead (1934) and Piaget (1926, 1932, 1970/1983), such situations challenge a person's capacity to view the world, as well as immediate problems, from multiple perspectives. This social cognitive capacity is developmental in much the same way as is one's capacity to grasp the physical properties of the world, but it can also be stimulated by experiences that involve taking the roles of others. Kohlberg's theory of moral development (1969, 1976, 1981, 1984, 1986) and Tapp and Levine's theory of legal development (Levine & Tapp, 1977; Tapp & Kohlberg, 1977) follow Piaget (1932) in interpreting this cognitive capacity to understand the social properties of the world in normative terms, i.e., encompassing prescriptive reasoning (moral and/or legal), attitudes toward the exercise of authority, and values such as fairness. Applied to our experimental conditions, cognitive developmental theory suggests that legal development level is the primary factor in the formation not only of legal reasoning but also of attitudes and behaviors with respect to rules and rule enforcement. Variations in rule-enforcing conditions should affect legal socialization by virtue of the role-taking opportunities they do or do not create, rather than through the controlling effect of consequences.

Our experimental manipulation established one role-taking opportunity. In the peer authority residence hall, residents formed an internal judicial board to decide all issues including cases of rule violation brought to it by the RAs. Residents of this hall referred to it as a "self-governing dorm" because of their judicial board. A stratified sample (by gender and floor) of residents was selected randomly to serve on the board. While there are probably numerous informal role-taking opportunities for anyone living in a residence hall, we established this formal mechanism as a means of implementing the experimental variation in rule-enforcing conditions. It also allowed us to observe closely the process of role-taking and to analyze the language and normative dynamic of these interactive deliberations. As this is a study of legal socialization, the internal judicial board provided an opportunity to observe how our subjects actually used their experiences, attitudes, and values in reasoning through issues of responsibility and blame and deciding whether and how to apply the rules. The findings that we have reported in Chapters 4 through 8, in which both legal development level and rule-enforcing conditions are seen to effect legal socialization, render our observations of the internal judicial board even more valuable because of its central role in relating the two predictor variables.

We analyze the cases heard and decided by the internal judicial board in the following pages, along with descriptions of surrounding behaviors and attitudes in the peer authority condition and comparable data from the external authority condition. In the process, we hope to illuminate important aspects of the interaction between legal development level and rule-enforcing conditions in legal socialization.

Comparing Activity in the Two Residence Halls

Data

The following description of activity under the two conditions is drawn from several sources. We had access to all of the incident reports, in-house warnings, and hall director duty logs for the entire residence system. Incident reports are formal reports of rule violation to the dean of students; in-house warnings were written but were not transmitted to the dean of students. An incident report would be filed, rather than an in-house warning, for a second offense or when a violation was serious. Each hall had a duty log in which all incidents were recorded on a daily basis by the RAs on duty. We interviewed a number of residents from each of the two experimental halls throughout the academic year. Members of a class in field research walked through the two experimental halls, as well as other residence halls, on a regular basis and wrote up field observation notes for the project. These reports covered any observed rule violations and/or enforcement activity and included characterizations of the kind and level of activity observed in the hall and its general atmosphere.

In addition, we held hour-long group debriefing meetings every other week with the hall director and RAs of each experimental hall, one week with the peer authority staff and the next with the external authority staff. The two hall directors bore the major responsibility for implementing and maintaining the experimental variation in rule-enforcing conditions, and these meetings gave them the opportunity to give a status report on their enforcement activities. The RAs used the debriefing meetings to discuss and analyze their experiences as peer enforcers as well as to report on rule violations and the general atmosphere of the hall. In addition, the RAs kept journals describing their activities and the attitudes and behaviors of the residents. These various sources provided a detailed picture of the nature and extent of both rule-violating and rule-enforcing activity campus-wide as well as in the two experimental halls through the entire academic year. We also had access to a special kind of data from the peer authority hall because we tape-recorded their internal judicial board hearings and the board deliberations. Consequently, our analysis of the peer authority condition allowed us to focus directly on the residents as well as on the RA enforcers.

Overview of Rule-Violation and Enforcement Patterns

As is clear from the data we have previously reported, most rule violation fell into the social disturbance category, somewhat less was disorderly, and relatively little was destructive. The social disturbance and disorderly behaviors were not only the most frequent but also the most widely distributed through the population. By the end of the spring semester, almost all respondents admitted to violating rules governing social disturbances and many admitted to engaging in disorderly behaviors. Our descriptions and case studies will focus on these behaviors because they reflect the kinds of experiences—of violating rules and observing rule violation and of being the target of and observing enforcement—that affected the vast majority of residents. They are also an appropriate focus because the norms of behavior and enforcement for these violations reflected genuine dissidence over the legitimacy of such rules. Consequently, the enforcement of these rules constantly provoked debate and comment as well as resistance among the residents. The rate of noncompliance was, not surprisingly, high across the residence system. In the natural socialization halls (freshman and control residence halls), enforcement was often sporadic. RAs would move in on parties and corridor hockey games only when these activities exceeded the tolerance of most residents or brought out the police.

In this atmosphere of inconsistency and resistance, the task of enforcement by peers is daunting if not impossible. University policy and training protocols require what is termed "confrontation." RAs are continually urged to "confront" violators. For example, they are supposed to stop anyone they see with an open alcohol container in the corridor or other public area of the hall and request that the violator leave the open area or pour out the alcohol; this is in contrast to making pronouncements about the open container rule at floor meetings and then looking the other way until a large party is underway or it is obvious that everyone is ignoring the rule. Likewise, they are supposed to request residents to turn down a blaring stereo during quiet hours as soon as the RA is aware of it rather than waiting until someone else on the floor complains. The clear implication of the confrontation policy is that the violators would not think to stop what they are doing unless reminded that they are violating a rule. They are being "confronted" not only with the exercise of authority but also with the rule itself. This kind of interaction between violators and enforcers does not occur in cases of fighting, smashing beer bottles in the corridors, or ripping sinks off the walls and throwing them out the windows. In such cases the violators know they are doing something wrong and do not need to be reminded of a rule. Where there is a disjunction between the norm and the rule, however, rule violators do not act as if they were doing something wrong. Their demeanor when "caught" does not indicate shame or chagrin, so the enforcer finds it difficult to confront them as violators. In fact, the onus of preserving the social balance of this interaction ceremony (Goffman, 1967) turns away from the violator and onto the enforcer when the violator maintains a demeanor of normality. This point illustrates a general feature of enforcing behavior, i.e., the demeanor of the violator controls the interaction to a large extent.

Rule Enforcement as an Interaction Ritual

Goffman's (1967) model of the interaction ritual provides a particularly insightful perspective on the relationship between enforcers and community members and a useful tool for analyzing the rule-enforcement process. Goffman's model is based on a "chain of ceremony" running through a mutuality of "deference and demeanor" (1967, p. 85) that he finds embedded in all human interaction. He argues that "Rules of conduct impinge upon the individual in two general ways: directly, as *obligations*, establishing how he is morally constrained to conduct himself; indirectly, as *expectations*, establishing how others are morally bound to act in regard to him" (1967, p. 49). The mutuality of interactions involving rules of conduct produces a closely woven and complex social fabric in which obligations and expectations become almost interchangeable, that is, "what is one man's obligation will often be another's expectation" (1967, p. 49). These obligations and expectations create a psychological pull for the individual because they commit him to a "particular image of self": "In the case of his obligations, he becomes to himself and others the sort of person who follows this particular rule, the sort of person who would naturally be expected to do so. In the case of his expectations, he becomes dependent upon the assumption that others will properly perform such of their obligations as affect him, for their treatment of him will express a conception of him" (1967, pp. 50–51). Because one's self-image is at stake in the interactions surrounding rule enforcement and because this is true for both rule followers and rule enforcers, "when a rule of conduct is broken we find that two individuals run the risk of becoming discredited: one with an obligation, who should have governed himself by the rule; the other with an expectation, who should have been treated in a particular way because of this governance. Both actor and recipient are threatened" (1967, p. 51).

Goffman's (1967) conceptualization of the interaction ritual surrounding rules of conduct leads to significant analytical insights when applied to the rule-enforcement process under study. The dilemma of the confrontation policy is that it is not necessary to "confront" the violator when the norm and the rule agree, and at the same time it is extremely awkward to do so when the norms of behavior are incongruent with the rules because enforcement then becomes a violation of social propriety. Following Goffman's analysis of interaction rituals, we can analyze these enforcement situations in terms of obligations to obey the rules, which impinge on the individual directly, and expectations about the behavior of others toward him, which impinge on the individual indirectly. The RA enforcers tend to view their situation less in terms of the substance of the rules than in terms of their duty to enforce them, and to interpret violations as attacks on their personal status since they are "just doing their job." Violators are resented because they force the RAs into a disciplinary role. On the other hand, violators differentiate between breaking *mala in se* rules, when they know they have done something wrong, and breaking *mala prohibita* rules, when they do not accept the prohibition. Both their behaviors and their attitudes toward enforcers reflect this differentiation.

Goffman's point about discreditation clearly characterizes the reactions of both enforcer and violator. When the norm and the rule agree, the violator knows he has done something wrong and in effect acknowledges the legitimacy of both the rule and the enforcer in his demeanor. In so doing, he shows himself willing to take the role of the other in the particular ritual of interaction that is rule enforcement. By contrast, when the norm and the rule disagree, as in most social disturbance and many disorderly violations, the violator challenges the legitimacy of the enforcer and shows himself unwilling to take the role of the other. What Goffman calls the "justice of ceremony" (1967, p. 85) is violated as well as the rule.

Ambiguities of Enforcement

It is clear, then, that the meaning of an enforcement event for participants on both sides of the rule depends on the relative congruence between the norms of behavior in the community and the substance of the rule. We have seen that this relative congruence can be high (destructive or *mala in se* behaviors such as assault or theft) or low (social disturbance or *mala prohibita* behaviors such as loud partying and drunkenness) or somewhere in between (disorderly behaviors such as hockey in the corridors). There is also some variation in norms across a community for each rule. Enforcement status generally varies inversely with the norms of behavior but, as we shall see in some cases later, there are enough differences to create considerable ambiguity in the ritual of interaction on occasion.

There can also be ambiguity in the enforcement process when RAs take the view that their goal is to induce responsible behavior. Sometimes RAs (like parents and teachers) will choose not to confront and correct minor violations, unless they become common or begin to produce serious effects on others, because they hope the violators will eventually correct themselves. Having experienced the ineffectiveness of this approach, one RA commented ruefully, "I guess people do respond best when the rules and guidelines are clear-cut. It seems to me, though, that it would be better to have people thinking themselves about what is right and wrong and making their decisions accordingly. This, of course, is unrealistic and could only work with people who are conscious of hurting or disturbing one another, and are keenly aware of their own feelings about the self." This comment illustrates a commonly held assumption that legal development occurs in a noncoercive atmosphere, but it also epitomizes the extent of social ambiguity that is necessary in order to create such an atmosphere. It is paradoxical that clarity and consistency, which are hallmarks of fairness (Fuller, 1964), might require an approach to enforcement that undermines the learning environment that is most conducive to legal development.

The first kind of ambiguity discussed earlier has to do with the social meaning of enforcement events. The second kind might be termed the ambiguity of nonintrusion because it illustrates that the other side of clarity and consistency in enforcement is the desire to withhold enforcement in order to induce people to see the wrongness of their actions for themselves. A third kind of ambiguity stems from the vagueness of the rules, which not only allows people on both sides of a rule to interpret it differently but also invokes differing interpretations among those on the same side. Whichever the effect, this kind of ambiguity has long been analyzed in the literature on enforcement (see, for example, Goldstein, 1960; Skolnick, 1966; White, 1974; Wilson, 1968). The usual focus of such analysis has been the exercise of official discretion, but the current study is more concerned with the kind of learning environment that this sort of ambiguity creates for legal socialization. What is learned about rules, fairness, and responsibility for one's actions through encounters with the ambiguities of rule enforcement? In our view, enforcement and the responses to it often have the instrumental effects of defining the norm for the group and revealing the values to be protected. Enforcement is not the simple encounter between enforcer and violator but rather the complex and lengthy process that begins with that encounter and reverberates past it through various stages of debate and judgment among all the members of the group who have been personally touched by the events or have observed and discussed them. It is this environment for legal socialization that we will analyze in the following descriptions and cases.

Focus on the Experimental Settings

The two experimental halls were chosen because they were generally representative of the residence system and similar to each other in important respects. Both are medium-sized and coeducational. Both are located on the main street of the town. Both have a mix of upper and underclassmen. The residence system as a whole ranges between two extremes: a few single-sex halls on the one hand, and three large, coeducational high-rise halls whose residents are predominantly freshmen on the other. The latter have a deserved reputation for excessive noise, partying, and vandalism. Most residents leave these halls for others or for off-campus housing after their first year, thus perpetuating the predominantly freshmen population. In contrast, the two experimental halls were reputed to be about average in rule-violating behavior. The external authority hall was slightly larger but had more upperclassmen and a returning staff. The peer authority hall had a new hall director and all but one of the RAs were new. In our judgment as researchers beginning a quasi-experimental field study, the external authority hall was larger but more stable, the peer authority hall smaller but less stable. On balance, there was no reason to expect the two halls to react differently to the experimental conditions.

Observers of the experimental halls reported major differences between the external authority and peer authority halls in the nature and extent of rule violation, however. These differences produced striking effects in the general atmosphere of the two residence halls and in the relationship between the RA enforcers and the residents. We believe these differences are related to the rule-enforcing conditions in each hall and that they significantly affected the learning environment for legal socialization in the two experimental settings. In what follows, we describe the two patterns of rule violation and their effects on the two communities.

External Authority Condition

There were 24 incident reports to the dean of students in the fall semester and 29 in the spring semester, most of which were recurrences preceded by in-house warnings. Many more incidents occurred that were dealt with by such warnings and then did not recur. The police were called three times during the fall semester and twice during the spring. In each of these incidents there were multiple problems including loud parties, brawls involving multiple participants, beer bottles being thrown from windows, interior damage, the use of fire extinguishers and underage drinking. A list of the kinds of behaviors that provoked rule enforcement by RAs includes the following: bottles thrown from windows, fights (e.g., over a poker game), doors ripped off, mirrors broken, sinks pulled out and smashed, phones ripped off walls (frequently), doors kicked, doors kicked in, "stomping the halls," verbal abuse of staff, "hall sports" (such as lacrosse played with bottles and waste baskets, hockey played with bottles and brooms, and assorted games with regular equipment), beer bottles smashed in stair wells and along corridors, water fights with fire extinguishers, drinking violations (such as under-age drinking, kegs, open containers, getting drunk, throwing up in the bathrooms and corridors), "cranking up the stereo," phone taps, "pen raids" (defacing doors), "flood-outs" (buckets of water thrown under doors to flood a room), and secret harassment campaigns against fellow residents.

The Rhythms of Rule Violation

These behaviors tended to concentrate on weekends, which begin on Thursday afternoon, but much occurred throughout the week as well. Examination of incident reports and duty logs indicates that the rate of occurrences was high in the first two weeks and then lower but gradually rising to another high around midterm, and lower again and rising to a crescendo by the end of term in mid-December. This same pattern was repeated in the second semester. The pattern clearly parallels the times of most pressure for the students. Each week began quietly as well, with low rates early and a gradual buildup to Thursday afternoon when most residents would begin serious drinking. The pattern seemed to have a dynamic rhythm to it, which tended to carry residents along as if they had no personal control but instead had abandoned themselves to the predictable force and flow of events. The RAs believed that the "blow-outs" near the end of each semester were also related to the fact that some residents were leaving the dorm, either to move off-campus or to graduate. According to this theory, such individuals no longer feared punishment or were actually hoping for the most common penalty, eviction from the residence system. The RAs in the external authority hall were so intimidated by the prospect of a blow-out by those no longer fearing punishment at the end of spring semester that they talked about it obsessively for a month in advance.

Getting Caught

The ebb and flow of activity seemed to sweep all residents along in its distinctive rhythm. Some said the only way to avoid becoming involved in the party atmosphere was to go away for the weekend. Since much of the activitity of partying was against the rules, the buildup toward a long weekend of partying inevitably created situations where enforcement would occur and thereby put many people at risk of being written up. But getting caught seemed to be a different socializing experience depending on the nature of one's violation. Instances of vandalism (pulling sinks out of the wall and smashing them), fighting, and smashing bottles were considered wrong, and residents generally supported enforcement of the rules in such cases even when they felt empathy toward the violators. Because these violations always grew out of partying situations, the residents' empathy was rooted in the sense that they could have been the culprits. The demeanor of the violators was hostile at first, primarily because they had been drinking, but it soon turned to embarrassment and most eventually apologized for their actions. The ritual of interaction in these cases affirmed the moral order by mutual acknowledgment of the residents' obligations and the RAs' expectations about such acts, thus restoring the justice of ceremony (Goffman, 1967).

The situation changed considerably when the violations were of the disorderly or social disturbance sort. Residents were generally hostile toward the peer enforcers and resentful of the enforcement policies. Those who were written up in connection with partying were usually the residents of the specific room where the party was held (having a keg, or "common source," was the major violation). The many others who were involved escaped enforcement if they dispersed without the police being called or were cited only for an open container violation or underage drinking. In these situations, those who were written up were angry and defensive, while those who were not written up were scornful of the policy and of the RAs who enforced it and generally resentful of authority. The justice of ceremony was violated for both sides of the interaction ritual. RAs were unhappy because residents had not only failed in their obligations to conduct themselves within the rules but had also violated the enforcers' expectations to be treated as bearers of moral authority. Residents felt the RAs were forcing them to take on obligations to obey illegitimate rules while at the same time denying the residents' expectations of being treated as responsible members of the community.

Responsibility

For the residents of the external authority hall, therefore, getting caught was largely unrelated to any moral context that would be conducive to taking responsibility for one's actions. Those who received written warnings (first offenses) tacked them on their doors defiantly, as a sort of badge of honor. This continued the pattern of attempting to restore the justice of ceremony by making the RA feel that s/he was in the wrong in writing up the violator and was, therefore, the deviant from the group. These citations were effective as a deterrent, however, because first offenders seldom repeated their offenses. Although effective, deterrence is based on invoking fear and therefore it lacked the moral context that would normally surround the legitimate exercise of authority. From their experiences, the violators (and observers) learned that punishment would follow getting caught, that their peers were on their side and considered the enforcement policy improper and unfair, and that nothing they could do or say would change the policy. From a social learning perspective, these individuals found their rule-violating behavior negatively reinforced by authority and positively reinforced by their peers. As a socializing experience, rule enforcement in the external authority hall taught the residents that responsibility is arbitrary because it has to do with getting caught and not with one's intentions to do harm.

The lack of moral authority in the enforcement process, or at least its ambiguous status, was clearly illustrated in the following case. One of the RAs graduated at the end of the fall semester and was replaced by someone who lived on the same floor. The new RA (Tom) was well thought of by the staff and popular among residents on the floor. In his second week on the job there was a large party on his floor with several kegs and many participants. He reported later that he had kept an eye on the party to make sure it was not too noisy but had not thought it necessary to police the numerous cups of beer (indicating a keg) that he saw being carried through the corridor despite the fact that people were going in and out of a locked room and many appeared to be drunk. Eventually, the RA who had responsibility for rounds that night (Joe) came into Tom's room and asked angrily why he had not shut the party down. Tom replied that he didn't think it was too noisy or out of hand. Joe reminded him that he was required to shut down any "common-source" party and write up those with kegs. He then called the residents in whose room the party was being held out into the hall and told them that they would be written up by Tom and to shut down the party.

This set of events had a number of repercussions, but the most pertinent for our purposes was the fact that the residents of the floor strongly supported Tom, even though he had to write them up, and tried in various ways to retaliate against Joe. They flooded Joe's room and covered his door with obscene messages for weeks, although he had been a very popular person in the hall. Tom's approach to enforcement was considered reasonable but Joe, who had been following the same procedure all year, was now blackballed by the floor. Tom was basing his decision on the outward effects of the party in relation to his understanding of the floor's tolerance of noise and other commotion, while Joe was enforcing the common-source policy. Every effort was made to discredit Joe, who complained bitterly that his reputation had been ruined, because the residents felt they had been discredited by his actions. In their treatment of Joe, the residents showed they were not only challenging the legitimacy of the enforcer but also that they were unwilling to take the role of the other in this interaction ritual. In short, the justice of ceremony had been violated. Tom, on the other hand, was given warm personal support from then on, which demonstrated the residents' willingness to accept the legitimacy of enforcement and to take the role of the other in the interaction ritual. This case illustrates how the enforcement process in areas of incongruence between the rule and the norm produced a confusing and even corrupting learning environment for legal socialization. Any notion of personal responsibility for one's actions was either obscured or distorted by the struggle to create reciprocity between the formal moral order and the normative structure of the community.

Retaliation

The residents' response to Joe was by no means the only instance of retaliation against RAs in the external authority hall. RAs, as well as the hall director, were the objects of various forms of retaliation throughout the year. These ranged from flood-outs and obscene messages to verbal abuse. Some RAs were subject to campaigns of harrassment. Several had their doors set on fire, and firecrackers in the hall outside the door were common. A favorite tactic of male residents was to urinate on the door of the RA, especially female RAs. Residents seemed to rest their own claims for status on their capacity to undermine the status of the RAs. Their only means for doing so was a combination of annoyance tactics directed at the RA personally and undermining the RA's role through ridicule. Thus the written warnings were posted on doors as if they were badges of honor and RAs were sometimes addressed in mock military fashion. The typical scenes of confrontation—open containers, noisy stereos—would sometimes begin with an attempt on the part of the residents to negotiate the way in which the rule would be enforced (for example, "but we're friends"). The RA would reply "you know it's my job," and the hostility was on. Once in a while the RA would, in the words of one, "act more like a neighbor than an RA" complaining about noise during quiet hours or garbage and vomit in the hall. This kind of verbal tactic would sometimes evoke an apology, but for the most part the RAs found it impossible to establish the obligation-expectation relationship in their favor.

There are three major conclusions one can reach about these responses to rule enforcement under the external authority condition. First, the prevalence of hostility, ridicule, and retaliation against the enforcers—despite the fact that the actual incidence of rule violation did not increase as it did throughout the rest of the residence system (excepting the two experimental halls)—provides a textbook case of defiance against what is considered to be the illegitimate exercise of authority. It is also important to note that this did not occur in instances of destructive behavior, where RA enforcement received support from the residents and (usually) apologies from the violators. Secondly, enforcement was closely associated with a continuing struggle to maintain a justice of ceremony between residents and enforcers. The ambiguities over the social meaning of the behaviors resulted in a constant reformulation of the relationship between two groups who were otherwise status equals. The enforcement relationship included obligations for constraining their behavior owed by the residents and the RAs' expectations about how they should be treated. The residents' expectations about how they should be treated by the RAs and what obligations the RAs owed them were equally at issue, justifying Goffman's comment about "the interpersonal, actor-recipient character of many rules: what is one man's obligation will often be another's expectation" (1967, p. 49). Finally, once a rule was invoked and enforced, the norms of behavior were defined for the residents—not by the official interpretation of the rule, but rather by their own responses to its enforcement. Through this group experience they discovered some common ground: defiance of the RAs, including concerted retaliation. The external authority condition was certainly a fertile, although not necessarily a positive, learning environment for legal socialization.

Peer Authority Condition

The peer authority hall differed from the external authority hall not only in its style of rule enforcement, which was dictated by the research design, but also in the nature and intensity of the rule violations committed by its residents. Because the experimental design precluded reporting incidents to the dean of students, we have no direct comparison of that measure. On the basis of continual reports by residents, RAs and observers to us, however, we can compare the pattern of rule violation in the two settings. There was one incident in which the police were called to the peer authority hall but it involved an attack on an RA by a nonresident who was drunk and trying to get in the locked side door after midnight. There were loud parties every weekend that observers said never got out of hand. Some residents engaged in varieties of "hall sports," although they stopped when asked to by an RA. There were numerous drinking violations, especially under-age drinking and open beer cans. Unlike the external authority hall two instances of drug violations (smoking pot) were the focus of action by the internal judicial board (see case studies later). On the basis of our campus-wide data, we believe there was no more drug use in the peer authority hall than elsewhere, however. In addition, there were no physical fights (brawls) among the residents, little damage to property, and little evidence of garbage, vomit and smashed bottles in the corridors. While the RAs were not universally beloved, there was no pattern of physical retaliation against them.

These behavioral differences between the two experimental settings cannot be explained easily by any of the individual level data we reported in Chapter 4, although the (nonsignificant) difference in direction of attitudinal change between the two resident populations certainly suggested that the experimental manipulation of rule-enforcing conditions was having legal socialization effects. The populations of the two halls were similar in background and gender, with the peer authority population somewhat smaller but also slightly less stable and mature. The rhythm of rule violation was the same across the residence system, as was the prevalence of social disturbance behaviors. We can only conclude that factors present in the group experience of each population shaped their attitudes and behaviors toward the exercise of authority, and ultimately determined the normative structures of the two communities. Our analysis of the response of external authority residents to their rule-enforcing conditions indicates a particular pattern of reaction to enforcement as well as a distinct pattern of rule violation. Therefore, we turn to the social interactions occasioned by rule enforcement to gain an understanding of the differences in legal socialization effects between the two experimental settings.

Our analysis of the social interactions under peer authority rule enforcement focuses on the cases that were brought before the internal judicial board. There were a number of verbal warnings about various first-offense violations and some written warnings about loud parties and smoking marijuana. Only three cases were brought to the judicial board, however. Two, brought during fall semester, charged violations of the rule prohibiting the use of marijuana. The third case was brought in April when an RA charged that there was a keg in a room that was hosting a party. It should be noted that the residents were well aware that they could have simply chosen anarchy by ignoring the board and the rules altogether. As the discussion of the cases will show, they did not choose anarchy but instead developed a strong sense of community control. Generally speaking, the interaction ritual of rule enforcement that we described in the external authority hall also occurred in the peer authority hall. That is, the senses of obligation and expectation in the interpersonal situation of rule enforcement fit Goffman's model of a justice of ceremony: when the norms of behavior agreed with the rules, violators appeared chagrined and apologized; but when the norms and rules conflicted, both violators and enforcers were angry and both attempted to restore the interpersonal balance inherent in the justice of ceremony. The three cases were instances of norm/rule conflict, but there were also several "noncases" involving norm/rule conflict in which the RAs backed off after the violators apologized (in the case of an extremely raucous party) or the evidence seemed insufficient to press a case before the judicial board. Finally, we will examine how the addition of the internal judicial board provided residents with an opportunity to go beyond the ritual interaction in a forum that obliged them to make judgments based on communitarian values rather than individual self-interest.

Case 1: The Public Forum

It was decided during a hall meeting that the internal judicial board should be composed of one member from each end of each floor (the floors are divided by gender in the center of the hall), chosen randomly but stratified by gender. As a result of this selection procedure, eight members were chosen representing the three floors, the "pit," and the "subpit." Various warnings were given out by the RAs in September and October, but none of these resulted in a judicial board case. The first case occurred in early November when two RAs charged two women residents with smoking marijuana. The two residents, Jill and Susan, had received a written warning for a previous incident in which the RA on rounds had noticed marijuana smoke in the corridor and traced the smell to Jill's room. When the RA knocked at the door, Jill answered and admitted that the smell was coming from her room. Both Jill and Susan, who was also in the room at the time, told the RA that they were sorry and would not do it again. Two weeks later another RA smelled marijuana on a different floor and traced it to a room that was holding a party behind locked doors. The RA broke up the party and wrote up each person present, including Jill and Susan. The others received first-offense warnings, but Jill and Susan were charged before the judicial board because of their prior warning.

While the judicial board was breaking completely new ground because this was their first case, they were working from what was by this time in the semester a well-established set of conventions about rule enforcement. Residents did smoke marijuana and drink when under age, but these activities were done behind closed (often locked) doors on the assumption that no one would be bothered by the act of rule violation itself as long as it was hidden. It was further assumed that blatant violations were wrong because they could be offensive to neighboring residents even if they did not disapprove of the behavior. From the residents' perspective, it was not the act itself or the violation itself that was wrong, but only the manner in which it was done. Several of the RAs had a different view, however, which directly clashed with the informal conventions of social control developed within the community. When these RAs smelled marijuana smoke in the corridor, they started after the culprits whether the doors were closed or not. The use of incense to hide the smell was considered a challenge rather than an attempt to mitigate the violation. These RAs believed that a rule violation must be confronted, that nothing could be overlooked. When someone pointed out to them that violations behind closed doors did no harm and were acceptable to the community, one RA replied, "I mean, so what if they're being responsible, they're still breaking the rules." Clearly, the stage was set for conflict when the internal judicial board began to hear its first case.

The hearing began in some confusion because no one had done it before, but the board members soon decided to follow the procedural outline that had been loaned to them by the university judicial board. Tension was high because both the accusers and the accused felt wronged. Jill and Susan were incensed because they had been charged with smoking pot when no one had seen them do so. They claimed that they had not been smoking, although some others in the room were smoking. The RAs, Nancy and

Jim, were equally indignant, first, because Jill and Susan had promised not to do it again, and second, because the whole floor was angry at them for writing Jill and Susan up for Jud Board. All four felt the social hurt of being discredited but believed the discreditation was unjust: Jill and Susan because they did not violate their obligation to obey the rule, and Nancy and Jim because their expectation of moral authority in the situation was turned upside down. Underlying this crisis in ritual interaction was the difficulty of enforcing the rule against smoking marijuana. Marijuana use was a basic fact of the social environment. Indeed, smoking pot was considered by many to be the quintessential social activity. Although not everyone indulged or approved, it certainly was a common activity in residents' rooms throughout the residence system and the rule against it was almost never enforced. The reason it was difficult to enforce was not because pot smoking was rare or hard to find but rather because of its sociable character: it was easy to find a party where a joint was being passed around, but almost impossible to identify who had or had not been smoking it. Consequently, the tension between the parties at the hearing was enhanced by the problematic nature of proof under these circumstances.

The board struggled to get the story out in the adversarial mode without the parties actually coming to blows. There were numerous reminders to both sides of the procedural ground rules ("you'll get your chance to tell your side next," "you're supposed to be asking questions, not making speeches"). But it was soon clear that the board members had found the issue that they wanted to grapple with, namely, how the rule should be enforced. In their questions of the RAs, the board members went over and over the problem of who could be charged under the wording of the rule against marijuana smoking. "Use of marijuana" was the operative term, and the board members noted that the rule made no mention of such legal phrases as "knowingly in the presence of." The hall director, who was present but not a party to the proceeding, was asked how the rule was enforced in other halls. She replied that being in the same room with pot smoking implied that you were smoking, so the RAs could assume that everyone was smoking whenever they found a room in which pot was being smoked. This statement of policy became known as the "assumption rule" in later discussions. The RAs were thoroughly questioned about what they had smelled, how they had traced it to that room, and why they had knocked on the door and entered the room. It was clear that the door had been closed, the music reasonably low, and that no other disturbance factors drew the enforcers to that room. After having ascertained from the RAs that they had assumed Jill and Susan were smoking but had not seen them do so (indeed, had not seen anyone smoking, but only smelled it), the board went into private session to deliberate.

As the deliberation began, it quickly became clear that the board members were divided. Two were outspokenly opposed to finding Jill and Susan guilty, "regardless of the evidence," because "the RA's shouldn't behave like that." Two others were unhappy with the notion that residents should "get away with anything they want to do when it's against the law." The rest were primarily concerned with the question of proof: "why should we assume that someone is guilty when we don't know?" The assumption rule became the primary focus of discussion. The group who were opposed to RA intervention argued that pot smoking was part of social life in the hall, and the board should not countenance enforcement against it unless the behavior was a blatant flaunting of a violation. In their view, responsibility for one's actions had to do with being discreet, and therefore anyone who was smoking pot with the door closed during a reasonably quiet party was being a responsible member of the community. If the RAs found out, they should use their discretion by asking people to end the party and giving everyone a warning rather than writing people up. The other side argued that the only responsible action for a resident was not to smoke pot at all and to leave a party if others were smoking. These board members felt that it was wrong for residents to do something that was against the law and they therefore believed the assumption rule was fair. The opposition then focused on the fairness question and argued that it was unfair to charge someone on the basis of an assumption rather than eyewitness knowledge. And so the argument moved naturally toward the kind of legal issue that plagues all law enforcement and is the basis of current legal policy debates.

Eventually, the argument over the fairness of the assumption rule hardened the division between the board members into two positions, which the participants themselves began to label "liberal" and "conservative." There appeared to be two areas of controversy underlying their disagreement over the assumption rule. The first area concerned the substance of the rule itself. The liberal view was that "smoking pot is something everybody does," while the conservatives believed that it was against the law and therefore wrong. The liberals pointed out that underage drinking was against the law, too, and the conservatives agreed that underage drinking did not pose a problem for them. This discussion led to further argument over "the kind of community environment" they wanted in their hall. The liberals felt that their residence hall had a relaxed and quiet social life relative to the rest of the system, and that pot smoking made a positive contribution to that kind of environment. They also contended that the residents themselves were able to "keep things under control" so outsiders would not be tempted to party there. "We've got a pretty good thing here at H-Hall. We don't attract a bad crowd because we don't have a lot of wild activities here." The conservatives agreed about the environment but felt that pot smoking could attract outsiders who were less "mellow." They all agreed that large parties with a lot of drinking were more likely to attract "wild-acting" outsiders, however, and that pot smoking among friends was less threatening to the community.

This meeting of minds did not resolve the conflict, however, because the conservatives felt that the RAs should be supported when they confronted behavior that was against the law: "It's not only their job, it's the law." The liberals countered that the RAs "are working for us" and they should "respect our ways." They felt that the incident would never have turned into a case if the RAs had been reasonable about it, since there had been no complaints from other residents. This disagreement about the RA role reached an impasse, however, and a member who had not argued either side of the debate suggested that they should establish guidelines for the future so that the RAs know what the residents felt was unfair. The focus of discussion then turned toward process: how could they control the RAs? It was eventually decided that the board should draw up guidelines for enforcement and then meet with the hall director and RAs to discuss them. They then turned to deciding the case. With some grumbling, the liberals agreed to uphold the assumption rule and find Jill and Susan guilty. All the board members believed that the two had in fact been smoking and that they would continue to do so. Jill especially had indicated that she did not know how she could avoid being charged again because she had so many friends who smoked. The conservatives talked about her attitude of "not taking this seriously" even when "it was against the law," and the liberals were hard pressed to find a way to support her. Their solution was to put the two on probation with the condition that another finding of guilty for smoking pot would mean automatic eviction (relocation to another residence hall). This left the focus on the assumption rule and its implementation. The issue of fair notice, which had arisen again and again and ultimately dominated the debate, provided a common ground for the remainder of the deliberation and for future discussion.

Four factors affecting legal socialization emerge clearly from this case. First, the residents had a view of what kind of community environment they wanted in their hall and of how it could be achieved and maintained, i.e., they wanted to socialize in a casual way, including alcohol and marijuana, but they would avoid engaging in "wild activities" that would attract "the wrong crowd." Therefore, they developed a pattern of informal social control based on the articulation of a set of values and specific strategies for realizing them. Second, the internal judicial board provided an opportunity to negotiate the protection of these values from interference by the agents of formal social control, and eventually to co-opt them into reinforcing the pattern of informal social control. Third, the residents found a common ground for debating their substantive differences in the issue of fair notice embodied in the assumption rule. While the liberals decried the rule as unfair, they bowed to the conservatives' view that some such rule was necessary in order to enable the RAs to uphold the law when they were confronted with clear violations. The conservatives in turn agreed to support the negotiations over the RAs enforcement practices, specifically with regard to "sniffing out" pot parties rather than waiting for complaints from other residents about noise or other offensive evidence of partying.

Fourth, the internal judicial board became a public forum for the airing of normative conflicts and for their resolution on grounds of community values. The hearings were not open to all residents, but both the substance of what was discussed there and the grounds on which the conflicts were resolved demanded that the participants adopt a perspective that went beyond that of individual self-interest. Ultimately, the debates in this public forum were about communitarian goals and the meaning of public values.

Case 2: Obligation and Responsibility

The negotiation between residents and RAs over enforcement practices began almost immediately after the first case, albeit in a rather tentative manner at first. The RAs felt threatened by the implied challenge to their authority and were reluctant to share the interpretation of university policy with any of the residents, while the residents generally felt it was their right to determine enforcement policy because they had an internal judicial board. The process of negotiation was in an early stage (the Board had a draft of some guidelines, but no meeting had yet been held with the RAs) when matters took a strange twist. Jeff, the chairman of the internal judicial board and one of those involved in the negotiation over the assumption rule, was caught smoking pot in his room with his roommate and some friends. An RA had smelled marijuana and traced it to Jeff's room. According to the RA, the room door was ajar. Jeff later denied that his door was open, but he admitted that he had been smoking. He was given a written warning. The very next night the RAs broke up a party at which Jeff was in attendance. The RAs alleged that pot was being smoked at the party and all present were given warnings except Jeff, who was "written up for Jud Board" because it was his second offense. The second case for the judicial board, then, involved an accused and accusers who had been parties to the negotiation over enforcement guidelines in addition to the other board members who now had an issue of precedent as well as a procedural stake in the outcome.

The resentment between the parties nearly boiled over as the second hearing began. Jeff believed that the RAs had been looking for him because of his role on the judicial board (he was one of the "liberals") and he wanted to challenge their method of enforcement in the second incident. He was stung by the attitude of the RAs toward him, in particular their indignant "how could you?" when they found out he was smoking. At one point in the hearing Jeff asked the RA, "Did you consider that at the time you were possibly exceeding your duties as an RA past the point of discipline through an excessive dialogue?" The RAs were upset because the chairman of the judicial board, who "should have known better," had violated the rule twice in two days. They felt this was a direct attack on their moral authority and rendered the judicial board illegitimate. In short, both sides felt discredited by the actions of the other and the "justice of ceremony" was seriously distorted as a result. This disruption of the normal ritual of interaction had clear consequences for the conduct of the hearing and for the social control function it would serve during the life of the project because it was obvious from the beginning of the hearing that the behavior of the RAs would be a central issue for the Board. The assumption rule as a matter of procedural fairness was colored by the residents' anger over the way the RAs had handled the second incident. The pot party presented a classic instance of applying the assumption rule, but the initial bone of contention was the RAs' decision to police the party in the first place.

The hearing began with a recital by the RAs of the circumstances of the first incident, for which Jeff had received a written warning. Jeff had admitted at the time that he was smoking and he did not deny it before the board. Asked if he had anything to say about it, Jeff replied, "Well, I would just like to comment on one thing on the first incident that we had been smoking and I, you know, accept that charge and the only point I really want to make is that I sense that Jim says that he suspected me the second night of having been smoking because I was so blatant smoking the first night and the conditions the first night were that about probably six people who don't live in this hall on their way home had come into the room, and people were going in and out and I was over in the far corner boxed away from the door by people and under no circumstances would I ever be casual enough to leave a door open. And secondly, there were a legal number of people in the room that was certainly under 10, and all of our behavior had been fine." In short, he had no problem admitting to the first violation, but he was protesting that he had not been irresponsible. He took the same line in discussing the second incident, although he would not admit that he had been smoking then. His approach was to attack the enforcement, particularly the application of the assumption rule. "The second charge assumes I was smoking pot because I was in a room where pot smoke was coming from. My first point is I was the person along with Nancy to open the door for Jim. In fact, we had just been getting ready to leave. We were standing up and we happened to be by the door. We both opened the door and we were the people that got the residents of the room for Jim. My second point is I was not aware that people at that time were smoking pot because the pot smoke had all been in the second room. There was a party that had been organized for a couple of days, a lot of people knew it was going to be there and so people were pretty cautious. They knew they were going to sit around smoking. There was no pot in the first room, and if Jim had inspected the room he would have noticed that there was no pot."

In short, Jeff was arguing that the assumption rule had no purchase in this situation. In addition, people were behaving in a responsible manner despite their intent to violate the rule and their rule-violating behavior at the party. Jeff revealed his thinking at the time in the following words: "I guess I figure that even if I should have known that there was pot being smoked in the room and I should've gotten out of there if I didn't want to be written up, is that still I think a warning would have been sufficient because there were not 20 people in the two rooms, which is legal. Nobody was belligerent and nobody gave Jim a hard time and the noise level was sort of in control and I don't know of any complaints from the residents." The real issue, according to Jeff, is "the duty of an RA. There's a question of whether RAs are policemen of the community to make sure everybody's being responsible or whether the RA is simply there to create the best environment possible and, you know, to keep personal liberty in control. In neither of the instances did I see that anybody's personal liberty was being infringed upon, and I don't think that the vices themselves are, you know, laws are to be interpreted and if we were blatant about it that would be a problem. But since we're basically renters as residents of this place we're not charges of the university and much as any other tenant would be responsible to their landlord it goes only to a certain degree. Community environment is not something to be ignored simply because people have what are known as vices. And I think the severity of the decision of the RAs to write people up in this case and in general has detracted more from the environment in this hall than the actual behavior or the actual crimes." Jeff's impassioned defense of his position was intended to indict the RAs and it succeeded. From this point on, the hearing would focus entirely on the behavior of the RAs, not on Jeff or his fellow pot smokers.

The RAs were completely taken aback by Jeff's criticism of their behavior. They seemed unable to engage in a debate over their activities and were easily backed into a defensive corner. As the hearing proceeded, one of the board members pulled out their draft of enforcement guidelines and suggested that they discuss them then and there. The guidelines included a statement that the assumption rule would be acceptable if the RAs were able to show that the accused was an active participant in a pot party and not simply that s/he had been in the room. The RAs agreed that this sounded fair, but one asked how they could prove active participation. Jeff replied that most people would tell the truth if caught fair and square. The board agreed, and the RAs nodded bleakly. Another guideline said the violation would have to be blatant. The board agreed that blatant meant in the corridor or with the door open and a very noisy or otherwise disruptive party. An RA asked if that implied that they should ignore all but blatant violations. A board member replied that she didn't think "their duty was to follow the rules to a degree that people have to alter their behavior beyond the mood of normal living." Jeff interjected that "I felt that I was in a safe environment" at the party because "I was not in the room where the pot smoking was going on." A board member said he felt Jeff had made a correct judgment and the RAs "shouldn't make us feel that we don't have a safe environment." The RAs seemed to agree, and suggested that Jeff receive a warning but no penalty. The Board then went into private deliberation.

The Board decided to accept the RAs' suggestion about Jeff. There was some discussion about whether or not he had smoked pot at the party, but even the conservatives seemed to feel that that issue was moot in the face of the RA's "shaky assumption." The fact that Jeff had been chairman of the board and still violated the rules provoked some discussion of how difficult it was to judge the conduct of others. One stated that "we can't ignore the rules altogether but we have to interpret them so they fit us and how we like to live." Another said, "the rules are there for us, just like the RAs work for us. If we aren't disturbing anyone, the RAs should leave us alone." A third suggested that "Jim should be talked to, but nice." In this way, the residents indicated their faith in the pattern of informal social control they had developed rather than an interpretation of the rules by RAs. In fact, the enforcement role of the RAs was severely and permanently undermined by these events. Two of them, including Jim, resigned at the end of the semester and the others largely withdrew from enforcement. There would be only one more judicial board case and that would not occur until the year was almost over.

But the second case had other implications as well. The assumption rule remained but its application was negotiated in favor of the residents' perspective on fairness. The pattern of informal social control initiated by the residents was now fully legitimized and would no longer be challenged by the agents of formal social control (with the one late exception that very much proved the rule). And finally, this case illustrated the fundamental distinction that had developed between one's obligation to obey the rules and being responsible for one's actions. The notion of an obligation to obey the rules is not only a logical part of the concept of a legal system (Hart, 1961, 1968) but is also closely tied to Goffman's (1967) social psychological concept of ritual interaction. Part of the "chain of deference and demeanor" when rules of conduct are involved is the obligation to obey, which is in turn tied to the expectation to be treated in a particular way (Goffman, 1967, p. 51; see pp.). Both of these concepts of obligation are deliberately devoid of substance, referring only to the relationship (either logical or empirical) between rules of conduct and the obligation to obey. Neither of them, however, conveys the sense in which the residents of the peer authority hall thought about being responsible for their actions. To them, being responsible meant an accountability to the communitarian norms of their social group. They viewed this accountability in moralistic terms, referring to the disruption of their neighbors and other kinds of social offensiveness. They believed that acts that violated the communitarian norms were wrong and that those who engaged in them deserved punishment and should apologize. To them, smoking pot behind closed doors was acting responsibly and the obligation to obey the rules had neither a logical nor an empirical connection to responsible behavior.

From the point of view of legal socialization, this disjunction between obligation and responsibility in one's experience with the exercise of authority has far-reaching implications.

Case 3: Privacy

The third and last case to come before the internal judicial board was a surprise to everyone involved. It occurred in early April when the semester was winding down (exams would start in a month) and social life was beginning to move outdoors. The hall had been relatively calm all year, although it was subject to the same rhythms of rule violation found throughout the campus. Weekends saw some rambunctious hall sports and loud parties, but these incidents were mild compared to most other halls and provoked no enforcement response from the RAs other than verbal warnings. A late snow storm disrupted the normal flow of events, however. It occurred in midweek and classes were canceled for one day. Residents began to party even though it was only Wednesday, and that evening the RA on duty had to contend with a loud stereo during quiet hours. She knocked on the door, loudly, for five minutes before the door was opened by someone leaving the party. The stereo was so loud that no one inside had heard her knock and she had to lean into the room to get anyone to hear her tell them to turn the stereo down because of quiet hours. As she did so, she heard one of the partyers say something like "I'll take care of the keg tomorrow." She also noticed a number of mugs and plastic cups in use, which were fairly reliable indicators of the presence of a keg. She did not see a keg. When she got someone's attention, she asked to speak with the residents of the room out in the hall. She told them they had to turn the stereo down and get rid of the keg and that she would be writing them up for a keg violation.

It was a week before the hearing could be scheduled and by that time the residents of the hall were thoroughly up in arms. They generally prided themselves on their ability to hide kegs, so part of their anger may have stemmed from hurt pride. The primary source of their anger, however, was the behavior of Ellen, the RA. The residents felt that she had invaded their privacy by gaining entrance to the room without their permission, and they focused the hearing on what they termed her abuse of authority. Despite the adversary format of the hearing, the defendants effectively played the role of victim and were able to deflect the accusations away from themselves and turn them against the RA. In effect, the hearing became a forum for blaming the RA, rather than an adversary arena for determining guilt or innocence. This was accomplished without abandoning the adversary format because the defendants refused to answer "yes" or "no" when asked if there had been a keg in their room. Instead, they repeatedly responded by questioning whether there was any direct evidence of a keg. This tactic had the effect of forcing the RA to explain what she had done over and over again, leaving many openings for the defendants to challenge her actions. The existence of the keg became a secondary issue, as the board began to debate whether an RA can gain entrance to a room by sticking her head in when someone opens the door to leave. One member asked a defendant, "If you were knocking on someone's door and the door opened right after you were knocking or a minute after, what would you do?" The defendant replied, "I'd probably wait until someone said come in. I mean that's the way I was brought up." Another defendant concluded, "I think it was really an invasion of our privacy to knock on our door or enter in the first place. It's too bad we don't have countercharges." In the end, the RA apologized to the residents for intruding into their room without being asked, although she did not withdraw the keg charge.

The board was clearly sympathetic to the position argued by the defendants, even though the conservatives were willing to take the keg issue seriously. They disposed of the keg charge quickly, however, agreeing that there must be direct evidence of a keg to hold someone guilty of violating the rule. They then turned their attention to the issue of enforcement guidelines again, particularly the question of room privacy versus RA prerogatives. No one on the board was concerned with the keg violation itself or with the party that provided the context. There was general agreement that they could control their own parties and no one suggested that this party or any other had been a problem for the residents. It was clear that the already-established and legitimized pattern of informal social control was working to everyone's satisfaction. The board members believed that, generally speaking, an RA would be going out of her way to find a violation because no one in their community committed blatant violations that really disrupted the lives of others. Even though most of them felt that the RA in this case had not been overzealous but rather had happened into an unwarranted intrusion on a party, they did see this more or less innocent act as something to be controlled and constrained for the future. In short, the hearing was perceived as being about RA enforcement behavior and not resident violations. The moral content of the hearing was blaming the RA and not accountability under the rules. The RA's actions amounted to a violation of privacy, and this was deemed the central moral issue of the incident.

This case also revealed a violation of the justice of ceremony in a new and significant form. The normal interpersonal balance inherent in Goffman's (1967) interaction ritual, as it is applied to situations involving rules of conduct, is composed of an individual who is under an obligation to obey the rule and another individual who has an expectation to be treated in a certain way as a result of the other's obedience. A person who obeys the rules is respectful not only of the rules but also of the one to whom the obligation is owed. Enforcers like RAs expect the respect that is due their role. In the same way, those who bear an obligation to obey the rules expect to be treated as responsible individuals who can be counted on to live up to their obligations. We have already seen that the residents who fail to obey what they consider legitimate rules will apologize to the RAs, thus restoring the justice of ceremony by fulfilling their obligation and showing that they will act as responsible individuals. By contrast, when the residents do not consider the rules to be legitimate, they will not apologize for violations or otherwise indicate that they feel an obligation. As a result, both residents and enforcers remain indignant and the justice of ceremony is not restored. Case 3 illustrates a different form of restoring the justice of ceremony. Here the demeanor of the violators controlled the interaction. Consequently, blame fell on the enforcers rather than the residents, the rules of conduct were the rules for RA enforcement behavior, and the enforcer was eventually led to apologize. In this way the judicial board hearing restored the justice of ceremony even though the normal authority relationship between the parties to this interaction ritual was reversed.

Conclusion

This description and analysis of the group experience in the two experimental settings yield several new insights about the interaction between individual and environment in the process of legal socialization. In the first place, our experimental manipulation of rule-enforcing conditions clearly produced two different kinds of learning environment. In both cases, however, the residents discovered they had something in common when the rules were enforced. For the external authority residents, that common ground was defiance of authority, acted out through various forms of retaliation against the enforcers. Peer Authority residents found their environment conducive to developing their own pattern of informal social control. When rules were enforced these residents discovered a common ground in the need to preserve the integrity of their community, both against inroads by outsiders and against intrusions by enforcers. Unlike the external authority residents, whose relationship to rules was entirely one-sided, the peer authority residents were able to negotiate guidelines for rule enforcement that fit the pattern of informal social control that they had developed for themselves and that reflected their sense of community. Those who were members of the judicial board displayed a capacity for taking the public viewpoint rather than pursuing narrow self-interest as they upheld the rules while negotiating guidelines for their enforcement. Consequently, peer authority residents were able to shape the rules to fit the community's sense of propriety, and thereby to serve communitarian values. It was clear to these residents from the beginning that they could have settled for anarchy if they chose, but they worked to pursue the community's interests instead. Discussion about the cases, the rules, and the work of the judicial board permeated the group, thus providing role-taking opportunities to a broad range of residents.

In addition to shedding light on the different learning environments for legal socialization, the group experience of rule enforcement reveals several other aspects of the interaction between the individual and the environment. It seems clear, for example, that rule enforcement can define a behavioral norm for the group by giving that behavior a social meaning. Sometimes the social meaning accords with the normative perspective of the enforcer, but it can also derive from negative responses to the enforcer. Whatever the normative direction of the definition, it results from the singling out of a piece of behavior as a violation of a rule. The behavior then takes on a particular social meaning that it did not have before. For example, drinking a beer in the corridor becomes an act of defiance, smoking pot becomes an affirmation of community, while pulling a fire alarm becomes dangerous and wrong. In the same way, an act of enforcing the rules takes on a social meaning that cannot be understood outside of its community context and the responses of members of that community. These responses in turn reveal to the community its members' sense of the values they want to protect, such as autonomy in social behaviors and privacy. In terms of the interaction between legal reasoning and the rule-enforcing environment, the group experience appears to mediate between an individual's existing conceptual categories and new rule content. In the case of norm/rule disagreement within the group (for example, social disturbance behaviors for our population), the new rule content cannot be assimilated into the conceptual categories that define the individual's established way of reasoning about fairness or the obligation to obey rules or being responsible for one's actions. Experiences with these behaviors and with enforcement against them, sometimes directly but most often vicariously through the group, are the points of departure for a learning process that eventually links the behaviors with legal reasoning (see Chapter 7).

The group experience of rule enforcement provides a three-dimensional normative structure that is often missing from dyadic exercises of authority. In dyadic situations, the moral authority of the enforcer is established by relative power and/or status and is maintained by convention. In many parent-child relationships, that moral authority is enhanced through love, but seldom do other dyadic relationships (teacher-student, employer-employee, police officer-citizen) achieve more than conventional legitimacy. In group situations, the moral authority of the enforcer derives from the group's willingness to accept the legitimacy of enforcement. This third dimension expands the moral content of the situation. By the same token, enforcement without legitimacy decreases the moral content of the situation and reduces the parties to a dyadic relationship. For example, a person with a capacity for postconventional legal reasoning may be reduced by these conditions to a preconventional state. In the external authority hall there were no opportunities to invest the social disturbance rules with moral content because there was no legitimate moral authority in their enforcement. By contrast, in the peer authority hall the residents did have opportunities to invest the social disturbance rules with the community's own normative meaning because the terms of their enforcement were defined in a way that was compatible with the community's informal rules of social control.

From the perspective of the interaction between the individual and the environment in legal socialization, this third dimension took the peer authority residents beyond simply seeing the situation from the viewpoint of others, as cognitive developmental theory would have it. Goffman suggests instead that "the individual must rely on others to complete the picture of him of which he himself is allowed to paint only certain parts" (1967, p. 84). This interdependence of individuals involved in an authority relationship produces Goffman's "chain of ceremony": "Each individual is responsible for the demeanor image of himself and the deference image of others, so that for a complete man to be expressed, the individuals must hold hands in a chain of ceremony, each giving deferentially with proper demeanor to the one on the right what will be received deferentially from the one on the left" (1967, pp. 84–85). In the case of social disturbance rules, this chain of ceremony was disrupted in both halls. Residents of both halls responded with expressions of outrage and indignation, while their RAs felt hurt as their moral authority was challenged or ignored. In the external authority hall the disruption was perpetuated, resulting in rule-enforcing conditions that precluded the legitimate exercise of authority. The disruption was resolved in the peer authority hall, resulting in a restored justice of ceremony. The difference lay in the peer authority group's capacity to revise the terms of its chain of ceremony, thus increasing the moral content of the situation. The interdependence of individuals involved in an authority relationship is an important social psychological component of legitimation. It illustrates the inadequacy of the often-used phrase "invisible glue" as applied to legitimacy, i.e., legitimacy is flexible and changing, not rigid and static. Furthermore, legitimacy does not appear to translate into a generalized concept of obligation, as has been argued or assumed by philosophers of law (Austin, 1954, Fuller, 1964; Hart, 1961, 1968; Kelson, 1945). Often, the sense of being responsible for one's actions is a matter of feeling accountable to the norms of a community and these group norms in some cases do and in other cases do not coincide with the rules as a whole.

Finally, this analysis of the group experience suggests some possibilities for conceptual expansion of both theories of legal socialization. The concept of a social contract, familiar to moral and legal development theories, does not always seem appropriate to describe the interaction between legal reasoning and the rule-enforcing environment. The social learning principle (Bandura, 1986) of control by consequences, although obviously in effect in some enforcement situations, was not always distinguishable from control through social bonding and normative interaction. What is it about the group experience that conflicts with these theories? Legal development theory explicitly uses the concept of a social contract to characterize Stage 5 of the postconventional level (Tapp & Kohlberg, 1977, pp. 91-92). The stress is on individual rights, a reliance on rational and social utility, and a rule-making rather than rule-maintaining perspective. All of these characteristics accord with the group experience in the peer authority hall, but the contract image implies a more individualistic group process than actually occurred. The role-taking opportunity provided by the judicial board had a procedural and legalistic focus that fits the social contract image. But the ritual interaction, both disrupted and restored, that surrounded the enforcement of the rules was fundamentally a matter of group norms. Likewise, the development of informal guidelines for social control was neither legalistic nor individualistic, but rather a communitarian process. We conclude that the distinction between conventional and postconventional legal reasoning, while it may hold in terms of reasoning in the abstract, does not make sense in the social context in which the interaction between reasoning and the environment takes place.

Conclusion

The purpose of this chapter is to summarize our findings and theoretical conclusions and to state their significance and implications for future methodological and theoretical work on legal socialization. We also discuss the import of our findings for possible application to contexts of legal learning and rule-enforcing environments.

Summary of the Findings

The empirical findings focused on the effects of legal development level, attitudinal variables (normative status of the rule-violating behaviors and enforcement status of the rules), and frequency of engaging in rule-violating behaviors. In Chapter 4, we focused on changes in these variables from fall to spring. We found that legal development level decreased for freshmen and the subjects in the control residence halls but stayed the same for the two experimental halls. In fact, legal development level increased slightly (not significantly) for participants living in the peer authority residence hall. The normative status of the rule-violating behaviors increased among freshmen (except for the dishonesty factor). In contrast, normative status did not change significantly among students living in either the peer authority or the external authority residence halls. A more fine-grained analysis revealed differences between the two experimental residence halls. The trends in the external authority hall, although not significant, were in the same direction as those for the the freshmen. In contrast, the trends in the peer authority hall, although not significant, were in the opposite direction with normative status decreasing from fall to spring. The changes in enforcement status were not consistent across all rule-governed behaviors for the freshmen sample (i.e., it increased for some rules, decreased for some, and stayed the same for others). In contrast, for the experimental samples, enforcement status did not change from fall to spring. Although not significant, a more fine-grained analysis showed that enforcement status decreased in the external authority residence hall and increased in the peer authority residence hall.

If we compare the two attitudinal variables, we notice that normative status has a more uniform effect than enforcment status across all the rule-governed behaviors in all rule-enforcing situations. The exception is in our two experimental residence halls where both normative status and enforcement status had the same effects on all rule-governed behaviors.

In Chapter 5, we compared the effects of our cognitive developmental factor (legal development level) versus our social learning factor (rule-enforcing condition) on our two main dependent variables: attitudinal factors (normative status and enforcement status) and behavioral factors. In these analyses conducted on the spring data from the two control and the two experimental residence halls, we found that legal reasoning level was a better predictor than rule-enforcing condition of both normative status and enforcement status. The only exception was that the rule-enforcing condition was a better predictor of the enforcement status of sex-related behaviors. Neither legal development level nor residence hall predicted the frequency of engaging in rule-governed behaviors.

In Chapter 6, we expanded the analyses conducted in Chapter 5 to include the interaction of the cognitive developmental factor (legal development level) and the social learning factor (residence hall) on the same dependent variables: normative status of the behavior and enforcement status of the rules and the frequency of engaging in the rule-governed behaviors. The interaction had a significant effect on the normative status of most behaviors (all except dishonest, crime, and sex-related behaviors) and the enforcement status of most rules (all except dishonest and crime behaviors). In addition, the interaction predicted the frequency of engaging in alcohol and dishonest behaviors.

We explored the meaning of the significant interaction in Chapter 6 in the analyses conducted in Chapters 7, 8, and 9. In Chapter 7, we explored the relationship between legal development level and the frequency of engaging in rule-violating behaviors separately for each of the rule-enforcing environments, including the freshman sample. In this chapter, we found that mediating path analytic models (which included the situational attitudes between the legal reasoning factor and the behavioral factor) better explained the relationship than a direct model between legal reasoning and the behaviors. The only exception was in the peer authority residence hall where there seemed to be more support for the direct model. We also explored the causal order of the path analytic models: a cognitive model in which legal reasoning came first and the behavioral factor came last or a behavioral model in which the behavioral factor came first and legal reasoning came last. There was support for each model, although more support for the behavioral model. Finally we compared the path analytical models for rule followers and rule violators and found no differences, i.e., the relationship between reasoning and behavior holds for both rule followers and rule violators.

In Chapter 8, we were interested in determining the importance of individual differences. Specifically we focused on whether rule followers and rule violators can be distinguished on the basis of the following personality and background variables: legal development level, Just World score, and demographic factors. We found no systematic differences between rule followers and rule violators in terms of these individual differences. The only differences we found were on the basis of our two situational attitudes (normative status of the behaviors and enforcement status of the rules). Rule violators reported higher normative status of the behaviors and lower enforcement status of the rules than rule followers.

Finally in Chapter 9, we explored the nature of the legal socialization process in the two experimental residence halls. The results of our qualitative analysis reinforced the fine grained differences between the external authority and the peer authority residence halls in Chapters 4 and 7. In the external authority residence hall, the rule-enforcing conditions led to resentment and retaliation against authority. Rule enforcement was one-sided with no involvement on the part of the residents. In the peer authority residence hall, where rule enforcement was not one-sided, residents developed a form of social control based on their views of the needs of their community. Rule enforcement was viewed as upholding the community standards—not those of the authorities, the hall staff. Members of the judicial board learned to represent the community's viewpoint—not just their own personal viewpoint. We conclude that role-taking opportunities in the context of enforcement have a positive influence on legal socialization.

Theoretical Conclusions

The three major theoretical conclusions concern the role of reasoning in legal socialization, the interaction beween cognitive developmental and social learning factors, and the mediating model between legal reasoning and behaviors. In Chapters 5 and 6, we found stronger support for the cognitive developmental explanation (Levine & Tapp, 1977; Tapp & Kohlberg, 1977) than for the social learning explanation (Akers, 1985; Akers et al., 1979; Bandura, 1969b, 1977). This finding provided the first indication of the significance of reasoning for legal socialization. We also found support for the interaction between the two factors, which we investigated further in the remaining chapters. In Chapter 7, we found that the two attitudinal variables—normative status of the rule-governed behaviors and enforcement status of the rules—mediate the relationship between the behaviors and legal reasoning. In addition, in most cases, the behavior leads to the two situational attitudes that lead to legal reasoning.

The empirical support for the interaction between cognitive developmental and social learning factors is of theoretical importance because most researchers assume either a cognitive developmental approach

(Levine & Tapp, 1977; Tapp & Kohlberg, 1977; Tapp & Levine, 1974) or a social learning approach (Akers, 1985; Akers et al., 1979; Bandura, 1969b, 1977), largely ignoring the effects of the other factor. Few have explored empirically the possibility and nature of an interaction between the factors representing each of the approaches. The findings of Chapter 6 demonstrate the importance of the interaction for predicting the attitudinal factors that reflect the legal environment about which individuals reason and within which they engage in rule-governed behaviors. The success of the mediating model in Chapter 7 suggests a third approach in which the focus is on how norms of behavior and rule enforcement mediate the relationship between cognitive and environmental factors.

We conclude that neither cognitive developmental nor social learning theory is sufficient by itself to account for the process of legal socialization. In Chapters 5 and 6, we analyzed the data with the situational factor, residence hall, as one of the variables. These analyses led to support for cognitive developmental theory over social learning theory as support for the interaction. In Chapters 7 and 8, we decomposed the interaction by developing path models for each of the rule-enforcing environments. In this analysis, we found more support for a behavioral model, in which behavior precedes reasoning, than for a cognitive model, in which reasoning precedes behavior. These findings suggest that both factors are important and that future work should focus on theoretical elaboration of their interaction. The relationship between legal reasoning and behaviors may take different forms under different conditions. It may be that reasoning simply provides a justification for behavior after the fact, or perhaps certain experiences must occur in order for a person to be able to form connections between reasoning and rule-governed behaviors. It may also be that behavior is a necessary catalyst for the kinds of cognitive processes we have characterized as legal reasoning.

Theoretical Implications

We argued in the opening chapter that a satisfactory account of legal socialization should include three factors: legal reasoning, attitudes toward the rule-enforcing environment, and rule-governed behaviors. We proposed a mediating model to describe their relationship and our empirical findings strongly support it. We now consider the implications of these findings for the future development of legal socialization theory.

The Three-Stage Model

The fact that reasoning, attitudes, and behaviors are related, and that they engage over time in a particular setting, implies that legal learning cannot be understood on the basis of one kind of variable alone. This suggests that both legal development theory and social learning theory are deficient as they are currently formulated. Those who criticized the study of abstract legal reasoning as narrow, tepid (Hogan, 1976), and irrelevant to the learning process (Bandura, 1986) are correct, at least to the extent that they suggest that such studies are incomplete. At the same time, those who would argue that social learning theory is inadequate to account for legal or moral socialization because it does not allow for the role of legal or moral reasoning (Kohlberg, 1969, 1976, 1984, 1986; Levine & Tapp, 1977; Tapp & Kohlberg, 1977) are correct to the extent that they identify a component of legal learning that is empirically independent of the effects of any particular legal environment. The three-stage model that we proposed in Chapter 1 more accurately reflects the process of legal socialization than does either theory.

We found, for example, that the three-stage model held regardless of whether the behaviors involved were rule-following or rule-violating or whether the individual was a follower or a violator. This suggests that the legal reasoning involved was broader than simple compliance decisions or even "moral regulation" (Bandura, 1986; Mischel & Mischel, 1976). Since it was also the case that background and personality characteristics were unrelated to following/violating behaviors, in contrast to the mediating role of situational attitudes, we can infer that a particular legal environment is important in forging a relationship among the three factors of the model. The fact that the attitudinal variable (enforcement status of the rules) is measuring a different aspect of legal socialization than is the cognitive variable (legal reasoning) was demonstrated in Chapter 7. All of these findings lead to the conclusion that legal learning involves three independent factors that engage or form connections during the process of legal socialization.

Further work is needed to clarify the relationships among these three variables, particularly that between legal reasoning and rule-governed behaviors. The predominance of the behavioral model suggests not only a causal sequence but also that behavior plays a primary role in the socialization process. Students of linguistics (Chomsky, 1972) and cognitive developmental psychology (Piaget, 1926, 1970/1983) might disagree, however, and argue that reasoning is not simply one more factor in a causal order but instead plays a generative role. The relationship between reasoning and behaviors might be more like that between the grammar of a language and a sentence spoken or written in that language than like the impact of one billiard ball upon another. In such a case, the statistical relationship implies a connection but the causal sequence is meaningless. Cognitive developmental theory does not provide an adequate response to the causal question. As it is applied to moral and legal reasoning, the theory has never been comfortable with the issue of causal order, probably because it verges on teleological rather than (Humean) causal explanation. Whatever the reason, a connection between reasoning and behaviors is asserted but seldom tested empirically. Our own empirical tests support the assertion, but do not fully clarify the nature of the causal relationship.

The Content of Legal Reasoning

We are not prepared to argue for a different explanatory logic solely on the basis of our findings, but we do contend that reasoning's important role in legal socialization, and especially its relationship to behaviors, should be a major focus of future work. We argued in Chapter 1 that content as well as process is important in studying legal socialization. The content we referred to was embodied in the rule-governed behaviors and the legal environment. We are now inclined to add the content of legal reasoning as well because its relationship to behaviors has raised intriguing questions. For example, our findings in Chapter 8 indicate that one's propensity to follow or violate rules is not related to one's legal development level. This finding runs counter to the cognitive developmentalists' assumption that preconventional reasoners are more likely to be rule violators (Blasi, 1980, 1983; Kohlberg, 1969, 1976, 1981, 1984, 1986). We are inclined to reject Kohlberg's rigid developmental scheme on these empirical grounds, which then raises questions about the accompanying philosophical structure as well. Is it possible to separate the developmental process from the philosophical content? And if so, what is there about the content of legal reasoning that links it to rule-governed behaviors?

The content of Kohlberg's three levels of reasoning about justice has been criticized extensively in the literature (Kohlberg, 1984; Weinreich-Haste & Locke, 1983) because of its individualistic flavor and its Kantian vision of liberal democracy. Legal development theory adopted a similar philosophical scheme, but tied its content specifically to the nature and function of rules (Levine & Tapp, 1977; Tapp & Kohlberg, 1977). There is more empirical justification for the legal developmental scheme, therefore, than for its moral developmental counterpart. But its basis remains a particular philosophical structure, one of a number that might be adopted rather than a universal scheme. In short, the content of legal reasoning as defined by legal development theory is not intuitively obvious but instead requires some kind of justification. In our view, that justification should be empirical. Kohlberg's "principles of justice" are not only philosophical principles; they also represent a particular view of what constitutes justice in the world which is rooted in a particular culture and a particular ideology.

The Empirical Basis for the Content of Legal Reasoning

We can identify three approaches to analyzing the empirical basis for the content of legal reasoning: reciprocity, the empirical source for "lay theories," and the production of ideology. The first is Piaget's (1970/1983) concept of diverse points of view, similar to Mead's (1934) view of social learning, which was adopted by Kohlberg (1969, 1976, 1981, 1984, 1986) as the basis for learning reciprocity. The capacity to understand reciprocity is reached developmentally, through experiences in taking the role of the other, and forms the basis for conceptualizing the principles of justice. This concept was discussed extensively in Chapter 2 and will not be reviewed here, but our findings suggest a nondevelopmental interpretation. The lack of a relationship between legal developmental level and rule-governed behaviors in our results and the support for the effectiveness of role-taking in the peer authority condition suggest that learning the capacity for reciprocity is not a matter of developmental stages, but instead comes from certain kinds of experiences. These experiences, and not developmental change, provide an empirical basis for Kohlberg's principles of justice, or something similar, to be the content of legal reasoning.

One important implication of the reciprocity approach is universality. Kohlberg (1969, 1976, 1981, 1984, 1986) based his claims for universality on the belief that human interaction ultimately produces a sense of reciprocity in everyone, unless prevented by social conditions. The philosopher John Rawls (1971) derived assertions about the generalizability of his principles of justice from the same belief, predicated empirically on Piaget's (1932) original theory. This universality claim has been roundly criticized on the basis of cross-cultural data (Sampson, 1977; Shweder, 1982; Simpson, 1974; Snarey, 1985; Sullivan, 1977), which, if valid, would undercut the claims for reciprocity as well. The critics are concerned that Kohlberg's philosophical structure—the normative content of his theory—is blatantly individualistic and a reflection of liberal democratic principles. This content fits reciprocity neatly, of course, but it excludes the communitarian values of other cultures. In some cultures, for example, the celebration of individual rights and autonomy that characterizes Stage 5 and 6 reasoning, and is therefore the "highest" level of reasoning for Kohlbergian theory, would never be honored above submission to the values and behavioral norms of the community or cultural group. According to the theory, members of such cultures can never reason beyond the conventional level. Furthermore, experiences of reciprocity, which is the empirical basis for stage development as well as for the principles of justice, cannot be universal across cultures. These implications form the basis for a critique that seriously undermines the empirical claims of the reciprocity approach.

A second approach to analyzing the empirical basis of the content of legal reasoning derives from recent social psychological literature concerning lay theories (Antaki, 1981; Furnham, 1988). Lay theories are beliefs used by ordinary people to explain natural events, their own or others' behavior, and social phenomena such as crime. Furnham (1988) recently described lay theories of psychology, psychiatry, medicine, economics, statistics, law, and education, and discussed how they structure belief systems and function as moral and explanatory frameworks. For example, most people have beliefs about crime and punishment, although these beliefs vary across cultures, class background, economic circumstances, and education. These beliefs allow people to explain the existence of crime and criminal events, to justify responses to perpetrators and victims, and to orient themselves to the risk of victimization. Each of these functions requires a somewhat different formulation of the basic set of beliefs. The varying uses even allow inconsistencies from one formulation to another, but yet an identifiable theory or "ordinary explanation" (Antaki, 1981) exists.

Legal reasoning, as we have used the term throughout this book, is just such an "ordinary explanation," e.g., a preconventional reasoner decides whether to follow or violate a rule in terms of the likelihood of punishment, a conventional reasoner in terms of the needs of the social group, and a postconventional reasoner in terms of the appropriateness and/or fairness of the rule. These are not the only possible formulations of lay legal theories, of course, as Furnham (1988) has demonstrated in his compilation from the literature. The range and variety of lay theories pose a fundamental issue: what is the empirical source for such formulations? Those who study lay theories tend to explain why someone uses a theory in terms of its function in protecting that person's self-esteem and/or sense of personal safety. For example, belief in a just world may lead people to blame victims (Lerner, 1980; Rubin & Peplau, 1975) and fear of crime may lead some people to apportion blame differently and offer different causal attributions about crime than do others (Kidder & Cohn, 1979). For these kinds of explanations, the content of legal reasoning has its empirical roots in the individual social psychological propensities or personality factors whose needs it serves.

In contrast, a dissenting perspective suggests that lay theories are not so much motivational devices as they are rhetorical expressions of interpretation that depend upon the categories of meaning available to the reasoner. This is an important contrast because it goes to the question of the role played by reasoning in the socialization process. Those who oppose the mainstream social psychological or positivist explanations (see, for example, Gergen, 1985; Gowler & Legge, 1981; Harre, 1981; Lalljee, 1981; Sampson, 1977; Shotter, 1981) argue instead that lay theories are the expression of attempts to make sense of the social environment in a context of social interaction. This process requires an ongoing exchange of accounts reiterating and elaborating shared social meanings. Its form typically falls into the category of offering "reasons for" one's actions, rather than providing causal explanations for them. Its purpose is the kind of communication that is necessary for the maintenance of social institutions and meaningful human interaction. Legal reasoning, understood in these terms, plays a fundamental interpretive role for individuals as they learn about rules and engage in rule-governed social practices. The content of legal reasoning, then, simply reflects the particular social practices that are its empirical source and the interpretive activities of the human beings who express it.

A third approach to analyzing the empirical basis of the content of legal reasoning is to assume that this content is ideological, and therefore the product of dominant social groups and/or political conflict. The categories of meaning in law reflect how dominant groups in a society view social and political life and how they define and apply the values of justice and fairness. Legal reasoning, on this account, becomes a matter of the manipulation of legal symbols by those in power to legitimize their authority and the acquiescent employment of these symbols by members of the community. The content of legal reasoning is ideologically determined because only certain categories of meaning are politically available to the reasoner. There is a strong tradition of sociolegal scholarship (Balbus, 1977; Brigham, 1980, 1987; Kennedy, 1980) that tends to synthesize legal and political cultures or at least assume that a society's legal culture is dependent on its political culture. A less political version of the ideology approach argues that the content of legal reasoning is culturally determined, which implies that a person understands the functions of law only through the categories of legal meaning that are culturally available.

Either version points research in a different direction than the previous two approaches. If the empirical basis of the content of legal reasoning is to be found in ideological forces, research must focus on social structure and relationships of political domination (Foucault, 1977; Pfohl, 1985). Lay theories would exist, but their interpretation would require one to identify the interests they enhance and undermine. Whose interests are served by a theory of personal accountability or by one of environmental determinism? What symbolic resources (Harrington & Merry, 1988) are brought to bear in the service of these interests and how are they reflected in legal reasoning? Whether one chooses a critical theory perspective or follows a positivist paradigm (Katz, 1988; Quinney, 1970, 1973; Scheingold, 1974, 1984; Turk, 1969), the linkage between group interests and their ideological expression can be detected in the content of legal reasoning. For example, Estrich (1987) analyzed state appellate court decisions on the issue of consent and other aspects of rape law and found that they abound in familiar lay theories about rape victimization that reflect an ideology of sexual relations growing out of male domination. In the most recent decisions, involving rape shield laws and similar attempts to challenge the ideology of male domination in sexual relations, Estrich finds some signs of the emergence of a different ideological perspective reflecting the growing power of women in our society. It is clear from this study and other explorations into the empirical bases of legal reasoning (see, for example, Kairys, 1982; Scheingold, 1974, 1984) that the legal content of reasoning has ideological sources.

Situational Content

The success of our mediating model implies that the situational content of the learning process should receive close attention. In the present study, the situational content was embodied in both attitudes and behaviors. Our measure of the normative status of the rule-violating behaviors was an attitudinal response to the rule-enforcing situation ("do you approve or disapprove of the following 24 behaviors?"), as was our measure of the enforcement status of the rules ("do you approve of enforcing rules against these behaviors?"). Each behavior was described using the idiomatic terminology of the community. The measure of frequency of behavior reiterated the 24 rule violations, again in the idiom of the community and the situation. These measures represented the kinds of experiences that naturally and commonly occurred within this community. They also reflected the issues, both of behavior and of rule enforcement, which the residents confronted and debated every day. We believe that the success of our mediating model demonstrates not only the importance of situational measures to socialization in general, but also the importance of the legal environment to legal socialization.

Referring again to the argument in Chapter 1, we suggest that the legal content of the learning situation is necessary to the process of legal socialization. Consequently, a generic theory of learning cannot adequately explain legal socialization. The situational content that contributed to the success of the mediating model included not simply norms of behavior but norms of rule-violating behavior and norms of rule enforcement. The analysis in Chapter 9 indicates the extent to which the situational content reflected fundamental legal/political values and issues. Members of the community were concerned about the *fair* enforcement of the rules, the *legitimacy* of the rules, and the role of *authority* in their lives. One cannot explain the reactions of residents in the two different experimental communities without reference to fairness and legitimacy and the role of authority. It is true that family and school settings raise similar issues, but that fact only underscores the fundamentally political nature of those institutions (Rousseau, 1960) and the legal learning that is acquired within them. We conclude that a theory of legal socialization must incorporate the salient features of the legal environment.

Conflict as a Condition for Legal Socialization

Conflict plays a central role in each of the two theories that informed this analysis. Cognitive developmental theory asserts that the experience of diverse points of view through taking the role of the other is a major feature of the developmental process (Kohlberg, 1969, 1976, 1981, 1984, 1986). Its legal development version (Levine & Tapp, 1977; Tapp & Kohlberg, 1977) suggests that participation in conflict resolution is a major means of producing significant developmental change. Role-taking opportunities, by definition, provide conflicting points of view. Social learning theory (Akers, 1985; Akers et al., 1979; Bandura, 1969b, 1977) also requires conflict as part of the learning process. For social learning theory, the conflict is provided by what might be termed feedback opportunities in the context of discipline. It is sometimes difficult to draw the empirical line between these two kinds of conflict because the experience of role-taking could conceivably include discipline situations, such as deciding whether or not to comply with a rule or questioning its legitimacy. We would argue, however, that the crucial form of conflict for legal socialization should be one that provides a fertile context for engagement between legal reasoning and rule-governed behaviors. Our findings afford a basis for identifying this form of conflict and for formulating its most telling theoretical role.

As we discussed in Chapter 7, there are several ways in which conflict was operationalized in our research design: (1) whether the rule was enforced by external authority or by peer authority, (2) whether one agreed or disagreed with a rule, and (3) whether one followed or violated a rule. The first operationalization can be used (broadly) to test the different effects of role-taking opportunities in the peer authority condition and feedback opportunities in the external authority condition. The second and third operationalizations may be either role-taking or feedback opportunities in that they refer to enforcing a rule in a discipline situation. To clarify the theoretical role of conflict in legal socialization and to draw the empirical line between role-taking and feedback opportunities, we can examine once again the findings of Chapter 7. Our data provided strong support for the first operationalization, clearly distinguishing between the peer authority and external authority conditions. Legal reasoning and rule-governed behaviors engage far more frequently when there are role-taking opportunities such as were present in the peer authority setting and absent in the external authority setting. By contrast, the second and third operationalizations did not reveal a distinct role for conflict, i.e., engagement occurred as frequently when respondents agreed with the rule as when they disagreed and for followers as well as violators.

These findings imply that role-taking opportunities provide the kind of conflict that forges connections between legal reasoning and rule-governed behaviors and thereby shapes legal socialization. They also imply that disagreeing with or violating a rule does not establish a similarly efficacious condition of conflict. There is a clear empirical line between these two situations, on the one hand, and the kind of role-taking opportunities afforded by the peer authority setting, on the other. It seems reasonable to conclude that disagreeing with or violating a rule are feedback rather than role-taking opportunities, a conclusion that narrows and clarifies the definition of conflict under legal development theory. One is also tempted to suggest that this empirical line and the negative findings with respect to disagreeing with and violating a rule allow us to define the theoretical role of conflict in terms of cognitive developmental theory rather than social learning theory. Since only the first of these operationalizations of conflict was formulated to test the competing hypotheses, however, we do not wish to overreach our research design. Our findings clearly imply a significant difference in the nature of conflict characterizing the role-taking opportunities of the peer authority condition and the feedback opportunities of the external authority condition. Further exploration of this difference is needed to delineate fully the theoretical role of conflict in legal socialization.

The Acquisition of Values

Since we have concluded that neither theory is adequate to account for legal socialization, it is clear that new theory building is necessary. We suggest that this effort should elaborate further on the relative weight of internal and external factors in the legal learning process. Our finding of an interaction between legal reasoning and the rule-enforcing environment led us to the mediating model that establishes the relationship between legal reasoning and rule-governed behaviors through situational variables. We then explored the formal and informal processes of social control in the two different rule enforcing environments in a qualitative analysis that raised provocative new questions. For example, a particularly intriguing question reframes some of the original debate, discussed in Chapter 1, over the acquisition of values. Natural rights theorists have often argued that individual autonomy is essential for democracy, while admitting that their individualistic assumptions make it difficult to accommodate communitarian values. Our findings with respect to legal development theory and the analysis of formal and informal social control processes in Chapter 9 bear directly on this question and should force consideration of the acquisition of legal/moral values in a new light.

The issue is both empirical and normative in that our empirical findings have normative implications, as we discussed in Chapter 1. We have concluded that the cognitive developmental paradigm is empirically invalid with respect to its theoretical postulation that sequential stages of reasoning are related to gradations in moral behavior. One of the attractions of this aspect of legal development theory, however, is the implication that those at the highest level of reasoning are constrained by values that lead to socially responsible behavior. If we reject this hierarchical model of values as our empirical findings suggest we should, we are left without any empirical grounds on which to base individual consent to communal authority. The analysis in Chapter 9 suggests a complex interplay of social forces and individual autonomy, the outcome of which was generally positive in the peer authority condition and generally negative in the external authority condition. We are not so naive as to assume that the existence of a peer conduct board or its equivalent would be sufficient to solve any community's (e.g., a neighborhood, school, prison, fraternity house) problems with social control while preserving a reasonable measure of individual autonomy. But we do think that the different processes of rule enforcement in our two conditions had a significant influence on community life. We also think that the influence lay in the complex interplay of social forces and individual autonomy mentioned earlier.

The role-taking opportunities available in the peer authority condition made an important contribution to the success of that community. It is also clear that effective informal processes of social control were at work in the peer authority condition but were absent in the external authority condition. We are not sure whether the presence or absence of these informal processes was a function of the presence or absence of role-taking opportunities. But it is apparent, on the one hand, that the style of rule enforcement used in the external authority condition had a pathological effect on human relationships and group morale, even though it probably contributed to a decrease in rule-violating behaviors relative to the total university community. On the other hand, the positive social consequences of the style of rule enforcement used in the peer authority condition suggests that devices for taking the role of the other deserve serious study as socialization strategies, as Tapp and Levine (1977) argued. Socially responsible behavior may have nothing to do with development or even with a hierarchy of values, but rather with role-taking experiences that create a sense of reciprocity. For these reasons, both empirical and normative, we are persuaded that further exploration of the interplay between informal processes of social control and their formalization is an important theoretical step in the study of legal socialization.

Methodological Significance

This study represents several methodological advances in the study of legal socialization. First, it demonstrates the usefulness of quasi-experimental studies. Second, the research emphasizes the importance of multiple methods (Campbell & Fiske, 1959). Third, the study measured the variables longitudinally. Fourth, new scales were developed to assess the normative status of the rule-violating behaviors and the enforcement status of the rules as well as the frequency of engaging in rule-violating behavior.

Cook and Campbell (1979) point out the importance of quasi-experimental designs. In this research, it would have been impossible to assign students randomly to residence halls. Therefore it was necessary to use a methodology that did not assume random assignment. The quasi-experiment allowed us to do this. We controlled for preexisting attitudes and behaviors by pretesting the participants before we introduced the experimental treatments. We also had two different comparison groups. First, we studied a group of freshmen who were not exposed to the experimental treatment over the course of the freshman year. Since our experimental group included both freshmen and upperclassmen, we also studied another control group from two residence halls that included a mix of freshmen and upperclassmen. This allowed us to compare the results from the experimental residence halls to both of these comparison groups.

In addition to the quasi-experimental design, we used both quantitative and qualitative methods. We administered a survey to the participants both before and after the treatment had been administered. This quantitative data provided us with the bulk of the information presented in this book (Chapters 4 through 8). In addition, we tape recorded our biweekly meetings with the hall staff in the two experimental residence halls. Observers reported on the behaviors and attitudes of the residents. We taped all the proceedings of the judicial board in the peer authority residence hall. In addition, the hall staff kept journals during the course of the experiment. These qualitative data are a rich source of information for Chapter 9.

Another important aspect of the study was the longitudinal nature of the design. Participants completed questionnaires their first night on campus in the fall semester and another questionnaire at the end of the spring semester. This aspect of the design was critical for a number of reasons. The pretest at the beginning of the fall semester allowed us to assess preexisting differences among the participants. Then we could interpret differences in the spring on the basis of the differences in the fall. The longitudinal nature of the research allowed us to assess whether our critical variables changed over time. For example, in the nonexperimental samples (the freshmen and the controls), the normative status of the rule-governed behaviors increased from the fall to the spring (Chapter 4). Most of the studies on legal socialization have been unable to assess whether the critical variables change over time; our design allowed us to make that assessment. The only other study that investigated change over time was the Wounded Knee study reported in Tapp et al., (1983). This study found that jurors in the Wounded Knee case reported higher legal development levels at the conclusion of the case than before the case began.

A final methodological aspect were the three scales developed for the study. These scales assessed the normative status of the rule-governed behaviors, the enforcement status of the rules, and the frequency of engaging in the rule-governed behaviors. The normative status scale assessed participants' approval of such rule-governed behaviors as stealing and being drunk. The enforcement status scale assessed approval of enforcing rules against the same behaviors. Finally the behavioral scale assessed the frequency of engaging in these rule-governed behaviors. The three scales allowed us to assess both attitudes toward rule-governed behaviors and the propensity to engage in the behaviors themselves. As can be seen in Chapter 3, the reliabilities for all three scales were very respectable.

These three scales were critical to the analysis of the data. For example, in Chapter 7, we found that the normative status of the behaviors and the enforcement status of the rules mediated the relationship between legal reasoning level and the behavioral scale. We factor analyzed the behavioral scale and found that the rule-governed behaviors fell into the following three factors: destructive behaviors, in which normative status of the behaviors was low and enforcement status of the rules was high; behaviors causing social disturbances, in which the normative status of the behaviors was relatively high and enforcement status of the rules was low; and disorderly behaviors, in which the normative status was in the middle and the enforcement status was fairly high. These three factors, along with four conceptual factors (alcohol, dishonest, crime, and sex-related behaviors), were included in all the quantitative analyses.

Possible Applications

Clearly, the study has implications for rule enforcement. The most obvious finding of the study has to do with the different effects of the two styles of rule enforcement in the two experimental conditions. Rule enforcement under the conditions of the external authority residence hall was clearly problematic. This is demonstrated most dramatically in Chapter 9, but also in negative attitudinal trends and the relatively weak showing of the mediating model under external authority conditions. Participants in the external authority hall demonstrated their discontent by their resentment of hall staff and their occasional open rebellion against the rules. In contrast, residents of the peer authority residence hall were proud of their status as a self-governing residence hall with their own judicial board. Other negative aspects of the external authority residence hall can be seen in the quantitative findings, particularly those reported in Chapter 4. Although not significant, the legal development level and the normative status of residents in the external authority condition decreased from the fall to the spring. In contrast, in the peer authority residence hall, legal development level and the normative status increased from fall to spring (although not significantly).

Another aspect of rule enforcement is the use of the judicial board in the peer authority residence hall. As described in detail in Chapter 9, the student members of the judicial board oversaw any rule infractions in the residence hall. The transcribed judicial board hearings demonstrate that the participants gained valuable experiences by their participation. They learned to broaden their perspective on rule enforcement and to see issues from the perspective of the hall staff as well as the perspective of the residents. They also learned to assert their own sense of responsible behavior regardless of the rules. Some of the issues in these cases were very difficult, but the students handled the deliberations in a mature way. This was a convincing demonstration of the social efficacy of "taking the role of the other" in resolving community problems. It was also apparent that informal processes of social control among the peer group were more effective than the rigid rule enforcement practiced under the external authority condition.

What are the implications of these findings for effective rule enforcement? We do not suggest that universities can solve their considerable problems with misconduct simply by instituting judicial boards in all of the residence halls and fraternity houses. As indicated in the previous discussion of theoretical implications, we do not yet know all of the factors that contributed to the effectiveness of the peer authority condition. And it is obvious that some groups are not ready to take advantage of role-taking opportunities or accept the responsibility of controlling themselves. We do suggest that universities can involve students in the discipline system on campus in a variety of ways, to the probable benefit of all concerned. Instilling positive community goals may be a sufficient point of departure for effective use of role-taking opportunities in a residence system.

We also want to highlight the extreme difficulty, indeed the near pathology, of the enforcement role played by student "resident assistants." This system of social control is pervasive on unversity campuses, but our study shows that it puts unreasonable stress on the students doing the enforcing. This problem is exacerbated by the fact that resident assistants are typically recruited to be "helpers" and "friends" rather than enforcers (Cohn & White, 1985). We hope that the present study, and particularly Chapter 9, will be read thoughtfully by university administrators.

More broadly, we think there are lessons in this study that can apply to any enforcement situation. Even in a democracy, we are seldom in a situation of generalized fidelity to law. It goes without saying that deliberate, serious law breaking requires a strong police response, but most enforcement situations do not fit that mold. Police officers, teachers, parents, and other figures in authority are often tempted to simply "lay down the law," as if that pronouncement and its accompanying threats will be sufficient to compel compliance. It is our view that this tactic is successful only in the short term, and then only by undermining the conditions under which individuals can hold themselves responsible for their actions. We are far from knowing all the answers to creating socially responsible behavior, but we think it is significant that residents not only resented what they viewed as the arbitrary exercise of authority but were also unable to take the role of the other under those circumstances. In fact, the situation seemed to impair their capacity to interact responsibly. When they thought the rule was legitimate and its enforcement fair, their attitude toward enforcement was wholly different. If we wish to advance toward a situation in which individuals are willing and able to hold themselves responsible for their actions, attention should be paid to these attitudinal dynamics and their implications for enhancing the capacity for socially responsible behavior.

In addition to rule enforcement, this study has also revealed some pathological effects of the college environment. Our data, particularly in Chapter 4, demonstrate the socializing effects of living in a college environment. Both the freshman and the control residents exhibited decreases in legal development level and increases in the normative status of the rule-violating behaviors from the fall to the spring. No interventions were introduced for these two groups of subjects. This suggests that something in the college environment had an effect on these students, independent of our intervention in the two experimental residence halls. In fact, the differences between the freshmen and control residents versus the experimental residents suggest that the natural socializing effects work against rule enforcement.

For example, the normative status of rule-violating behaviors increased in the two control groups (freshmen and control residents). Although the changes were not statistically significant, the normative status of rule-violating behaviors decreased slightly in the peer authority condition and increased slightly in the external authority residence hall. These findings suggest that universities should attend to the impact of their own rule-enforcing environments. More attention should be given to the negative experiences of students, particularly in the freshman year. Some universities have freshman courses to influence the socializing process. Our findings suggest that such efforts could be effective, especially if they are based on realistic information about the natural socialization process.

Concluding Note

We close with a strong sense of how little we know about legal socialization and of what work is left to be done. This study has resolved some issues and raised many new questions. The research that remains is not only extensive but also difficult to design and implement. We are convinced of its importance, however. As the present study suggests, there is no generalized fidelity to law in this society, and probably not in any society despite Durkheim's (1984) views on consensus. The study of the enforcement process is, therefore, an intriguing and rewarding enterprise.

Epilogue

"And I think the severity of the decision of the RAs to write people up in this case and in general has detracted more from the environment in this hall than the actual behavior or the actual crimes."

"We can't ignore the rules altogether but we have to interpret them so they fit us and how we like to live."

The student judicial board met on Tuesday to hear the case of Bob and Joe, who were charged with smoking marijuana at a party in their room the previous Thursday night. The RAs, Carol and Steve, told how they had followed the trail of odor to Bob and Joe's room, how the music from the stereo had drowned out their knocking, and how someone finally opened the door to leave. Bob and Joe argued that they had not invited Carol and Steve into their room so there was no basis for any charges.

Members of the board asked Carol and Steve if they had seen either anyone smoking or a joint being passed around. The RAs admitted that they had seen nothing but that the odor was strong in the room. "We know the rule was broken. We had to charge someone and it was their room. They were responsible." Bob and Joe were asked if they were smoking that night. Bob replied, "We're not going to say one way or the other." Joe argued that the RAs should not have looked in the room unless they were invited in. "We were being responsible," Joe said. "No one was complaining. It was just a group of friends unwinding after a tough week. We weren't doing anything to disrupt the hall."

Two board members thought Bob and Joe should be found guilty because they probably were smoking. "We have to uphold the law." Others disagreed, arguing that the RAs had gone too far, given that there was no clear evidence that a rule had been broken. "It's not as if this was a real problem."

In the end, the board decided to find Bob and Joe not guilty. The RAs were told they couldn't assume someone was smoking simply because they smelled it. "If you see the rule broken, we'll give them a penalty. But it has to be blatant, really irresponsible. Otherwise the rule does more harm than good".

References

Abelson, R. (1972). Are attitudes necessary? In B. T. King & E. McGinnes (Eds.), *Attitudes, conflicts, and social change* (pp. 19–32). New York: Academic Press.

Adelson, J., & O'Neil, R. P. (1966). The growth of political ideas in adolescence: The sense of community. *Journal of Personality and Social Psychology, 4*, 295–306.

Akers, R. L. (1985). *Deviant behavior: A social learning approach* (3rd ed.). Belmont, CA: Wadsworth Publishing Co.

Akers, R. L., Krohn, M. D., Lonza-Kaduce, L., & Radosevitch, M. (1979). Social learning and deviant behavior: A specific test of a general theory. *American Sociological Review, 44*, 635–655.

Allinsmith, W. (1960). The learning of moral standards. In D. R. Miller & G. E. Swanson (Eds.), *Inner conflict and defense* (pp. 141–176). New York: Holt, Rinehart & Winston.

Almond, G., & Verba, S. (1965). *The civic culture*. Boston: Little, Brown.

Antaki, C. (Ed). (1981). *The psychology of ordinary explanations of social behaviour*. London: Academic Press.

Argyle, M., & Little, B. R. (1972). Do personality traits apply to social behavior? *Journal of the Theory of Social Behavior, 2*, 1–35.

Aronfreed, J. (1968). *Conduct and conscience*. New York: Academic Press.

Aronfreed, J. (1969). The problem of imitation. In L. P. Lipsitt & H. W. Reese (Eds.), *Advances in child development and behavior* (Vol. 4, pp. 209–319). New York: Academic Press.

Asch, S. E. (1955). Opinions and social pressure. *Scientific American*, Nov., 31–35.

Asch, S. E. (1956). Studies of independence and conformity: A minority of one against a unanimous majority. *Psychological Monographs, 70*(9).

Austin, J. (1954). *The province of jurisprudence determined*. (Ed.) London: Weidenfeld and Nicolson.

Balbus, I. (1977). Commodity form and legal form: An essay on the relative autonomy of law. *Law and Society Review, 11*, 571.

Bandura, A. (1969a). *Principles of behavior modification*. New York: Holt, Rinehart & Winston.

Bandura, A. (1969b). Social-learning theory of identificatory processes. In D. A. Goslin (Ed.), *Handbook of socialization theory and research* (pp. 213–262). Chicago: Rand McNally.

Bandura, A. (1973). *Aggression: A social learning analysis*. Englwood Cliffs, NJ: Prentice-Hall.

Bandura, A. (1977). *Social learning theory*. Englewood Cliffs, NJ: Prentice-Hall.

Bandura, A. (1986). *Social foundations of thought and action: A social cognitive theory*. Englewood Cliffs, NJ: Prentice-Hall.

Barker, E. (1960). Introduction. In *Social contract: Essays by Locke, Hume and Rousseau*. New York: Oxford University Press.

Becker, W. C., Peterson, D. R., Luria, Z., Shoemaker, D. J., & Helmer, L. A. (1962). Relations of factors derived from parent-interview ratings to behavior problems of five-year olds. *Child Development, 33*, 509–535.

Bem, D. J. (1972). Self-perception theory. In L. Berkowitz (Ed.), *Advances in experimental social psychology* (Vol. 6, pp. 2–62). New York: Academic Press.

Bem, D. J., & Funder, D. C. (1978). Predicting more of the people more of the time: Assessing the personality of situations. *Psychological Review, 85*, 485–501.

Benn, S. I., & Peters, R. S. (1959). *The principles of political thought*. New York: Free Press.

Black, D. (1976). *The behavior of law*. New York: Academic Press.

Blasi, A. (1980). Bridging moral cognition and moral action: A critical review of the literature. *Psychological Bulletin, 88*, 1–45.

Blasi, A. (1983). Moral cognition and moral action: A theoretical perspective. *Developmental Review, 3*, 178–210.

Bowers, K. S. (1973). Situationism in psychology: An analysis and a critique. *Psychological Review, 80*, 307–336.

Brigham, J. (1987). Rights, rage, and remedy: The construction of legal discourse. *Studies in American Political Development, 2*, 303.

Brigham, J. (1980). Law as symbolic and modern jurisprudence. *Polity, 12*, 481.

Brim, O. G., & Wheeler, S. (1966). *Socialization after childhood*. New York: Wiley.

Brodbeck, M. (1968) (Ed.). Models, meanings and theories. *Readings in the philosophy of the social sciences*. New York: Macmillan.

Broughton, J. M. (1986). The genesis of moral domination. In S. Modgil & C. Modgil (Eds.), *Lawrence Kohlberg: Consensus and controversy* (pp. 363–385). Philadelphia: The Falmer Press.

Burgess, R. L., & Akers, R. L. (1966). A differential association-reinforcement theory of criminal behavior. *Social Problems, 14*, 128–147.

Campbell, D. T., & Fiske, D. W. (1959). Convergent and discriminant validation by the multitrait-multimethod matrix. *Psychological Bulletin, 56*, 81–105.

Carlson, R. (1971). Where is the person in personality research? *Psychological Bulletin, 75*, 203–219.

Chomsky, N. (1972). *Language and mind*. New York: Harcourt, Brace, Jovanovich.

Cohn, E. S., & White, S. O. (1986). Cognitive developmental versus social learning approaches to studying legal socialization. *Basic and Applied Social Psychology*, 7(3), 195–209.

Cohn, E. S., & White, S. O. (1985, June). *Doing justice: Under the rug or on the table*. Paper presented at the annual meeting of the Law and Society Association, San Diego.

Connell, R. W. (1972). Political socialization in the American family: The evidence re-examined. *Public Opinion Quarterly, 36*, 323–333.

Cook, T. (1985). The bear market in political socialization and the costs of mis-

understood psychological theories. *American Political Science Review, 79*(4), 1079–1093.
Cook, T. D., & Campbell, D. T. (1979). *Quasi-experimentation: Design and analysis issues for field settings*. Chicago: Rand McNally.
Dennis, J. (Ed.). (1973). *Socialization to politics*. New York: Wiley.
Deutscher, I. (1973). *What we say/What we do: Sentiments and acts*. Glenview, IL: Scott, Foresman.
Dillehay, R. C. (1973). On the irrelevance of the classical negative evidence concerning the effect of attitudes on behaviors. *American Psychologist, 28*, 887–891.
Durkheim, E. (1952). *Suicide*. New York: Free Press.
Durkheim, E. (1984). *The division of labor in society*. (W. D. Halls Trans.) New York: Free Press.
Easton, D. (1965). *A systems analysis of political life*. New York: Wiley.
Easton, D., & Dennis, J. (1969). *Children in the political system: Origins of political legitimacy*. New York: McGraw-Hill.
Edwards, A. L. (1984). *An introduction to linear regression and correlation* (2nd ed.). New York: W. H. Freeman & Co.
Emler, N. P. (1983). Morality and politics: The ideological dimension in the theory of moral development. In H. Weinreich-Haste & D. Locke (Eds.), *Morality in the making: Judgement, action and social context*. New York: Wiley.
Emler, N. P., & Hogan, R. (1981). Developing attitudes to law and justice: An integrative review. In S. S. Brehm, S. M. Kassin, & F. X. Gibbons (Eds.), *Developmental social psychology* (pp. 298–314). New York: Oxford University Press.
Eron, L. D., Walder, L. O., Toigo, R., & Lefkowitz, M. M. (1963). Social class, parental punishment for aggression, and child aggression. *Child Development, 34*, 849–867.
Estrich, S. (1987). *Real rape*. Cambridge, MA: Harvard University Press.
Farrington, D., & Tarling, R. (1985). *Prediction in criminology*. Albany, NY: State University of New York Press.
Fiske, D. W. (1974). The limits for the conventional science of personality. *Journal of Personality, 42*, 1–11.
Foucault, M. (1977). *Discipline and punishment*. New York: Random House.
Freud, S. (1925). Instincts and their vicissitudes. In S. Freud, *Collected papers* (Vol. 4). London: Institute for Psychoanalysis and Hogarth Press.
Fuller, L. L. (1964). *The morality of law*. New Haven, CT: Yale University Press.
Funder, D. C. (1983). The "consistency" controversy and the accuracy of personality judgments. Journal of Personality, *51*, 346–359.
Funder, D. C. (1987). Errors and mistakes: Evaluating the accuracy of personality judgments. *Psychological Bulletin, 101*, 75–90.
Furnham, A. (1988). Lay theories. Oxford, England: Pergamon Press.
Geertz, C. (1973). *The interpretation of cultures*. New York: Basic Books.
Gelman, R. & Baillargeon, R. (1983). A review of some Piagetian concepts. In J. H. Flavell & E. Markman (Eds.), *Handbook of Child Psychology Vol. III*. New York: John Wiley & Sons.
Gerbasi, K. C., & Zuckerman, M. (1975, April). *Experimental investigation of jury biasing factors*. Paper presented at the annual meeting of the Eastern Psychological Association, New York.

Gergen, K. J. (1985). The social constructionist movement in modern psychology. *American Psychologist, 40*(9), 266–275.

Gerstein, R. S. (1972). The practice of fidelity to law. In S. Krislov, K. O. Boyum, J. N. Clark, R. C. Shaefer, & S. O. White (Eds.), *Compliance and the law* (pp. 35–50). Beverly Hills, CA: Sage.

Gewirtz, J. L. (1969). Mechanisms of social learning: Some roles of stimulation in early human development. In D. Goslin (Ed.), *Handbook of socialization theory and research.* Chicago: Rand McNally.

Gibbs, J. C., & Schnell, S. V. (1985). Moral development versus socialization: A critique. *American Psychologist, 40*, 1071–1080.

Gibbs, J. P. (1981). *Norms, deviance and social control.* New York: Elsevier.

Gilligan, C. (1982). *In a different voice: Psychological theory and women's development.* Cambridge, MA: Harvard University Press.

Goffman, E. (1967). *Interaction ritual.* New York: Pantheon.

Goldstein, J. (1960). Police discretion not to invoke the criminal process: Low-visibility decisions in the administration of justice. *The Yale Law Journal, 69*, 543–589.

Goode, W. J. (1986). Individual choice and the social order. In J. F. Short, Jr. (Ed.), *The social fabric.* Beverly Hills: Sage.

Goslin, D. A. (1969), (Ed.). *Handbook of Socialization theory and research.* Chicago: Rand McNally.

Gowler, D., & Legge, K. (1981). Negation, synthesis and abomination in rhetoric. In C. Antaki (Ed.), *The psychology of ordinary explanations of social behavior.* London: Academic Press.

Greenstein, F. I. (1965). *Children and politics.* New Haven, CT: Yale University Press.

Hamilton, V. L. (1978). Who is responsible? Toward a social psychology of responsibility attribution. *Social psychology, 41*, 316–328.

Haney, C., & Zimbardo, P. (1977). The socialization into criminality: On becoming a prisoner and a guard. In J. L. Tapp & F. L. Levine (Eds.), *Law, justice and the individual in society: Psychological and legal issues* (pp. 198–223). New York: Holt, Rinehart and Winston.

Harre, R. (1981). Expressive aspects of descriptions of others. In C. Antaki (Ed.), *The psychology of ordinary explanations of social behaviour.* London: Academic Press.

Harrington, C., & Merry, S. (1988). Ideological production: The making of community mediation. *Law and Society Review, 22*, 709–734.

Hart, H. L. A. (1961). *The concept of law.* New York: Oxford University Press.

Hart, H. L. A. (1968). *Punishment and responsibility.* Oxford, England: Clarendon Press.

Heider, F. (1958). *The psychology of interpersonal relations.* New York: Wiley.

Hess, R. D., & Easton, D. (1960). The child's changing image of the president. *Public Opinion Quarterly, 24*, 632–644.

Hess, R. D., & Torney, J. V. (1967). *The development of political attitudes in children.* Chicago: Aldine.

Hirschi, T. (1969). *Causes of delinquency.* Berkeley, CA: University of California Press.

Hobbes, T. (1960). *Leviathan.* Oxford, England: Basil Blackwell.

Hogan, R. (1976). Legal socialization. In G. Bermant, C. Nemeth, & N. Vidmar

(Eds.), *Psychology and the law* (pp. 65–80). Lexington, MA: Lexington Books.
Holmes, O. W., Jr. (1897). The path of the law. *Harvard Law Review, 10*(8), 457–478.
Hull, C. L. (1943). *Principles of behavior*. New York: Appleton-Century-Crofts.
Hume, D. (1955). *An inquiry concerning human understanding*. C. W. Hendel (Ed.). New York: Liberal Arts Press.
Humphries, D., & Greenberg, D. S. (1984). Social control and social formation: A Marxian analysis. In D. Black (Ed.), *Toward a general theory of social control* (Vol.2). Orlando, FL: Academic Press.
Jzzett, R. (1975). Personal communication. Cited in Rubin, Z. & Peplaas, A. Who believes in a just world? *Journal of Social Issues, 31*, 65–90.
Jaros, D. H., Hirsch, H., & Fleron, F. J. Jr. (1968). The malevolent leader: Political socialization in an American subculture. *American Political Science Review, 62*, 564–575.
Jennings, M. K., & Niemi, R. G. (1974). *The political character of adolescence: The influence of families and school*. Princeton, NJ: Princeton University Press.
Jennings, M. K., & Niemi, R. G. (1981). *Generations and politics*. Princeton, NJ: Princeton University Press.
Kairys, D. (Ed.). (1982). *The politics of law*. New York: Pantheon Books.
Kant, I. (1949). *Fundamental principles of the metaphysics of morals*. New York: Liberal Arts Press.
Kant, I. (1965). *The metaphysical elements of justice*. (J. Ladd, Trans.) New York: Library of Liberal Arts.
Katz, J. (1988). *Seductions of crime*. New York: Basic Books.
Kelman, H. C. (1958). Compliance, identification and internalization: Three processes of attitude change. *Journal of Conflict Resolution, 2*, 51–60.
Kelman, H., & Hamilton, V. L. (1989). *Crimes of obedience*. New Haven, CT: Yale University Press.
Kelson, H. (1945). *General theory of law and state*. (A. Wedberg, Trans.) New York: Russell and Russell.
Kennedy, D. (1980). Toward an historical understanding of legal consciousness. *Research in Law and Sociology, 3*, 3.
Kidder, L., & Cohn, E. (1979). Public views of crime and crime prevention. In I. Frieze, D. Bar Tal, & J. Carroll (Eds.), *New approaches to social problems* (pp. 237–264). San Francisco: Jossey-Bass.
Klein, E. D. (1984). *Gender politics: The rise of the contemporary feminist movement*. Cambridge, MA: Harvard University Press.
Kohlberg, L. (1969). Stage and sequence: The cognitive-developmental approach to socialization. In D. A. Goslin (Ed.), *Handbook of socialization theory* (pp. 347–480). Chicago: Rand McNally.
Kohlberg, L. (1976). Moral stages and moralization. In T. Likona (Eds.), *Moral development and behavior* (pp. 31–53). New York: Holt, Rinehart & Winston.
Kohlberg, L. (1981). *Essays on moral development, 1: In the philosophy of moral development*. New York: Harper and Row.
Kohlberg, L. (1984). *The psychology of moral development: The nature and validity of moral stages*. San Francisco: Harper and Row.
Kohlberg, L. (1986). A current statement on some theoretical issues. In S. Modgil & C. Modgil (Eds.), *Lawrence Kohlberg: Consensus and controversy* (pp. 485–546). London: The Falmer Press.

Kornhauser, W. (1959). *The politics of mass society*. Glencoe, IL: Free Press.

Krislov, S., Boyum, K. O., Clark, J. N., Shaefer, R. C., & White, S. O. (Eds.), (1972). *Compliance and the law*. Beverly Hills: Sage.

Lalljee, M. (1981). Attribution theory and the analysis of explanations. In C. Antaki (Ed.), *The psychology of ordinary explanations of social behavior*. London: Academic Press.

Lane, R. E. (1962). *Political ideology*. Glencoe, IL: Free Press.

Langton, K. P. (1967). Peer group and school and the political socialization process. *American Political Science Review, 61*, 751–58.

LaPierre, R. T. (1934). Attitudes vs. actions. *Social Forces*, 13, 230–237.

Law Enforcement Assistance Administration – U.S. Department of Justice. (1974, February 14). *Guideline: Use of LEAA Funds for psychosurgery and medical research*.

Lemert, E. M. (1972). *Human deviance, social problems and social control*. 2nd Ed. Englewood Cliffs, NJ: Prentice-Hall.

Lerner, M. (1980). *The belief in a just world: A fundamental delusion*. New York: Plenum Press.

Lerner, M. J., & Miller, D. T. (1980). Just world research and the attribution process: Looking back and ahead. *Psychological Bulletin, 85*(5), 1030–1051.

Levi, E. (1948). *An introduction to legal reasoning*. Chicago: University of Chicago Press.

Levine, F. J. (1979). *The legal reasoning of youth: Dimensions and correlates*. Unpublished doctoral dissertation, University of Chicago.

Levine, F. J., & Tapp, J. L. (1977). The dialectic of legal socialization in community and school. In J. L. Tapp & F. J. Levine (Eds.), *Law, justice and the individual in society: Psychological and legal issues* (pp. 163–182). New York: Holt, Rinehart & Winston.

Lipset, S. M. (1960). *Political man*. Garden City, N. Y.: Doubleday.

Lipset, S. M., & Rabb, E. (1970). *The politics of unreason*. New York: Harper & Row.

Lipsitz, L. (1964). Work life and political attitudes: A study of manual workers. *American Political Science Review, 58*, 959.

Locke, J. (1960). *Social contract: Essays by Locke, Hume and Rousseau*. New York: Oxford University Press.

Loevinger, J. (1986). On Kohlberg's contribution to ego development. In S. Modgil & C. Modgil (Eds.), *Lawrence Kohlberg: Consensus and controversy* (pp. 183–193). London: The Falmer Press.

Mancuso, J. C., & Sarbin, T. R. (1976). A paradigmatic analysis of psychological issues at the interface of jurisprudence and moral conduct. In T. Lickona (Ed.), *Moral development and behavior: Theory, research and social issues* (pp. 326–341). New York: Holt, Rinehart & Winston.

McCartney, K., Robeson, W., Jordan, E., & Mouradian, V. (1989, April). *Mothers' language with first- and second-born children: A within-family study*. Paper presented at the biennial meeting of the Society for Research in Child Development, Kansas City, MO.

McClosky, H. (1964). Consensus and ideology in American politics. *American Political Science Review, 58*, 361–382.

McClosky, H., & Brill, A. (1983). *Dimensions of tolerance: What Americans believe about civil liberties*. New York: Russell Sage Foundation.

Mead, G. H. (1934). *Mind, self and society*. Chicago: University of Chicago Press.
Merelman, R. M. (1969). The development of political ideology: A framework for the analysis of political socialization. American *Political Science Review, 63*, 750–767.
Milgram, S. (1963). Behavioral study of obedience. *Journal of Abnormal and Social Psychology, 67*, 371–378.
Milgram, S. (1974). *Obedience to authority: An experimental view*. New York: Harper & Row.
Mill, J. S. (1950). *John Stuart Mill's philosophy of scientific method*. New York: Library of Liberal Arts.
Miller, A. G. (1986). *The obedience experiments: A case study of controversy in social science*. New York: Praeger.
Mischel, W. (1968). *Personality and assessment*. New York: Wiley.
Mischel, W. (1973). Toward a cognitive social learning reconceptualization of personality. *Psychological Review, 80*, 252–283.
Mischel, W., & Mischel, H. N. (1976). A cognitive social-learning approach to morality and self-regulation. In T. Lickona (Ed.), *Moral development and behavior* (pp. 84–107). New York: Holt, Rinehart & Winston.
Modgil, S., & Modgil, C. (Eds.), (1986). *Lawrence Kohlberg: Consensus and controversy*. London: The Falmer Press.
Monahan, J. (1978). The prediction of violence criminal behavior. In A. Blumstein, J. Cohn, & D. Nagen (Eds.), *Deterrence and incapacitation*. Washington, DC: National Academy of Sciences.
Monahan, J. (1981). *Predicting violent behavior*. Beverly Hills, CA: Sage.
Morris, H. (1976). *On guilt and innocence*. Berkeley, CA: University of California Press.
Owen, D., & Straus, M. (1975). The social structure of violence in childhood and the approval of violence as an adult. *Aggressive Behavior, 1*, 193–211.
Parke, R. D. (1977). Socialization into child abuse: A social interactional perspective. In J. L. Tapp & F. J. Levine (Eds.), *Law, justice and the individual in society: Psychological and legal issues* (pp. 183–197). New York: Holt, Rinehart & Winston.
Parsons, T., & Shils, E. A. (1951). *Toward a general theory of action. Cambridge*, MA: Harvard University Press.
Patterson, O. (1982). *Slavery & social death*. Cambridge, MA: Harvard University Press.
Pepitone, A. (1975). Towards a normative and comparative biocultural social psychology. *Journal of Personality and Social Psychology, 34*(4), 641–653.
Peters, R. S. (1958). *The concept of motivation*. London: Routledge & Kegan Paul.
Peterson, D. S. (1968). *The clinical study of social behavior*. New York: Appleton-Century-Crofts.
Pfohl, S. (1985). *Images of deviance and social control*. New York: McGraw-Hill.
Piaget, J. (1926). *The language and thought of the child*. London: Routledge & Kegan Paul.
Piaget, J. (1932). *The moral judgement of the child*. New York: Harcourt, Brace & World.
Piaget, J. (1970/1983). Piaget's theory. In P. H. Mussen (Ed.), *Handbook of child psychology*. (Vol. I, pp. 103–128). New York: Wiley.
Quinney, R. (1970). *The social reality of crime*. Boston: Little, Brown.

Quinney, R. (1973). *Critique of legal order*. Boston: Little, Brown.
Rawls, J. (1971). *A theory of justice*. Cambridge, MA: Harvard University Press.
Renshon, S. A. (1974). Personality and family dynamics in the political socialization process. *American Journal of Political Science, 19*, 63–80.
Renshon, S.A. (1977). *Handbook of political socialization theory and research*. London: Collier Macmillan.
Rosenberg, S. W. (1985). Sociology, psychology and the study of political behavior: The case of research on political socialization. *Journal of Politics, 47*, 715–731.
Rossi, P. H., & Berk, R. A. (1985). Varieties of normative consensus. *American Sociological Review, 50*(3), 333–347.
Rousseau, J. (1960). The social contract. In *Social contract: Essays by Locke, Hume and Rousseau*. New York: Oxford University Press.
Rubin, Z., & Peplau, A. (1975). Who believes in a just world? *Journal of Social Issues, 31*, 65–89.
Sampson, E. E. (1977). Psychology and the American ideal. *Journal of Personality and Social Psychology, 35*, 767–782.
Sanders, J., Regulus, T., & Hamilton, V. L. (1980, June). *Class and consequences: Two experiments on the effects of social status on responsibility judgements*. Paper presented at the annual meeting of the Law and Society Association, Madison, WI.
Sarason, I. G., Smith, R. E., & Diener, E. (1975). Personality research: Components of variance attributable to the person and the situation. *Journal of Personality and Social Psychology, 32*, 199–204.
Sarat, A. (1977). Studying American legal culture: An assessment of survey evidence. *Law and Society Review, 11*(3), 427–488.
Scheingold, S. A. (1974). *The politics of rights*. New Haven, CT: Yale University Press.
Scheingold, S. A. (1984). *The politics of law and order: Street crime and public policy*. New York: Longman.
Schwartz, D. C., & Schwartz, S. K. (Eds.), (1975). *New directions in political socialization*. New York: Free Press.
Searing, D. D., Schwartz, J. J., & Lind, A. E. (1973). The structuring principle: Political socialization and belief systems. *American Political Science Review, 67*, 415–432.
Sears, D. O. (1975). Political socialization. In F. I. Greenstein & N. W. Polsby (Eds.), *Handbook of political science*. Reading, MA: Addison-Wesley.
Sears, R. R., Maccoby, E. E., & Levin, H. (1957). *Patterns of child rearing*. Evanston, IL: Row, Peterson.
Sechrest, L., White, S. O., & Brown, E. D. (Eds.). (1979). *The rehabilitation of criminal offenders*. Washington, DC: National Academy of Sciences.
Shotter, J. (1981). Telling and reporting: Prospective and retrospective uses of self-ascriptions. In C. Antaki (Ed.), *The psychology of ordinary explanations of social behavior*. London: Academic Press.
Shweder, R. A. (1982). Liberalism as destiny. *Contemporary Psychology, 27*, 421–424.
Simpson, E. L. (1974). Moral development research: A case study of scientific cultural bias. *Human Development, 17*, 81–106.
Skinner, B. F. (1938). *The behavior of organisms*. New York: Appleton-Century-

Crofts.
Skinner, B. F. (1953). *Science and human behavior*. New York: Macmillan.
Skolnick, J. (1966). *Justice without trial*. New York: Wiley.
Snarey, J. (1985). The cross-cultural universality of social-moral development: A critical review of Kohlbergian research. *Psychological Bulletin, 97*, 202–232.
Snyder, M., & Ickes, W. (1985). Personality and social behavior. In G. Lindzey & E. Aronson (Eds.), *The handbook of social psychology* (Vol. II, pp. 883–947). New York: Random House.
Stouffer, S. A. (1955). *Communism, conformity & civil liberties*. New York: Wiley.
Straus, M. A. (1980). *A measure of socioeconomic status*. Unpublished manuscript, University of New Hampshire, Durham.
Straus, M. A., Gelles, R., & Steinmetz, S. K. (1980). *Behind closed doors: Violence in the American family*. Garden City, NY: Doubleday/Anchor Press.
Sullivan, E. V. (1977). A study of Kohlberg's theory of structural development: A critique of liberal social science ideology. *Human Development, 20*, 352–376.
Sutherland, E. H. (1947). *Principles of criminology* (4th ed.) Philadelphia: J. B. Lippincott.
Sutherland, E. H. & Cressy, D. R. (1978). *Criminology* (10th ed.) Philadelphia: J. B. Lippincott.
Sykes, G. M., & Matza, D. (1957). Techniques of neutralization: A theory of delinquency. *American Sociological Review, 22*, 664–670.
Tapp, J.L. (1970). What rule? What role? *Reacting to Polier's Rule of law and role of psychiatry. UCLA Law Review, 17*, 1333–1344.
Tapp, J. L. (1970). Methodology. In L. Minturn & J. L. Tapp (Eds.), *Authority, rules and aggression: A cross-national study of children's judgments of the justice of aggressive confrontations: Part II*. Washington, DC: United States Department of Health, Education, and Welfare.
Tapp, J. L. (1980). Psychological and policy perspectives on the law: Reflections on a decade. *Journal of Social Issues, 36*(2), 165–192.
Tapp, J. L., Finckenauer, J., & Yakovlev, A. (1988, June). *A cross-cultural study of legal socialization among and between American and Soviet youth*. Paper presented at the annual meeting of the Law and Society Association, Vail, CO.
Tapp, J. L., Gunnar, M., & Keating, D. (1983). Socialization: Three ages, three rule systems. In D. Perlman & P. C. Cosby (Eds.), *Social psychology* (pp. 42–74). New York: Holt, Rinehart & Winston.
Tapp, J. L., & Kohlberg, L. (1977). Developing senses of law and legal justice. In J. L. Tapp & F. J. Levine (Eds.), *Law, justice and the individual in society*. New York: Holt, Rinehart & Winston.
Tapp, J. L., & Levine, F. J. (1970). Persuasion to virtue: A preliminary statement. *Law and Society Review, 4*, 565–582.
Tapp, J. L., & Levine, F. L. (1974). Legal socialization: Strategies for an ethical legality. *Stanford Law Review, 27*, 1–72.
Tapp, J. L., & Levine, F. J. (Eds.), (1977). *Law, justice and the individual in society*. New York: Holt, Rinehart and Winston.
Tedin, K. L. (1980). Assessing peer and parental influence on political attitudes. *American Journal of Political Science, 24*, 136–154.
Torney, J. V. (1971). Socialization of attitudes toward the legal system. *Journal of Social Issues, 27*, 109–136.
Torney, J. V. (1977). Socialization of attitudes toward the legal system. In J. L.

Tapp & F. J. Levine (Eds.), *Law, justice and the individual in society: Psychological and legal issues* (pp. 134–144). New York: Holt, Rinehart & Winston.

Turiel, E. (1983). *The development of social knowledge: Morality and convention.* Cambridge, MA: Cambridge University Press.

Turiel, E. (1989). Commentary. *Human Development, 32*, 45–52.

Turk, A. (1969). *Criminality and the legal order.* Chicago: Rand McNally.

Weber, M. (1939). *Max Weber on law in economy and society*, M. Rheinstein (Ed.). New York: Simon & Shuster.

Weinrich-Haste, H., & Locke, D. (Eds). (1983). *Morality in the making.* New York: Wiley.

Wheeler, S. (1961). Socialization in correctional communitites. *American Sociological Review, 26*, 697–712.

White, S. O. (1972). A perspective on police professionalization. *Law and Society Review, 7*, 61–85.

White, S. O. (1974). Controlling police behavior. In D. MacNamara & M. Reidel (Eds.), *Police: Perspectives, problems & prospects.* New York: Praeger.

White, S. O., & Cohn, E. S. (1989, June). *What do we mean by legal reasoning?* Paper presented at the annual meeting of the Law and Society Association, Madison, WI.

White, S. O., & Straus, M. (1981). The implication of family violence for rehabilitation strategies. In S. Martin (Ed.), *New directions in the rehabilitation of criminal offenders* (pp. 255–288). Washington, DC: National Academy of Sciences.

Wilson, J. Q. (1968). *Varieties of police behavior.* Cambridge, MA: Harvard University Press.

Winch, P. (1958). *The idea of a social science and its relations to philosophy.* London: Routledge & Kegan Paul.

Zeldich, M., Jr. (1986). The problem of order. In J. F. Short, Jr. (Ed.), *The social fabric.* Beverly Hills, CA: Sage.

Zellman, G. L., & Sears, D. O. (1971). Childhood origins of tolerance for dissent. Journal of Social Issues, 27, 109–136.

Appendix

Questionnaire Used in the Study

Demographics

1. What is your class rank?
   Fr._______
   So._______
   Jr._______
   Sr._______
2. (a) Have you always lived in your present dorm?
   Yes_______ No_______
   (b) If your answer is *no*, please list other dorms you have lived in.
   ____
   ____
3. What is the main reason for your living in a dorm?
   1. Parents wishes
   2. Own choice
   3. Financial reasons
   4. Don't know
4. Would you rather live off-campus?
   1. No
   2. Not sure
   3. Yes
5. What do you think the purpose of a dorm should be?
   a. A place that encourages study and academic concerns.
   Not at all Neutral Completely
   0 1 2 3 4 5 6
   b. A place to gain close friendships and to develop emotionally and socially.
   Not at all Neutral Completely
   0 1 2 3 4 5 6
   c. A place to party, relax and have a good time.
   Not at all Neutral Completely
   0 1 2 3 4 5 6
6. How much guidance and structure should a dorm provide?
   Not at all Neutral Completely
   0 1 2 3 4 5 6
7. To what extent do you think a dorm should be a place where you are left completely alone to do as you want?
   Not at all Neutral Completely
   0 1 2 3 4 5 6
8. To what extent do you usually make decisions completely on your own?
   Not at all Neutral Completely
   0 1 2 3 4 5 6
9. What do you think the role of the Resident Assistant in a dorm should be?

	Not at all		Neutral			Completely
a. Counselor	0	1	2	3	4	5 6
b. Enforcer rules	0	1	2	3	4	5 6
c. Source of information	0	1	2	3	4	5 6
d. Looks after building (eg. tends to repairs, hands out keys, etc.)	0	1	2	3	4	5 6

Tapp and Levine Rule-Law Interview

Please answer the following questions in your own words.

1. What if there were no rules?

2. What is a rule?

3. What is a law?

4. Why should people follow rules?

5. Why do you follow rules?

6. Can rules be changed? Why?

7. Are there times when it might be right to break a rule?

Rubin and Peplau Belief in a Just World Scale

Please circle the number which expresses your feeling regarding the questions below.

Completely Agree			Undecided			Completely Disagree
0	1	2	3	4	5	6

1. I've found that a person rarely deserves the reputation he has.	0	1	2	3	4	5	6
2. Basically the world is a just place.	0	1	2	3	4	5	6
3. People who get "lucky breaks" have usually earned their good fortune.	0	1	2	3	4	5	6
4. Careful drivers are just as likely to get hurt in traffic accidents as careless ones.	0	1	2	3	4	5	6
5. It is a common occurance for a guilty person to get off free in American courts.	0	1	2	3	4	5	6
6. Students almost always deserve the grades they receive in school.	0	1	2	3	4	5	6
7. People who keep in shape have little chance of suffering heart attack.	0	1	2	3	4	5	6
8. The political candidate who sticks up for his principles rarely get elected.	0	1	2	3	4	5	6
9. It is rare for an innocent man to wrongly be sent to jail.	0	1	2	3	4	5	6
10. In professional sports, many fouls and infractions never get called by the referee.	0	1	2	3	4	5	6
11. By and large, people deserve what they get.	0	1	2	3	4	5	6
12. When parents punish their children, it is almost always for a good reason.	0	1	2	3	4	5	6
13. Good deeds often go unnoticed and unrewarded.	0	1	2	3	4	5	6
14. Although evil people may hold political power for a while, in the general course of history the good wins out.	0	1	2	3	4	5	6
15. In almost any business or profession, people who do their job will rise to the top.	0	1	2	3	4	5	6
16. American parents tend to overlook the things most to be admired in their children.	0	1	2	3	4	5	6
17. It is often impossible for a person to receive a fair trial in the USA.	0	1	2	3	4	5	6
18. People who meet with misfortune have often brought it on themselves.	0	1	2	3	4	5	6

Indicate the degree to which you agree or disagree with each statement using the following scale:

Completely Agree			Undecided			Completely Disagree
0	1	2	3	4	5	6

19. Crime doesn't pay.	0	1	2	3	4	5	6
20. Many people suffer through absolutely no fault of their own.	0	1	2	3	4	5	6
21. Basically, UNH is a fair place.	0	1	2	3	4	5	6
22. In general, UNH students who are written up for breaking rules deserve it.	0	1	2	3	4	5	6
23. In general, UNH students who are brought before Judicial boards are treated equally.	0	1	2	3	4	5	6

Continued.

Indicate the degree to which you agree or disagree with each statement using the following scale:

Completely Agree			Undecided			Completely Disagree
0	1	2	3	4	5	6

24. In general, the rules at UNH are not enforced consistently.	0	1	2	3	4	5	6
25. In general, the penalties given students who break rules at UNH "fit the crime."	0	1	2	3	4	5	6
26. In general, UNH rules are reasonable.	0	1	2	3	4	5	6
27. When I get "lucky breaks" it's usually because I've earned my good fortune.	0	1	2	3	4	5	6
28. I almost always deserve the grades I receive in school.	0	1	2	3	4	5	6
29. By and large, I deserve what I get.	0	1	2	3	4	5	6
30. When I meet with misfortune, it is often because I brought it on myself.	0	1	2	3	4	5	6

Cohn and White Rule-Violating Behavior and Attitude Scale

Here is a list of things you might have done during your last semester at college. Please circle the answer number which is most appropriate for each item.

0=never 2=2-3 times 4=6-9 times 6=20 or more times
1=once 3=3-5 times 5=10-19 times

1. Writing a paper for a friend in the dorm.	0	1	2	3	4	5	6
2. Taking a test for a friend in the dorm.	0	1	2	3	4	5	6
3. Drinking in public areas of dorm (not authorized party) by those under 20.	0	1	2	3	4	5	6
4. Drinking in dorm room by those under 20.	0	1	2	3	4	5	6
5. Being drunk in dorm.	0	1	2	3	4	5	6
6. Smoking marijuana in dorm.	0	1	2	3	4	5	6
7. Using hard drugs.	0	1	2	3	4	5	6
8. Using a dorm bathroom intended for opposite sex.	0	1	2	3	4	5	6
9. Refusing to leave when your roommate wants to have girl/boyfriend overnight.	0	1	2	3	4	5	6
10. Asking your roommate to leave when you want to have a girlfriend/boyfriend overnight.	0	1	2	3	4	5	6
11. Having your boyfriend/girlfriend move into your room.	0	1	2	3	4	5	6
12. Having a stereo or TV playing loud enough to be heard in the corridor.	0	1	2	3	4	5	6
13. Having a loud party in your room at any time.	0	1	2	3	4	5	6
14. Yelling or making noise in the corridors.	0	1	2	3	4	5	6
15. Playing "hall sports."	0	1	2	3	4	5	6
16. Shooting off fire extinguishers for fun.	0	1	2	3	4	5	6
17. Setting off fire alarms or smoke detectors for fun.	0	1	2	3	4	5	6
18. Breaking up furniture and/or damaging the building.	0	1	2	3	4	5	6
19. Removing lounge furniture to your own room.	0	1	2	3	4	5	6
20. Having a physical fight with another person in the dorm.	0	1	2	3	4	5	6
21. Cursing or yelling at another person in the dorm.	0	1	2	3	4	5	6
22. Stealing from others in the dorm.	0	1	2	3	4	5	6
23. Making remarks & joking with sexual overtones.	0	1	2	3	4	5	6
24. Making sexual advances when they aren't wanted.	0	1	2	3	4	5	6
25. Being hassled sexually without physical force used.	0	1	2	3	4	5	6
26. Being harrassed sexually, including use of physical force.	0	1	2	3	4	5	6
27. Reporting to dorm staff student who is breaking a rule and causing you a problem.	0	1	2	3	4	5	6
28. Reporting to Dean of Students Office another student who is breaking a rule and causing you a problem.	0	1	2	3	4	5	6
29. Complaining directly to a student who is breaking a rule and/or causing you a problem.	0	1	2	3	4	5	6

	To what extent do you approve or disapprove of the following behaviors?							To what extent do you approve or disapprove of enforcing rules against the following behaviors?						
	Completely Disapprove			Neutral			Completely Approve	Completely Disapprove			Neutral			Completely Approve
1. Writing a paper for a friend in the dorm.	0	1	2	3	4	5	6	0	1	2	3	4	5	6
2. Taking a test for a friend in the dorm.	0	1	2	3	4	5	6	0	1	2	3	4	5	6
3. Drinking in public areas of dorm (not authorized party) by those under 20.	0	1	2	3	4	5	6	0	1	2	3	4	5	6
4. Drinking in dorm room by those under 20.	0	1	2	3	4	5	6	0	1	2	3	4	5	6
5. Being drunk in dorm.	0	1	2	3	4	5	6	0	1	2	3	4	5	6
6. Smoking marijuana in dorm.	0	1	2	3	4	5	6	0	1	2	3	4	5	6
7. Using hard drugs.	0	1	2	3	4	5	6	0	1	2	3	4	5	6
8. Using a dorm bathroom intended for opposite sex.	0	1	2	3	4	5	6	0	1	2	3	4	5	6
9. Refusing to leave when your roommate wants to have girl/boyfriend stay.	0	1	2	3	4	5	6	0	1	2	3	4	5	6
10. Asking your roommate to leave when you want to have a girl/boyfriend overnight.	0	1	2	3	4	5	6	0	1	2	3	4	5	6
11. Having your girl/boyfriend move into your room.	0	1	2	3	4	5	6	0	1	2	3	4	5	6
12. Having a stereo or TV playing loud enough to be heard in the corridor.	0	1	2	3	4	5	6	0	1	2	3	4	5	6
13. Having a loud party in your room at any time.	0	1	2	3	4	5	6	0	1	2	3	4	5	6
14. Yelling or making noise in the corridors.	0	1	2	3	4	5	6	0	1	2	3	4	5	6
15. Playing "hall sports".	0	1	2	3	4	5	6	0	1	2	3	4	5	6
16. Shooting off fire extinguishers for fun.	0	1	2	3	4	5	6	0	1	2	3	4	5	6
17. Setting off fire alarms or smoke detectors for fun.	0	1	2	3	4	5	6	0	1	2	3	4	5	6
18. Breaking up furniture and/or damaging the building.	0	1	2	3	4	5	6	0	1	2	3	4	5	6

Continued.

	To what extent do you approve or disapprove of the following behaviors?							To what extent do you approve or disapprove of enforcing rules against the following behaviors?						
	Completely Disapprove			Neutral			Completely Approve	Completely Disapprove			Neutral			Completely Approve
19. Removing lounge furniture to your own room.	0	1	2	3	4	5	6	0	1	2	3	4	5	6
20. Having a physical fight with another person in the dorm.	0	1	2	3	4	5	6	0	1	2	3	4	5	6
21. Cursing or yelling at another person in the dorm.	0	1	2	3	4	5	6	0	1	2	3	4	5	6
22. Stealing from others in the dorm.	0	1	2	3	4	5	6	0	1	2	3	4	5	6
23. Making remarks & joking with sexual overtones.	0	1	2	3	4	5	6	0	1	2	3	4	5	6
24. Making sexual advances when they aren't wanted.	0	1	2	3	4	5	6	0	1	2	3	4	5	6
25. Being hassled sexually without physical force used.	0	1	2	3	4	5	6	0	1	2	3	4	5	6
26. Being harrassed sexually, including use of physical force.	0	1	2	3	4	5	6	0	1	2	3	4	5	6
27. Reporting to dorm staff a student who is breaking a rule and causing you a problem.	0	1	2	3	4	5	6	0	1	2	3	4	5	6
28. Reporting to Dean of Students Office another student who is breaking a rule and causing you a problem.	0	1	2	3	4	5	6	0	1	2	3	4	5	6
29. Complaining directly to a student who is breaking a rule and/or causing you a problem.	0	1	2	3	4	5	6	0	1	2	3	4	5	6

Author List

Subject Index

MIX
Papier aus verantwortungsvollen Quellen
Paper from responsible sources
FSC® C105338

If you have any concerns about our products,
you can contact us on
ProductSafety@springernature.com

In case Publisher is established outside the EU,
the EU authorized representative is:
Springer Nature Customer Service Center GmbH
Europaplatz 3, 69115 Heidelberg, Germany

Printed by Libri Plureos GmbH
in Hamburg, Germany